Praise for *Ty and The Babe*

"[Stanton's] research and wide-ranging interviews render each of them more human. . . . it's definitely a fresh perspective."
—*The Detroit News*

"Tom Stanton has beautifully re-created the most romantic period of American sports, provided new and powerful insights into a pair of greatly misunderstood figures . . . and given baseball and golf fans everywhere something to cheer lustily about."
—James Dodson, author of *Final Rounds* and
Ben Hogan: An American Life

"A book about the relationship between Ty Cobb and Babe Ruth . . . is great drama . . . and Stanton tells that story with flair and telling detail."
—*Booklist*

"The wardrobe mistress of baseball history seems to have assigned the white hat to Babe Ruth and the black hat to Ty Cobb for all time. . . . Now Tom Stanton comes along to rearrange the roles in his terrific new book, *Ty and The Babe*, which chronicles the relationship between the two baseball icons. He takes off the hats and tells us about the real people. And it all is great fun."
—Leigh Montville, author of *The Big Bam*

ALSO BY TOM STANTON

The Final Season

The Road to Cooperstown

Hank Aaron and the
Home Run That Charged America

TY AND THE BABE

Baseball's Fiercest Rivals:
A Surprising Friendship
and the 1941 Has-Beens
Golf Championship

~

Tom Stanton

THOMAS DUNNE BOOKS | *St. Martin's Griffin* ✹ *New York*

THOMAS DUNNE BOOKS.
An imprint of St. Martin's Press.

www.thomasdunnebooks.com
www.stmartins.com

Book design by Michael Collica

Library of Congress Cataloging-in-Publication Data

Stanton, Tom, 1960–
    Ty and the babe : baseball's fiercest rivals : a surprising friendship and the
1941 has-beens golf championship / Tom Stanton.
        p. cm.
    Includes bibliographic references and index.
    ISBN-13: 978-0-312-38224-7
    ISBN-10: 0-312-38224-3
    1. Cobb, Ty, 1886–1961. 2. Ruth, Babe, 1895–1948. 3. Baseball players—
United States—Biography. 4. Male friendship—United States. 5. Golf. I. Title.

GV865.A1 S725 2007
796.357092'2—dc22

                                                                        2007008926

First St. Martin's Griffin Edition: July 2008

10 9 8 7 6 5 4 3 2 1

For Mike Varney,
an uncommon friend

Contents

A Note

THE EVIDENCE BEGAN TO MOUNT A FEW YEARS BACK WHEN I came upon an old baseball fan, Fred Smith, who had met Ty Cobb during his playing days. Smith bristled at the way contemporary journalists portrayed Cobb. It didn't mesh with his memories. "He was beautiful—wonderful," said Smith. "It always made me mad when you'd read these stories about how miserable he was, because these guys who wrote about him never saw him. They weren't alive when he was playing."

Months after, in the final days at Tiger Stadium, one of Cobb's granddaughters appeared at the ballpark. I asked her about Cobb's torrid image. She had heard the stories and seen the damning portrayals. But it wasn't what she remembered. "My grandfather was very good to his family and to a lot of people," she said. People like Bill Glane and Jimmy Lanier, upon whose paths I would stumble a half decade later.

Glane was a hot prospect back in 1945 when selected to play in *Esquire*'s East-West Classic. One team was to be coached by Ty Cobb, the other by Babe Ruth. The players gathered in New York City for ten days of practice. "When I went there," Glane recalled, "I wanted to meet Ruth. I had come there expecting Ruth to be the friendly one and Cobb to be the nasty one. But Ruth didn't pay no attention to us ball players. Cobb was the nice guy. He had patience with us. He worked with us. The two guys were opposites." Cobb even invited Glane up to his hotel suite for a private chat one evening.

Jimmy Lanier grew up in Augusta, Georgia, a few streets over from Ty Cobb's children. He and redheaded Herschel Cobb were best friends. "Mr. Cobb was just Herschel's daddy," said Lanier. "I didn't realize he was such a famous man." In 1925, Cobb asked Lanier to be his personal batboy. Lanier went north to Detroit and lived in Cobb's home for two summers. He likes to say that they knew each other from the day Lanier was born until the day Cobb died. As a boy, Lanier was witness to the famous men who came to the Cobb home. Bobby Jones, Bill Tilden, Grantland Rice, Tris Speaker, Knute Rockne, Connie Mack—the names astounded. They comprised a living who's who of American sports. Occasionally, Lanier found himself at the dinner table with them. "I'd always sit to the right of Mr. Cobb," he said. "He'd ask me to say the blessing. I was shy but I'd mumble something."

Now well into his nineties and no longer able to drive, Jimmy Lanier shook his head at how time had withered Ty Cobb's reputation. "So many things were said about Mr. Cobb that weren't true," he said. "The image of him is highly exaggerated, blown out of proportion. He did a lot of very kind things. He was very fond of ragtag fellows. He could spot a little boy whose family couldn't afford anything and he'd give him a ball. He was a gentle, considerate man to me. He was like a second father. 'Jimmy, my boy'—that's what he called me. 'Jimmy, my boy.' I loved Mr. Cobb and he loved me."

And then there's Ernie Harwell, the famed baseball broadcaster. He met both Ruth and Cobb. He appreciated their abilities and got on fine with each.

"If you had to spend an hour with one, who would you prefer?" I asked him over lunch in the senior complex where he and his wife, Lulu, live.

"Cobb," he said. "Most people would probably like Ruth better. He was a partygoer, a hail-fellow sort of guy. I know all the ball players loved Ruth. He was a blustery kind of man, profane, a loud-mouth. Cobb was a little more cerebral. A little more dignified, at least to me."

Which isn't to say Cobb was a saint and Ruth a Satan. You could just as easily—more easily, actually—find a legion of folks to vouch for Ruth; and I did. There was Rip Collins, a 1930s clubhouse boy who admired Ruth. "True to legend, he always seemed to be eating hot dogs when he came into the clubhouse," said Collins. "He was a barrel-chested guy with a deep voice. Kind of scary until you met him. A man's man. A decent guy. He did a lot of good things for people." And there was Elden Auker, who pitched against Ruth, played golf with him, and enjoyed his company: "He was just a big kid. He laughed and joked all the time."

But that fits with how we view the Babe, doesn't it? As the playful, mischievous Santa Claus of baseball—the antithesis of that devil incarnate Ty Cobb, right?

Cobb and Ruth towered over their peers as the most famous players of their century. They reigned as the undisputed kings of the American pastime, men whose celebrity exceeded the boundaries of sport and whose personalities and achievements stirred millions and swayed society.

They were emblematic of the decades they dominated. Tyrus represented the 1900s and the 1910s. He was the Wright Brothers and Henry Ford and Theodore Roosevelt—ingenious, industrious, and vigorous. He embodied the unwavering determination of soldiers at war in Europe. He was scrappy and diligent, a zealous fighter, a man of drive and action who took to heart his father's admonition that he make something of himself. Ruth personified the Roaring Twenties. He exemplified the rags-to-riches dream. He was wild and free-spirited, a live-for-the-moment soul, a party unto himself, the grand marshal of a parade of larger-than-life characters that included Capone, Lindbergh, Dempsey, and Valentino. Bombastic and flamboyant, Ruth fit perfectly in the age of speakeasies, Prohibition gangsters, short-skirted flappers, Hollywood scandals, and Ziegfeld showgirls. He hit home runs as big as the times.

For fourteen seasons, Cobb and Ruth played on the same fields, facing one another in more than two hundred games. Both felt the rivalry intensely. It wasn't coincidence that Ruth stroked more home runs against Cobb's team than any other—or that during Cobb's six seasons as a manager no one defeated the Yankees more often than Tyrus's Tygers. At the height of their competition, as the spotlight faded on Cobb and brightened on Ruth, their clubs rated as the top draws in baseball. In those years, almost every game between New York and Detroit featured achievements by one or the other and often both. It was a raucous, rollicking time that saw one aging hero struggling to preserve his place in a game being radically transformed by a popular newcomer.

Decades after their deaths and generations since their final games, their names still conjure vivid caricatures: of the ice-veined, deceptively nicknamed Georgia Peach, an angry genius in spikes; and of his younger nemesis, the fun-loving, barrel-bellied Babe, a jovial man-child in pinstripes. Their burnished portraits thrive yet in the national consciousness, and some truth flourishes in each. But they provide only a hint of the larger, wildly colorful, and deeply textured story that swirls beneath—the story of the most intense rivalry ever known to baseball, the battle between the two men who for a half century afterward were still contenders for the title of "greatest player ever." And, too, the nearly unfathomable friendship that blossomed between them later in life and revealed itself to the public in the 1941 golf tournament that brought them back into headlines. Although some of their records have been toppled, Ty Cobb and Babe Ruth remain among the most monumental figures in sports history. Seventy years on, they continue to inspire, intrigue, and entertain.

If I bring any bias to these pages, it is one born of the belief that the passing years have been unkind and unfair to both men. They have been reduced to stark and shallow clichés—a fate that serves neither them nor us. Cobb especially lives on only as a wicked apparition, a mere shadow of himself, a figure whose current image would be unrecognizable to those who lived in his time. I would be pleased if in some small way this book helps bring to life a more complete picture of him.

—TOM STANTON
New Baltimore, Michigan

———————————●———————————

Part I

Cooperstown 1939

∾

Cobb's Send-off

Fans pack Main Street in Cooperstown for the first
Baseball Hall of Fame induction. NATIONAL BASEBALL HALL OF
FAME LIBRARY, COOPERSTOWN, N.Y.

O N AN OVERCAST SUNDAY IN JUNE 1939, A TRAIN CARRY-
ing Ty Cobb arrived at Detroit's bustling depot. Cobb and
his youngest children, seventeen-year-old Jimmy and nineteen-
year-old Beverly, had come to spend the day in the Motor City. It
was a precoronation of sorts, a brief stopover en route to Cooperstown, where Cobb would be inducted—first of his class—into

the newly unveiled National Baseball Hall of Fame. Their cross-country trip had begun in California, where the Cobbs now lived, and it would eventually take them to New York City, Washington, Cleveland, and Chicago.

In his ball-playing prime, Cobb would have been spotted instantly among the rush of passengers at Michigan Central. He was then one of the two most recognizable figures in the burgeoning city, Henry Ford being the other. People had always noticed Cobb. At six-foot-one, he stood a few inches taller than the average man. His portrait, appearing frequently in publications across the country, had made his face familiar. His guarded grin—tight-lipped as if embarrassed by his teeth—often gave him away. If not, his eyes usually did. Everyone noticed Cobb's blue eyes: intense, piercing, pulsing, steely as a battleship, some said; the color of robin eggs or Courier and Ives china, according to others. They radiated from beneath narrowed lids. Energy surged from them.

More than a decade had passed since Cobb had played the game, and it had been several years since his last visit to Detroit, when he threw out a ceremonial first pitch before a Detroit Stars Negro league game. Cobb was fifty-two now, and he blended easily in a crowd. If you weren't expecting him, if you weren't casting about for famous folks or giving more than a passing glance, you would have thought him just another middle-aged businessman in an overcoat. You wouldn't have noticed him—not there, anyway.

Down Michigan Avenue from the hulking, eighteen-story depot stood the ballpark where Cobb had once thrilled crowds, frustrated opponents, and clawed his way to unparalleled success. The park had changed considerably since his playing days, not only in ownership and name—from Navin Field to Briggs Stadium—but in size, with a new double-decked grandstand that swelled capacity to fifty-five thousand. Cobb had changed, too—physically, yes, with the addition of a few pounds and the subtraction of much hair, but also in demeanor. That afternoon, as the Tigers battled Washington, Cobb showed a side many had never seen.

Cobb looked dapper in the stands in a stylish straw hat and tailored gray-blue suit, and he still turned heads there. At the ballpark, they knew him. There, word spread quickly that the Georgia Peach was in town. There, fans, photographers, players, and friends clamored yet for his attention. Seated with Walter Briggs in the owner's box beside the Tigers' third-base dugout, Cobb felt the admiring gazes as he smoked a cigar. He signed autographs—for Edsel Ford's children, someone told him—tipped his cap at older women, and reminisced with outfielder-turned-pharmacist Davy Jones, who tried to ignore the pain in his ready-to-burst appendix. Cobb waved to old pals who called his name, joked with goofy Nick Altrock, the famous ball-juggling, googly-eyed clown of the visiting Senators, and basked in the moment. Occasionally, a player would steal a look at him.

It must have gratified Cobb that his youngest children were getting a sense of what it was once like for him. They were too young to appreciate his days in a uniform, and maybe seeing the respect and the adulation he received would provide a different view of their daddy. They knew dissension in their fragile household. Their mother had filed for divorce several times, and their oldest brother, Ty Junior, had a strained relationship with Cobb. Young Ty had rebelled strongly against his strict, demanding father. He disliked baseball, lived a fast life in college, dropped out of Princeton, and failed to graduate from Yale. Though he had since matured and begun work on a medical degree, Ty Junior still did not get along well with his famous father. Cobb had been a ballplayer throughout his namesake's childhood, gone for weeks and months on end, and that hadn't strengthened their bond.

Cobb had vowed it would be different with the two youngest of his five children. Jimmy was six when his dad retired from baseball. He had seen him golf frequently but didn't remember much of his baseball career. Born prematurely, he stood several inches smaller than his father, who sometimes affectionately called him Fido or Snake. Jimmy considered himself his dad's favorite, and decades later would fondly remember him as the loving man who would tuck him into bed and kiss him goodnight.

Cobb's pledge to be a better father figured into this trip. It was a graduation gift to his daughter. They would be visiting an East

Coast finishing school that she might attend in autumn, and the three of them would be going to the futuristic World's Fair and to a couple of Broadway plays. Cobb wanted to see Raymond Massey in *Abe Lincoln in Illinois* and maybe Katharine Hepburn in *The Philadelphia Story.*

"I had twenty-five years of baseball, and I had all the baseball I wanted," he said. "I had to be away from my family six months a year. I hardly saw my children all summer and in the winter they were in school. . . . You're not living the life of a martyr when you play baseball but there's a lot of things you can't do."

During a rain delay, Cobb appeared in the Detroit locker room, a pack of reporters trailing him. The air crackled with electricity. He greeted the quiet veteran Charlie Gehringer, one of his batting protégés, a star second baseman, and the last remnant of Cobb's 1926 team. Flashbulbs popped and sizzled as Cobb gripped his hand and locked his eyes on him. Gehringer averted his stare. Gehringer sat on a stool, one shoe on, the other off. His right foot had been sliced on a slide by George Washington Case.

"You aren't going to quit, are you?" Cobb asked.

"No," said Gehringer, "I'm just going to get another pair of shoes."

As good as Gehringer was—and several writers ranked him among the best ever at his position—Cobb always felt Gehringer could have been better. With a bit more fire and exuberance, he might have been as fine as Eddie Collins, Cobb believed.

The team's freshest talent was Barney McCosky, and Jimmy Cobb didn't linger long before heading to the locker of the rookie center fielder, who had already been nicknamed Belting Barney by *The Sporting News.* "That kid of mine has made up his mind that McCosky is the greatest player in baseball," Cobb remarked. "He talks of him all the time."

The other Tigers—and not just the Southern boys, though there were plenty of them—gathered around Cobb. Tommy Jefferson Davis Bridges, a noted curveball pitcher from Tennessee, shook his hand. Fellow Georgian Rudy York, a hard drinker prone to charring mattresses with untended cigarettes, quizzed Cobb about his bird dogs. Bobo Newsom, the colorful ace of the staff, invited him to go hunting in South Carolina.

"I might do that, Buck," Cobb replied, his words as smooth and stretched as taffy.

Everyone wanted to see the Peach.

Slicker Coffman, a relief pitcher, presented himself.

"Sounds like an Alabama drawl," Cobb guessed.

"Sure is," he replied. "I'm from Veto, Alabama."

Cobb talked with Bing Miller about their days with Connie Mack's Philadelphia Athletics, and he gave a verbal boost to Red Kress, a struggling utility man who had begun his career as Cobb was ending his. "If you can hit like you did when you first got in this league, you're okay," said Cobb.

After the game, Cobb's homecoming continued at his suite in the Hotel Statler, looking out over busy Grand Circus Park. Cobb shared memories with seventy-year-old Bobby Lincoln Lowe, who had been a fifteen-year veteran when Cobb debuted in 1905. And then Cobb rang up a dozen friends, including an auto executive hospitalized in Ann Arbor.

"They've got three balls and two strikes on me," Don O'Keefe told him.

"Then you'll hit a home run," Cobb said.

Cobb seemed possessed of one mission: to reconnect with as many friends as time would allow. Perhaps it was just the distance. Or his long absence. He had been living near San Francisco since 1932 and hadn't been back to Detroit much since retiring in 1928. Or maybe a grander epiphany had struck him. Maybe he was coming to realize that the fierce competitiveness that had served him so well on the ball field had deprived him of an abundance of close friendships. Maybe that helped explain his demeanor. Mild, mellow, relaxed—in his playing days people rarely described him with such words. One pal even said he was now as "sedate as a school-marm."

Of all the acquaintances Cobb renewed during his twelve-hour stop in Detroit, it was the one with Alex Rivers that touched him most. Cobb had sent a friend to search for Rivers, whom he had known for thirty-three years, since 1908, when Rivers was toiling as a clubhouse man in New Orleans. Cobb took a liking to him immediately and invited him to Detroit.

"I would be happy if I could see him," Cobb said.

Moments before departing for his train, Cobb got his wish. Alex Rivers, a black man, appeared in his suite. The sight affected Cobb, and he grew emotional, patting Rivers warmly on the back.

"Mister Ty, you are still my man," said Rivers, who had worked as Cobb's personal locker-room assistant, chauffeur, and handyman and who had honored him by naming his firstborn Ty Cobb Rivers. They reminisced about days gone by, and caught up on family matters. After Cobb left baseball, Rivers had parlayed his baseball celebrity into a job as messenger for Detroit mayor Frank Murphy.

"Keep in touch with me, Alex," Cobb said. "You're still my man, too."

Emotions came easily to Cobb, and this journey promised to be nostalgic and sentimental. Cobb must have been flush with tender feelings when he left by train that evening. He had been celebrated in Detroit, and now he was heading toward Cooperstown to help dedicate the National Baseball Hall of Fame and to be officially enshrined as the first member of the game's most elite class. Life was grand.

2

Aboard the Centennial Special

I N NEW YORK CITY, BABE RUTH PREPARED TO BOARD THE CEN-
tennial Special, a string of thirteen Pullman cars that would
ferry dozens of current and former stars, dignitaries, and press and
radiomen to Cooperstown for the next day's festivities. Honus
Wagner and Walter Johnson were there. So were seventy-six-year-
old Connie Mack, Dizzy Dean, Eddie Collins, Casey Stengel, Commissioner Kenesaw Mountain Landis, and Postmaster General James
Farley, an FDR confidant and cabinet member. But of all the bright
figures aboard those railcars, not one could approach the popularity of the Babe. Four years removed from his playing days, Ruth still
evoked cheers and drew fans wherever he went.

For that very reason, Larry MacPhail, an innovator who had introduced night baseball to the majors, had signed him to a $15,000
contract as a Brooklyn Dodgers coach the previous June. Ruth had
hoped the position would lead to a managerial job. He wanted to
lead the Yankees, and if not the Yankees then another major-league

team. The Dodgers hoped Ruth would boost attendance; they got their wish. Attendance jumped by 38 percent at Ebbets Field. Fans came to see Ruth coach first base and hit a few balls in batting practice. "He knew what his position was and he was a very fine gentleman with it," said teammate Buddy Hassett. "He didn't try to put on airs." But the experiment lasted only through the season, after which Brooklyn fired manager Burleigh Grimes and replaced him with disagreeable Leo Durocher. Once again, Ruth, forty-four, was out of baseball.

Babe and Claire, his second wife, lived in a high-rise apartment at Riverside Drive and Eighty-ninth Street, several blocks west of Central Park. The Ruths loved the neighborhood. Over time, they resided in three apartments in the vicinity, raising Julia (Claire's daughter from her first marriage) and Dorothy (Babe's daughter from an extramarital fling during his first marriage). On occasion, when boys would bring his daughters home, Ruth would drop beer bottles from the apartment windows—his way of letting them know he was watching. In 1939, Julia was in her early twenties and Dorothy in her teens. Both would marry in 1940.

The spacious Ruth apartment included a household bar, where Babe entertained friends. Decorative beer kegs dotted the room, and framed photos and cartoons covered the walls. Cigar smoke scented the air. The place looked out over the Hudson River toward New Jersey—a view that Ruth had studied in near panic on the night of October 30, 1938, when the radio carried reports of an invasion by warriors from Mars.

"Get under the bed," yelled Ruth, peering out the window, unaware that the radio broadcast was Orson Welles's dramatization of *The War of the Worlds.* Ruth, like a million others, thought the planet was under attack.

Ruth lived comfortably. He didn't need money. Someone was always floating opportunities his way—endorsement deals, radio jobs, a chance to referee wrestling matches for $25,000 a year (hell no, he said). In March, he had helped teach at the Roy L. Doan Baseball School in Jackson, Mississippi, coaching kids and leading a youth ball team. (His boys beat a group from New Orleans in extra innings.) But if he couldn't manage in the major leagues, Ruth preferred most of all to spend his days on golf courses, a pastime he had discovered in his early years with Boston. He played all of the New York–area courses: St. Albans, Fresh Meadow, Leewood, Metropolis, Wykagyl, and more. Weeks before his journey to Cooperstown, he had helped a Long Island contingent reclaim the Louis B. Stoddard Bowl, a minor golf cup, at Apawamis by defeating squads from New Jersey and Westchester. It wasn't the Masters or the World Series, but it tickled Ruth, who on a good day could shoot in the mid-70s. Ruth was as crazy about golf as was his old adversary, Ty Cobb.

The Centennial Special chugged through the picturesque Susquehanna Valley and toward Cooperstown on Monday morning, the first passenger train the local tracks had borne in half a decade. The village had been preparing for the big event for months. A few residents probably had been anticipating it since 1907, when a gullible, patriotic-minded committee embraced sketchy testimony from one aged man and concluded that baseball had been invented in Cooperstown in 1839 by Abner Doubleday, who later became a hero of the Civil War. It had taken town boosters quite a while to figure out what specifically to do with this nugget. But in the 1920s, they built a ballpark, Doubleday Field. That was a start. The village's wealthy benefactor, an heir to the Singer Sewing Machine fortune, accumulated a few artifacts over time, and ever so slowly plans took shape for a museum and a hall of fame. When league officials finally lent their support, the idea blossomed. In 1936, baseball writers chose the first class of inductees: Cobb, Ruth, Honus Wagner, Christy Mathewson, and Walter Johnson. More followed in the years after, and now all of those chaps—the breathing ones, anyway—were coming to town for the sport's alleged one-hundredth birthday. They were accompanied by one or two current players from every team, who would compete in an all-star exhibition.

The Yankees sent Arndt Jorgens and George Selkirk. Fans no doubt would have preferred young Joe DiMaggio and veteran Lou Gehrig, but DiMaggio had just returned to the lineup after a lengthy injury, and Gehrig was heading to the Mayo Clinic to figure out what was wrong with his lethargic muscles. "I don't know what is the matter with me, if anything is," he said. "It doesn't seem logical to me I should have slipped back so swiftly."

Headquartering the National Baseball Hall of Fame in Cooperstown had not been without controversy. The choice spawned two camps of critics: those who recognized as dubious the claim that Doubleday fathered the sport, and those who ridiculed the wisdom of locating the shrine in an out-of-the-way hamlet. While most writers willingly winked at the notion that baseball began in Cooperstown, Joe Williams of the *New York World-Telegram,* one of the nation's best-known sports columnists, refused to abide "the myth of Cooperstown" or to play along with its "fine, rousing joke." He pointed out that no evidence existed that Doubleday had anything to do with baseball. Doubleday's prime connection was longtime friend A. G. Mills, a former National League president. Mills chaired the commission that gave Doubleday credit. That body's report, wrote Williams, "was about as factual as a misty love sonnet." Time would prove Williams right, but it wouldn't be as kind to another syndicated titan of the sports pages, the *Boston Post*'s Bill Cunningham, who predicted doom: "If you're alive fifty years from today and haven't anything more pressing to do, just for the hakes [hell] of it, take a ride over through the little town of Cooperstown, New York, and ask somebody whatever became of the baseball museum. . . ."

Cooperstown was beautiful. The village—amid a rolling evergreen landscape, nestled by forested hills and snug against the placid waters of Lake Otsego—had been pioneer territory. The town was founded in the late 1700s by the enterprising William Cooper, whose youngest son, James Fenimore, would become a renowned author, capturing the region in his Leatherstocking tales of Mohicans, trappers, settlers, and adventurous spirits. Even in 1939, the village qualified as quaint. Many buildings along Main Street and its intersecting roads predated the Civil War, and some were remnants of the century prior to it.

It was a dewy, glistening morning, the air fragrant and fresh, when the Centennial Special rolled into Cooperstown, its engine and cars dwarfing the kids running beside them. Hundreds of local folks swarmed the platform of the Delaware and Hudson station and flooded onto the tracks to greet and glimpse their distinguished guests. They spotted craggy-faced Commissioner Landis, with his shock of stubborn white hair, and the statuesque Connie Mack, looking as hard as a shaft of peanut brittle. Their faces were synonymous with the sport. But others, absent their uniforms, presented challenges. In full living color, they defied the gray-tone photos of the Sunday rotogravures and sepia-stocked Playball gum cards. Was that Lloyd Waner of the Pirates or Jimmie Wilson of the Reds or Billy Jurges of the Giants? Maybe Cookie Lavagetto of the Dodgers? In the days before television, even some ardent fans couldn't distinguish the Johnny Vander Meers from the Cecil Travises.

But everyone recognized one man. When Babe Ruth stepped into the cool morning air, he found himself enveloped in a wave of oohs and ahhs and cheers. There was no hiding or disguising his circus-bear presence. Uniform or not, they knew him. They knew his grinning round mug and his flattened nose. They knew his from-the-gut smile, his shoulder-shaking laugh, and his wavy dark hair and the way it crested on the right side just above his forehead. They knew the Bambino, and they loved him.

Ruth made himself comfortable in town, buying cigars at a Main Street store and summoning a barber to the colonial Cooper Inn for a private shave after finding the line too long at the tonsorial shop. Everywhere he went, he autographed scorecards and baseballs. "I didn't know," he thundered, "that there were so many people left who didn't have my John Hancock."

Cooperstown hummed as more trains arrived throughout the morning. Automobiles poured in from all points, bringing thousands of spectators, who would soon outnumber the village of two thousand by five to one. Hank Greenberg, one of several sluggers nominated as Ruth's successor, declined a ride to the hotel, walking instead, a pied piper surrounded by a band of children. Boston's Moe Berg, a brilliant linguist and mediocre catcher, filmed the merriment with his own moving-picture camera.

On park benches, over late breakfasts, at street corners, the immortals revisited dusty memories and gloried in their achievements. Cy Young laughed about a trick play he had pulled off nearly four decades earlier. Grover Cleveland Alexander, the beloved Old Pete whose alcoholism and epilepsy had sent his life spiraling downward, humbly shared stories about his current occupation as a sideshow attraction in a Forty-second Street flea circus. "I'm right next to the hootchie-cootchie dancers," he said. Outside the Mohican Garage, Walter Johnson recalled the time a police officer stopped Ty Cobb for speeding. "I made the mistake of ribbing Ty about it," Johnson confessed. Cobb pummeled Johnson's Senators the next day.

Where was Ty Cobb, anyway? All of the other inductees had arrived. "Where's Cobb?" Surely someone had asked the question. Maybe Johnson, Eddie Collins, Tris Speaker, or another of his friends. It would have crossed the mind of his last employer, Connie Mack, the noble man who had helped restore Cobb's dignity by signing him to a generous contract in 1927 in the wake of a gambling controversy. Certainly Mr. Mack would have wondered, Where is Tyrus?

3

The Challenge

Ty Cobb misses the formal portrait at the first induction
ceremony but ten honorees make it: (back row) Honus
Wagner, Pete Alexander, Tris Speaker, Nap Lajoie,
George Sisler, and Walter Johnson; (front row) Eddie
Collins, Babe Ruth, Connie Mack, and Cy Young.
NATIONAL BASEBALL HALL OF FAME LIBRARY, COOPERSTOWN, N.Y.

T HE OFFICIAL CEREMONIES BEGAN AT NOON UNDER A
bright sun on a dais in front of the red-bricked Hall of Fame,
directly across from the post office, which was selling commemo-
rative three-cent stamps. Schools and stores had closed early for the

gala, and Main Street was a sea of people, some sitting on roofs of vehicles that had been swallowed by the crowd, others securing shade beneath leafy maple trees. Baseball officials peppered the audience with brief speeches, interrupted occasionally by a small band's thumping renditions of "My Country 'Tis of Thee" and "Take Me Out to the Ball Game." The honorees were called one by one, beginning with the founders and continuing with the ballplayers, each name followed by a roll on the bass drum. The band played "Taps" for Wee Willie Keeler and Christy Mathewson, and then the living immortals got their introductions.

"Ty Cobb," said the announcer.

But when Cobb did not walk through the Hall of Fame doors, murmurs spread across the stage.

"He's not here," someone whispered.

"Ty Cobb has not arrived yet, folks," the announcer noted.

After an awkward pause, he continued.

"Honus Wagner . . ."

Wagner stepped forward amid the ovation, his legs so bowed that, according to one observer, you could roll a keg between them. Wagner recalled hitchhiking on a buggy to see Connie Mack play. "This is a wonderful little town or village or whatever we call it," he said. "It puts me in the mind of Sleepy Hollow."

Nap Lajoie and Cy Young followed, and then Walter Johnson and George Sisler, the latter having skipped his son's college graduation to be there. "This is about the proudest day of my life," said Eddie Collins. "I'd be proud to be the batboy for this team." Tris Speaker and Pete Alexander got their due, as well. All of them wore suits and ties, except the last one.

"Babe Ruth—the Bambino."

The audience erupted as Ruth wobbled to the podium in a Palm Beach blazer, his shirt collar wide open, his socks pushed to his ankles, his complexion a golfer's bronze.

"Thank you, ladies and gentlemen," he said, his resonant voice booming into the microphone. Ruth sounded like a radio detective, strong and manly, his words rich with inflection.

"Just because this celebration has been staged to pay tribute to the players of the past, I don't see why the kids of today shouldn't be included, too," Ruth said. "We started something years ago and right now the kids are keeping the ball rolling. They deserve all the help we can give them. Incidentally, this is sort of an anniversary for me also. Twenty-five years ago yesterday, I pitched my first major league baseball game for the Red Sox. . . ."

Ruth was playing to his audience, the fans, and they loved it. Couldn't the heads of baseball—and they were all there—see that he belonged in the game? Couldn't someone appreciate what he would bring to a team as a manager? Ruth might have become leader of the Detroit Tigers in 1934 if not for an impending trip to Honolulu. He likely assumed there would be other offers over the years. He dreamed of managing the Yankees. But the Yankees insisted that Ruth prove himself by getting his seasoning in the minor leagues. Anyone surveying the stage outside the Hall of Fame, however, could see the phoniness in that demand. Speaker, Collins, Johnson, and Sisler had all been given a chance. Even Young and Wagner had shepherded a few games. Every ex-player on the platform except for Ruth and Alexander had been given the opportunity to manage in the majors.

After the speeches had concluded and the red, white, and blue ribbons had been snipped and the official portrait snapped—minus Cobb—the crowd began to disperse, heading into the museum to admire the exhibits, to the post office for celebratory postcards proclaiming AMERICA PREFERS BASEBALLS TO CANNONBALLS, and to picnics, restaurant lunches, and a Democratic party clambake in honor of Postmaster Farley, who was plotting to challenge his friend Franklin Roosevelt for the party's presidential nomination. It was then that Ty Cobb emerged from the crowd and appeared on the podium, setting off a slight frenzy. Word spread quickly, and fans began flooding back to the stage. Cobb would tell everybody he had been delayed by a stomach ailment when in fact he had arrived late intentionally to avoid being photographed with Commissioner Landis (who as it turned out wasn't in the official picture anyway). Cobb had never forgotten how Landis embarrassed him during the 1926 gambling controversy.

Cobb's eyes welled with tears as he hugged a bony Connie Mack. Despite his reputation, which would grow more severe after his death, Cobb was admired by most of the men on the platform. Lajoie referred to him as "the cream of the crop." Wagner praised him, too. Walter Johnson and he had played poker with presidents. Collins and Speaker had hunted with him. Even Babe had shared drinks and meals with Ty.

When he spotted Cobb, Ruth offered his hand. "Hello, rookie," he said as they shook.

Later, at Doubleday Field before the all-star scrimmage, Cobb paid a price in humility for not having been formally introduced from the induction stage: Many failed to recognize him. It took convincing before the ticket taker would let him into the park, and then New York Giants groundskeeper Henry Fabian, a once-familiar acquaintance, responded with indifference when Cobb called his name.

"You don't know who I am, do you, Henry?" asked Cobb.

"No, I don't."

Moe Berg was stunned. He turned to Jimmy Cobb. "I'll bet that's the first time your dad ever had to introduce himself to anybody," Berg said.

"No, it isn't," responded Jimmy, who was not phased by the un-intentional slight. Jimmy had missed his dad's glory days. He knew his father best not as a baseball star but as a former star. And while the name "Ty Cobb" remained celebrated, the face that went with it was much less familiar. Cobb's appearance had never lent it-self to memorable caricature. But Ruth's features—bulbous nose, rounded cheeks, plump lips—certainly had. Cartoonists and writers seemed in constant competition to trump each other with their depictions of Ruth. (One reporter covering the induction de-scribed Ruth as "a weather-beaten, spade-nosed gargoyle with a crescent-moon grin.")

Such instant and intimate recognition eluded Cobb. Removed from the game, he had gradually become more anonymous, more ordinary. Whenever given the opportunity, Cobb advised veteran ballplayers to stay in the sport as long as possible.

The passing years hadn't impacted Ruth's standing. He had long ago surpassed Cobb in the popularity contest, and the size of his victory was increasing with time. Cobb realized he would never be more popular than Ruth. But he hoped to hold on to his claim as the better player.

At the ball field, Cobb was one of the few legends who didn't suit up for the scrimmage. He watched honorary managers Honus Wagner and Eddie Collins select teams from the crop of current stars. Collins took Lloyd Waner, Hank Greenberg, Mel Ott, Dizzy Dean, and others. But Wagner won with Arky Vaughan, Charlie Gehringer, Ducky Medwick, Lefty Grove, and more. The highlight came in the fifth when Babe Ruth pinch-hit for Danny MacFayden. Ruth took mighty swings but ended up walloping a high pop in front of the plate. The crowd howled for catcher Arndt Jorgens to drop the ball, but he snagged it instead, retiring Ruth.

Sometime that day—maybe during lunch at the Cooper Inn or in the dugout at the ball field or during the Cavalcade of Baseball with Mel Ott carrying the banner or in the gymnasium at Knox Girls' School, where the players put on their uniforms—Ty Cobb acted on a thought that had been tickling him for at least two years. In 1937, at a golf tournament in Oakland, California, mischievous PGA tour manager Fred Corcoran, a longtime baseball fan, had struck up a conversation with Cobb, who was competing as an amateur. Remembering the grand diamond battles of Cobb and Ruth, Corcoran challenged Cobb's ego. "Say, do you think you can beat Ruth at golf?" he asked. Cobb, sipping a highball, snapped, "I can beat Ruth at anything. . . . I'll play him any time, anywhere, and for any amount."

Nothing had come of that original conversation, but Cobb had never forgotten it. (Cobb didn't forget anything.) He liked the idea of meeting Ruth in golf, of taking their competition into a new arena, of giving the fans another taste of one of the spiciest rivalries the sporting world had ever seen. But it was more than that. He liked Ruth, too. Babe enlivened the whole affair at Cooperstown. Although Ruth hadn't gotten the most votes, he did get the most attention. Without him, the festivities would have had a gaping hole.

The celebration reminded Cobb that he liked being in Babe's company. He liked shooting the bull with him.

In the glowing goodwill and warm camaraderie of Cooperstown, Cobb decided that he really did want to meet Babe on the golf course. At some point, he slipped a note to Ruth challenging him to a contest on the fairways: I CAN BEAT YOU ANY DAY IN THE WEEK AND TWICE ON SUNDAY AT THE SCOTTISH GAME.

The prospect intrigued Ruth as well.

That evening on the train out of Cooperstown, plans and strategies began taking shape amid the reminiscing. Cobb and his two youngest would be staying in New York for a few days. He and Ruth would play a round then, they agreed.

Cobb had been out of the spotlight for years, and he savored the flood of attention. In a drawing car, he shared drinks with Walter Johnson as Moe Berg quizzed them.

"Ty, did you ever get into a batting slump?"

"Sure I did. Lots of times."

"What did you do when you were in a slump?"

"I hit the ball back to the pitcher," Cobb explained. "When you're in a batting slump it is because your stroke is off—and you're not going to get any base hits until you readjust it. That's all I tried to do. Just keep hitting the ball back swinging straight and short."

"I'll never forget something you said to me, Ty. I was catching for the White Sox one day and you made three hits the first three times up. The next time up, you were bearing down as hard as ever, and I said to you: 'What are you trying so hard for? You got three hits already.' And you looked down at me and said, 'That's how I get .380.' . . . How did you hit against Walter?"

"Not much," Cobb said.

"I wouldn't say that," Johnson interjected. "I did pretty well against you the first two years, but after that you pounded me just like you pounded everybody else."

"Here I've been talking about what I did to the Highlanders," said Cobb. "Walter, tell them what you did. How about those three games in a row you beat them—three days in a row."

"Four days," corrected Johnson.

And it went like that late into the night on the Pullman car, the scotch and whiskey flowing freely, the smoke hanging heavy in the air, Cobb talking to his pals, Ruth nearby laughing with his, their conversations blending and spilling into one another as the train clicked along the tracks and the lights of the passing towns flickered on the landscape.

Cobb had heard that Ruth—both men were left-handers in golf as well as baseball—possessed a wicked slice. "Babe," he called out, "what I want to play on is a course with long, narrow fairways."

Ruth had an answer to that. How about St. Albans? In proposing they play at the private Queens course, Ruth probably didn't let on that it was his favorite. St. Albans had its share of wide fairways, but Cobb wouldn't have known that golfing in California.

"Babe probably is a better golfer than I am but I think I can beat him," Cobb admitted quietly to a reporter. "I have to get him upset. That's the way I'll beat him. I know he slices pretty bad. . . . I bet he's worrying about that slice already.

"I like the Babe," he continued. "I always did."

Always? Hell, did Cobb think he'd get away with that one? His pals must have mustered all their self-restraint to keep their eyes from reeling back into their heads. Cobb always liked Ruth? Sure. And Ruth always liked Cobb. What about all their on-field confrontations, their skirmishes, the riot in Detroit? What about the years when the only words that passed between them were insults and vulgarities? What about the beanballs? And how about those times when they refused to autograph the same baseball or those games in which it seemed their sole motivation was to show up the other? Were those all signs of how much Ty liked Babe and Babe liked Ty?

"He's been a wonderful fellow," Cobb added, "and the greatest long-distance hitter baseball ever had. But I could always get him mad. I'll get him mad and beat him."

Ruth, meanwhile, was downing a substantial meal, assuring his companions that he would defeat Cobb.

"I'll fix him good," he said with a wink. "I always did."

"I'll get him so burned up," Cobb countered, "he'll shoot 90."

The train pulled into Manhattan about midnight. Ruth departed at 125th Street with golf on his mind. "I'll call you Wednesday and let you know the time," he told Cobb.

They made a joint appearance at the World's Fair on Tuesday, but the golf match failed to materialize. Cobb, who left little to chance, canceled, claiming he had business to handle. Perhaps he suspected a setup, or maybe he just wanted to spend the time with his children, as he had promised. A playful air had kissed the talk of their golf match. Friends had marveled at how both men lit up over the idea and how they acted like long-separated pals. Cobb and Ruth chums? Go figure. It hadn't always been that way.

Part II

The Baseball Years

4

1915: The Greatest Ever

Cobb with a load of lumber. ERNIE HARWELL COLLECTION, DETROIT PUBLIC LIBRARY

I T WAS AN AGE OF NICKNAMES, AND EVERY GOOD, COLORFUL, or noteworthy ballplayer had one. Reds and Rubes abounded: Red Ames, Rube Benton, Red Faber, Red Doolan, Rube Marquard, Rube Foster (when he wasn't being called Little Sureshot), Rube Robinson, Red McKee, Red Smith of Boston, and Red Smyth of Brooklyn. There were more Reds than you could shake a Stick or a Slick or a Slim at. There was a Tubby, too, and at some point a Blimp, a Fats, and a Jumbo. There were plenty of Docs: Ayers, Crandall, Lavan. There were Leftys and Whiteys, Rips, Bucks, and Kids, a regiment of Chiefs and Generals, a congregation of Deacons and Preachers, and a barnyard of Turkeys, Mules, Gooses, and Duckys.

St. Louis had Dots Miller and Pancha Snyder; Brooklyn, Wheezer Dell. In Chicago, Pants Rowland managed. Shoeless Joe Jackson, and in New York John "Little Napoleon" McGraw could bear witness to a baseball lifetime that included Pud Galvin, Bones Ely, Noodles Hahn, Charlie "Piano Legs" Hickman, Cozy Dolan, Cannonball Crane, Boileryard Clarke, Cupid Childs, Piggy Ward, Buzzy Wares, Chappy Charles, Oyster Burns, Shorty Fuller, and a whole mess of Peps, Pops, and Dads.

There had been a Spittin' Bill, a Wild Bill, and a Big Bill, and over the years a string of Joneses too difficult to keep up with—among them, Binky, Broadway, Bumpus, Cowboy, Jumping Jack, Sad Sam, and Angel Sleeves. Everyone, save for Homer Smoot and Fielder Jones, seemed to have a baseball nickname. Clifford Carlton Cravath had three of them: Cactus, Gavvy, and by 1915 Old Man. And let us not forget the stars: Christy "Big Six" Mathewson, Mordecai "Three Finger" Brown, Honus "the Flying Dutchman" Wagner, Tris "the Grey Eagle" Speaker ("Spoke," to friends), and Walter "Big Train" Johnson, who might have been immortalized as the Blond Shrapnel, had writer Grantland Rice had his way.

Detroit fielded Wahoo Sam Crawford, Hooks Dauss, Harry "the Giant Killer" Coveleski ("the Big Pole," if you preferred), Tioga George Burns, Chauncey Dubuc, Slim Lowdermilk, and Ralph "Pepper Boy" Young. And, of course, Ty Cobb, the Georgia Peach. Say that nickname anywhere in baseball and folks recognized it instantly. Once Cobb was anointed with it—and there were other possibilities like Tyrus the Terrible, the Georgia Phantom, and Damon Runyon's the Jewel of Georgia—it belonged to him alone.

In Boston, young George Herman Ruth—who played with Zip Collins, Duffy Lewis, Dutch Leonard, Doc Hoblitzel, Hick Cady, and Pinch Thomas on a team led by Rough Bill Carrigan—was increasingly being called Babe. But he didn't yet own the name. Babe Adams in Pittsburgh was more famous. Plus, there were Babes in Detroit and St. Louis and probably elsewhere.

~

When he first met Ruth, on a sparkling Michigan day in the spring of 1915, Ty Cobb reigned as the unconquerable king of baseball. He was the game's premier warrior, fiercest competitor, smartest hitter, most ingenious player, strongest drawing card, highest-paid performer, and brightest base-path terror and an inspiration to boys throughout the nation. He also was the owner of one finely shaped head, the beauty of which could not be easily appreciated, one admirer would lament, because of "the way he wears his cap on the ball field—down over his eyes."

Cobb was twenty-eight and beginning his eleventh season, once again the defending batting champion of the American League. The year prior, he had won his eighth straight title, though limited by a thumb injury sustained in a fight with an unrepentant butcher's assistant. The scuffle had occurred after Cobb stormed into a Detroit meat shop, demanding an apology on behalf of his wife, who claimed the store had sold her spoiled fish. Cobb's explosive temper set off a number of such unfortunate encounters, but it didn't keep baseball observers from trumpeting his talents.

"Cobb has no superior," said Walter Johnson, the much-loved pitcher. *Baseball Magazine* agreed. "There is no player on the diamond today, there has never been a player of any age, to equal Cobb in versatility, in all around excellence," its pulpy pages proclaimed. Tobacco manufacturers and bat makers and purveyors of products of all types clamored for Cobb's endorsement, and he obliged for a sum: THE WORLD'S GREATEST BALL PLAYER SMOKES THE

WORLD'S BEST TOBACCO . . . I DRINK COCA-COLA REGULARLY THROUGHOUT ALL SEASONS OF THE YEAR . . . TY COBB, SUPER-MAN, WORLD'S GREATEST BASEBALL PLAYER, TELLS HOW NUXATED IRON GAVE HIM NEW LIFE. Cobb had starred in a traveling stage production, had been celebrated in song ("They All Know Cobb" and "King of Clubs"), and would soon be show-cased in a feature film, *Somewhere in Georgia.* Presidents invited him for visits, newspapers paid him to share his expertise in guest columns, and newspaper poets, like John H. McGough, heralded his qualities in rhyme: ". . . A whip of steel, eye for the pill, en-durance, forcsight, strength, and skill / A perfect player, nobly planned, to belt the bulb, to beat the band . . ."

On a sun-kissed May 11 afternoon in Detroit, as latecomers fil-tered in to Navin Field from the streetcars along Michigan and Trumbull avenues, the sprite Donie Bush stirred the crowd by opening the first inning with a single. Manager Hughie Jennings, a once-sharp leader now dimming in the grip of alcoholism, stood along the first-base line, where he often raised his fists and let loose his familiar rally cry. "Ee-yah!" Jennings would call, and in-evitably fans would parrot him: "Ee-yah! Ee-yah!"

After Oscar Vitt, a snazzy dresser and a survivor of the San Fran-cisco earthquake, moved Bush to second, the on-field announcer bellowed the name of the next hitter through his megaphone. As if Ty Cobb needed any introduction. As if they didn't know him instantly, didn't realize who batted third, didn't recognize him twirling three bats as he strutted to the plate—a routine that served two purposes: to lighten his swing and to intimidate the pitcher, on this day a cocky kid from Baltimore.

The mind's eye pictures such moments in the gray palette of the black-and-white photos of the era. But the scene burst with color: the yellow slat seats of three-year-old Navin Field, the forest green fence in center, the red-banded socks tight around George Herman Ruth's muscular calves, the blue Old English *D* across Cobb's heart, the kaleidoscopic panels advertising taxi services and chewing to-baccos and shaving creams along the outfield walls, the sunlit sky streaked with streams of smoke from nearby stacks, the brick church towers rising beyond home plate along Michigan Avenue, the speckled fabric of the audience, some 4,385 fans, mostly men, their heads topped in checked caps, brown derbies, beige panama hats, and an occasional burgundy bowler.

Cobb nailed his eyes on the pitcher, a platter-faced, gray-flanneled twenty-year-old. Though roughly Cobb's size, George Ruth wore a broader build, with wide shoulders and a globe of a head that balanced precariously on his neck. He looked like a grown street urchin, not a Herculean figure destined to alter the history of the game. The left-hander was making only his fourth start in his first full season. To Cobb, he was just another kid, a prospect who might fizzle like wet fireworks.

Ty Cobb and George Ruth were contrasts in almost every way. One sprung from the red clay of the rural South, the other from the seaside grit of the urban Northeast. One was Baptist, the other Catholic. One came from a family deeply rooted on the continent, the other from immigrant grandparents. One benefited from a comfortable childhood; the other suffered poverty. Cobb's six-two, college-educated father, now dead, savored history and science; could read Greek and Latin; served as a mayor, a state senator, and a school superintendent; and expected great achievements from Tyrus in medicine, law, or military service. George Herman Ruth Jr. grew up around seedy saloons run by a roughneck, nearly illiterate father who gave him his own name and not much else. With his miniscule mother plagued by worries, the younger Ruth spent years in a parochial industrial school for orphans, delinquents, and neglected children. Ruth was virtually abandoned by parents incapable of raising him. He was deemed incorrigible.

Cobb could not have imagined at that moment that George Ruth would become his primary rival, transform the nature of baseball, and challenge him for eternal glory. What he did know was that Donie Bush was on second base waiting to score. Gripping his bone-burnished ash bat inches above the knob and with his hands spread apart, Cobb faked a bunt that unsettled a rookie third baseman and allowed Bush to steal third. Cobb followed with a single to Tris Speaker in center, and the Tigers were on their way.

After Sam Crawford popped to strong-armed Duffy Lewis in

left, Cobb stunned the Red Sox by tagging and taking second. He should have been an easy out, but the ball escaped a flustered fielder. Cobb had that effect on opponents. He made them anxious. He rattled them like maracas.

In the third, Cobb singled again and later got a free base when Ruth turned wild and walked a trio of batters. Ruth forced in a run, thus ending his day. It was an unimpressive outing, not the kind that would endear him to manager Bill Carrigan and certainly not of a caliber to trouble the great Tyrus. But Ruth did provide a glimpse of something more pleasing: his hitting prowess. Ruth pounded a double off the scoreboard, giving the Red Sox their only run. Days earlier, he had smacked a home run at the Polo Grounds. Veteran reporters were beginning to murmur about the mounds-man who could handle a bat. "Ruth seems to be considerable of a hitter," noted Detroit journalist E. A. Batchelor. But no one had a clue just how "considerable" he would become.

Soon, Boston would begin to use Ruth in occasional pinch-hit appearances.

~

Ty Cobb could clout long balls, too. But his came in golf, not baseball. Raised in Royston, Georgia, not far from Augusta, on a landscape scented with magnolias, Ty Cobb became smitten by the Scottish game early in his career. Augusta rated as a golf resort long before Bobby Jones began to imagine the dream course that would make the town internationally famous. Since the turn of the century, the city had been a vacation spot, with luxurious hotels, grand courses, and irresistible winter weather. The amenities drew privileged folks south. By age twenty-three, Cobb was turning up regularly on the fairways of the Augusta Country Club and learning to putt on the hard-packed, sand-covered surfaces that preceded grass greens. President William Howard Taft was a regular as well, with a wide swing that accommodated his substantial belly. After Cobb moved his young family to Augusta, the temptation to play a round never left him.

Cobb had a stormy relationship with golf. He loved the sport, as did many star ballplayers, including Christy Mathewson and Chief Bender. And he also hated it. In the spring of 1913, he boasted of playing thirty-six holes a day during the off-season. "That gives you plenty of walking and exercises the leg muscles," he said. But the relationship curdled months later when he suspected the game was affecting his play on the ball field. Cobb let nothing come between him and success on the diamond. He ate two meals a day, convinced it gave him just the right amount of energy. During winter, he hunted with fitted weights in his shoes to keep his legs limber. He limited his trips to movie houses, fearing that watching films in a dark room might be harmful to his eyes. Coffee with cream or sugar was fine, but not coffee with both cream and sugar. If Cobb got it in his mind that something was hindering his performance, he steered clear of it. Cobb won the batting title comfortably in 1913, but his average dropped nineteen points—to .390. He blamed golf and vowed to avoid it during the season. But its lure proved too strong, and soon he was back on the fairways. But then, two years later, he again accused the sport of impeding his batting eye and upsetting his swing. He was hitting over .400 at the time. "I'll have to quit golf," he announced. "I will play one more match, in Washington, and then I am through until after the season ends in October." Just one more game. One more, that's all.

On August 29, 1915, Cobb watched in wonder at Navin Field as three golfers put on a demonstration after the fifth inning. Amateur champion Francis Ouimet, Max Marston, and Jesse Guilford took turns driving balls from home plate over the center-field fence and onto the roofs of the homes beyond. No batter had ever hit a baseball to that region—yet. Cobb watched with more than casual interest. But when spectators called for him to give it a try, he declined. Cobb knew his limits.

The day after the ballpark exhibition, Cobb followed Guilford, Ouimet, Jerome Travers, Chick Evans, and others as they competed in the final qualifying round for the U.S. Golf Association crown. He admired their play; the feeling was mutual. "Golf is a funny game," said Ouimet. "If Ty Cobb played golf instead of baseball and if he opposed me in a match and I had him ten up and ten to play, I would not feel safe. As a matter of fact, I would hate to oppose Cobb more than any man that I have met in golf. His determination, that indomitable spirit, and his never-beaten attitude would make him a most dangerous opponent anywhere and at any time. A man with that determination could do most anything in sport."

Cobb's devotion to baseball limited the time and attention he could give his golf game. He wouldn't begin entering official competitions for two decades, and it would take another few years after that before Cobb would engage in his most famous golf match.

5

In Pursuit of Immortality

Tris Speaker and Ty Cobb. ERNIE HARWELL COLLECTION,
DETROIT PUBLIC LIBRARY

~

THE RED SOX BATTLED THE TIGERS FOR FIRST PLACE
throughout the 1915 season, with Tris Speaker leading on
offense and Ruth, Rube Foster, Ernie Shore, Joe Wood, and Dutch

Leonard sharing the glory on the mound. The Boston clubhouse, like others, was fractured by religious and regional differences: Catholics versus Protestants (or KCs versus Masons, as some framed it), Southerners versus Northerners, Confederates versus Yankees. The Civil War had ended a half century earlier, but some players had grandfathers who had fought. The divisions remained real and raw, particularly on the Southern side.

Speaker and Joe Wood, from Texas and Missouri respectively, had become tight friends early in their careers. Both were descended from cowboy stock and freely vocalized their profuse prejudices. They roomed together throughout Wood's career. They were confirmed stars, though Wood had fallen off since his impeccable 34-5 pitching performance in 1912. Wood disliked Babe Ruth. They were enemies, and any adversary of Wood was, by extension, an adversary of Speaker. In their eyes, Ruth had several glaring faults: He was coarse, he was cocky, and he was a Catholic convert.

Away from the team, Speaker's closest pals included Ty Cobb, a Masonic brother. They arrived in the majors within years of each other and frequently found themselves among the league leaders in hitting, with Speaker almost always behind Cobb—though Speaker was the better fielder, as everyone quickly acknowledged. Before Boston-Detroit games, the two often chatted near the batting cage or off to the side, sometimes sitting on milk crates with bats in hand. Speaker certainly shared his distaste for Ruth, and likely repeated the tale of Ruth's uncouth postgame habit of taking a shower and then stepping back into the same sweaty underwear, a practice for which he was unmercifully teased. For Cobb, baseball amounted to psychological warfare, and this—excuse the imagery—juicy rag provided him much ammunition. On the field, when Ruth walked near him, Cobb liked to remark about the arrival of a strong odor, a shorthand reference to the humiliating practice. Around the cage, while Ruth took batting practice, Cobb would always ask other players, "What smells?"

In mid-September, the Detroit club headed to Fenway Park for the final showdown between the teams. Fenway, like Navin Field, was one of a new breed of concrete-and-steel ballparks. Nestled against Lansdowne Street, just beyond the railroad tracks, Fenway's left field then featured a twenty-five-foot wall covered with advertising panels. The turf, sloping up toward the fence, was nicknamed Duffy's Cliff for Duffy Lewis, who patrolled it.

The Tigers were two games out of first. Earlier in Detroit, led by Cobb, they had given the Red Sox a rough time. Five times in one contest, Cobb—suspecting that Ernie Shore was scuffing the ball with emery paper—insisted the umpire inspect the ball. Unsatisfied, Cobb even went to the Boston dugout to register his suspicions with Sox manager Carrigan. Boston players caught Cobb scanning the ground for clues. Cobb also contributed mightily to the profane bench jockeying, a fact not lost on the partisan Boston press.

"Tyrus Cobb was the leader at all times, egging the crowd on and bothering the Boston men in every way, as well as intimidating the umpires," reported *The Boston Globe*. "If the Tigers can win by clean methods, such as the Red Sox always use, they will receive the praise of the good baseball sports, but they should not have it all their own way on their own grounds and expect the Boston fans to treat them with the consideration due players who use only fair methods."

Writers considered it their privilege to rally local fans. The notion that sports reporters should be objective witnesses had yet to take hold. "A little help from the fans will go a long way toward inspiring the men," added the *Herald*. And the *Post:* "It is up to Boston fans to root as they have never rooted before. Concerted, consistent, and persistent rooting is the order of the day. Start in at the beginning of the game. Don't wait until the seventh. And keep it up throughout the whole series."

Boston was wilting amid a torrid heat wave that had claimed lives, closed schools, and dropped draft horses to the scorching pavement. The suffocating heat even prompted two city residents to seek relief by suicide. One jumped from a window and fell to her death; another leaped into the Charles River. At Fenway, a clubhouse worker stood before the dugout bench, fanning players with a sheet of canvas. Still, more than twenty-one thousand fans turned out for the midweek contest. All seats, save those in the sun-drenched bleachers, were sold. It promised to be a lively, crucial series, and Cobb's presence helped the gate, as always. His drawing power made Frank Navin the envy of other team owners. A year prior, Connie Mack had been asked why his first-place Athletics were being outdrawn on the road three-to-one by fourth-place Detroit. "You'll find the answer in center field," he said, pointing his scorecard at Cobb.

The Bostonians booed Cobb from the beginning. But it only inspired him. He drove in the first run and scored the second. When they jeered him in his next at bat, he tipped his cap. The Tigers handled the Sox easily. Ruth watched from the bench as the jabbering Jungaleers took a commanding 5–1 lead into the eighth. By then, the Sox had gotten their fill of Cobb's antics.

Feisty Carl Mays, mastering his underhand delivery, opened the inning by retaliating against Cobb with two pitches aimed at his unprotected head. Cobb grew furious. On the third pitch, Cobb swung and missed and let his bat sail toward Mays on the mound, which riled the home-team boosters. Mays and Cobb traded insults and challenges. But umpires Bill Dinneen and Dick Nallin prevented a fight. Boston fans were livid. It was blistering hot, the stands were rich with the stench of cigars and body odor, and their team was losing. They wanted revenge. Mays blazed a third ball at Cobb. It nicked Cobb's elbow, but he took first peacefully. Cobb stole second on the next pitch, moved to third on a sacrifice, and scored on a grounder, plowing into catcher Pinch Thomas on a close play. When the call went his way, Cobb looked to the stands and grinned.

Throughout the eighth and ninth innings, Boston fans showered Cobb with taunts, tonic bottles, rocks, and pieces of coal as he stood in center field. A bit of restraint might have been helpful. Instead, Cobb, conspicuous as a cardinal in snow, pointed to the scoreboard, which showed his team ahead 6–1. Cobb's gesture made the fans even angrier. The game ended when Larry Gardner lofted a fly to center. As Cobb snagged the last out, furious fans hurdled the fences and charged toward him. Hundreds tightened around him like a noose. But Cobb did not flee.

Cobb hadn't run in Philadelphia years before when snipers were said to be targeting him after a spiking incident involving Home Run Baker, and he wouldn't run now. "You can't let crowd psychology lick you," he would say. "If a crowd thinks you are afraid, they'll do anything." He walked coolly toward the infield. Soon, he was a lone figure in a knotting mass of animosity. He pushed unhurriedly through the crowd toward second base. He was jostled and elbowed but refused to dash for the dugout. From the stands, thousands more watched him glide across the field, the calm eye in a swirling storm. One fan hurled a bottle over the crowd. It pegged Cobb on the shoulder. Cobb turned to confront the man. As the mob grew bolder, baton-wielding police officers rushed to Cobb's side, along with members of the Detroit club. It took several moments before he could be escorted from the field. On his way to the clubhouse, Cobb had words for the men in the press box, blaming them for antagonizing the spectators. Long after the game, troublemakers remained outside the gates, fidgeting for a fight. Officers took Cobb to his hotel.

If nothing else, the incident should have impressed upon George Herman Ruth one fact: When challenged, Ty Cobb did not back down.

For the next three games, police feared a riot and fielded a strong deterring presence at Fenway. The stands were jammed as if it were the World Series. Scalped tickets sold for up to eight dollars apiece, and spectators flooded into the roped overflow sections of the outfield. Even Woodrow Wilson's vice president, Thomas Marshall, witnessed a game.

The famed Royal Rooters, hundreds strong, marched onto the diamond from center field, singing their anthem, "Tessie," and a newer song, "Dublin Bay." The Red Sox responded by sweeping the Tigers: 7–2 on Friday, in what would have been a shutout if not for Cobb's ninth-inning home run; 1–0 in a twelve-inning contest on Saturday; and 3–2 in the Sunday finale, pitched by George "Babe" Ruth.

The three-game streak crushed Cobb's World Series hopes. The

Tigers finished two and a half games behind Boston, the closest they had come since taking the pennant six years earlier. Cobb captured his ninth straight batting title and led the league in hits, runs, and total bases. He also set a new record, with ninety-six stolen bases. But the Red Sox and Ruth got the real prize: the championship.

And anyone who thought Cobb didn't notice simply didn't know Cobb. Nothing in baseball escaped his attention, and nothing bothered him more than his lack of a world championship. Cobb's critics liked to spotlight that void in his list of accomplishments. The "greatest player ever," they pointed out, had never won the world title. He had appeared in three championship series, 1907 to 1909, and each time his team had lost. In the last one, veteran star Honus Wagner had shown up the raw, twenty-two-year-old Cobb.

The Sox and Ruth were world champions. Damn right Cobb noticed.

~

During the off-season, Ferdinand Lane of *Baseball Magazine* journeyed to Augusta by train to spend a day with Cobb. A cold evening had frosted the morning landscape near Cobb's Williams Street home. Lane, who postponed a career in biology to cover baseball, found the ballplayer in a reflective mood, pondering his place in the annals.

"Baseball is a new game and you don't read in history of any men who became immortal by becoming great players," Cobb said. "But any bid to anything out of the ordinary in my own case will be won on the diamond or not at all. And I know enough of fame on the diamond to realize that it lasts just as long as the ability is there to win it. I shall have my day like all the rest, and whatever I have done will be forgotten just as other records have been forgotten before."

Cobb's words may have been tinged with false modesty, but they didn't hide his desire to be more than merely remembered.

Not that anyone would soon be forgetting Ty Cobb, not with nine consecutive titles. No other player, after all, had come close. Honus Wagner's eight crowns were scattered over a span of twelve seasons, and Cobb was still relatively young and absolutely driven.

Cobb rarely spoke of what motivated him, but the shooting death of his father by his mother burned his psyche. William Herschel Cobb was killed—accidentally, a jury decided—weeks before Ty ascended to the American League. He had initially advised his son against a career in baseball but then encouraged him with one bit of advice: Don't come home a failure.

Cobb didn't want simply to be remembered; he wanted to be remembered as the best. "I always was ambitious, I guess," Cobb told Lane. "I used to think that if I were ever able to make a record on the diamond I would be satisfied. But people have been good enough to claim I have done no less and I am not satisfied."

6

A Green Pea

George Herman Ruth prepares for his Navin Field
debut. ERNIE HARWELL COLLECTION, DETROIT PUBLIC LIBRARY

~

F OR ALL THE PROMISE HE HAD SHOWN WINNING EIGHTEEN
games, Babe Ruth wasn't considered the star of the Red Sox
in the spring of 1916. There were, for starters, Tris Speaker, Harry

Hooper, and Duffy Lewis, baseball's Golden Outfield. Speaker would soon be sent to Cleveland, but Lewis and Hooper, the humble, college-educated gentleman, would remain. Ruth couldn't even be considered the top pitcher in Boston. Ernie Shore, Dutch Leonard, or Rube Foster would be as likely to claim the honor. (Speaker's buddy Joe Wood was a financial holdout.) But fortunes changed quickly in March and April, and Ruth pitched well enough to secure the opening-day assignment.

Barely two years free from the confines of St. Mary's Industrial School and the watchful eyes of the Xaverian Brothers who ran the place, Babe Ruth savored his status and independence and enjoyed much of what had been prohibited, discouraged, or unavailable at the institution: women, beer, gambling, gluttony, and silk shirts. He was twenty-one and flush with money, freedom, and the public acclaim that came from playing professional ball. Ruth spent as if there would always be more. "He was a green pea," Harry Hooper recalled. In July 1914, Ruth had met Helen Woodford, a young waitress. They married within three months. It wasn't long, however, before he found himself hunting for the company of other women. Among ballplayers, he certainly wasn't alone in that quest.

Ruth got along well with most teammates. Though gruff, crude, brash, and uneducated, he had an outgoing, roughhousing, one-of-the-gang personality that fit with the all-male atmosphere of the locker room and the ball field. He possessed traits that Ty Cobb lacked, among them an ability to laugh about the game and a willingness to engage in the good-natured, back-and-forth teasing of teammates. But he did not have Cobb's sophistication. Cobb was articulate and socially polished; he liked to read; and he enjoyed classical music, once turning up late for a ball game in New York after becoming enthralled at a pipe organ concert in Manhattan's Aeolian Hall (where in 1924 George Gershwin would debut *Rhapsody in Blue*).

If Ruth had somehow escaped Cobb's competitive gaze in 1915—a suggestion bordering on fantasy, given Cobb's ability to register variations in the eyebrow movements of pitchers—he certainly drew it in the next two seasons.

Ruth shut out the Tigers in May, July, and August of 1916. On September 21, he was going for a fourth shutout. Cobb—recently depicted chatting with fans in his wool team cardigan in a sketch on the cover of a national magazine—faced Ruth with the Tigers behind in the seventh inning. Babe wasted no pitches. He promptly struck out Cobb. It was a noteworthy achievement because Cobb averaged only one strikeout every four games or so. But the way it happened made it even more memorable. Ruth disposed of Cobb with embarrassing ease. He scorched three straight strikes past him. Pitchers rarely handled Cobb in such a humiliating fashion. Ruth did the same to Bobby Veach. Six pitches, two outs.

And then on May 11, 1917, Ruth showed up Cobb again. As America prepared to send its young men to join the war against Germany and its allies, Babe Ruth was storming through the ranks of the American League. By the time he reached Detroit in May, the twenty-three-year-old had won six straight and was undefeated. On a frigid Friday, fans in overcoats clustered in the stands to watch him work. All afternoon, Ruth was stingy with hits.

The Tigers were down 2–1 in the ninth when Cobb tossed aside two of his three bats and approached the plate with one out. Catcalls thundered from the Boston bench, reminding him that he had fanned earlier. But Cobb wasn't easily fazed. He dropped a bunt and beat the throw for a single. On the next play, Veach grounded to the left side of the infield, and Cobb moved to second. Suddenly, noticing that both the third baseman and short-stop were out of position, Cobb raced toward third, gambling that Ruth—whose intelligence Cobb found deficient—wouldn't cover the open base. It was the kind of daring, alert play that had earned Cobb his reputation. But Ruth surprised him. Babe raced for third, snagged the throw, and pinned Cobb, completing a rally-ending double play. Ruth "tagged Ty so viciously in the ribs that the Georgian could not get up for a couple of minutes," reported the *Boston Post.*

When Harry Heilmann—who once rescued a drowning driver en route to a ball game—followed with a double, on which Cobb would have scored from second, incensed fans questioned Cobb's brazen base running. Detroit journalists defended Cobb. "He made a good play that went wrong . . . ," said Joe Jackson of *The Detroit News.* "Instead of blaming Cobb, the thing to do is to give the southpaw credit for both quick thinking and also for good mechanical execution." Harold Wilcox of the *Detroit Times* agreed, noting that Ruth defied rumors that "his head is made of the stuff with which Wayne County frequently paves its highways."

Ruth was not done sticking it to Cobb.

On a chilly, threatening July 11 Wednesday, he again took the mound in Detroit, hoping for his first victory since being suspended June 24 for slugging umpire Brick Owens. Aided by the darkened sky, Ruth stymied Tiger hitters. His curves broke sharply, and his fastballs roared over the plate. In the third, he struck out Cobb with a runner in scoring position. Ruth was pitching impressively. One imagines Cobb's tongue feverishly flicking distractions at Babe, trying to derail him. "What smells? . . . What smells?" In the eighth, Donie Bush got an infield single and broke up his no-hitter. Cobb came to bat again. This time, one of Ruth's pitches conveniently found Cobb's rib cage.

By now, Ty Cobb was well aware of Babe Ruth.

After the regular season, Ruth and Cobb faced each other again in an all-star memorial benefit for the Silver King, the late, gray-haired *Boston Globe* sports editor Tim Murnane. A treasured figure in baseball and Beantown, Murnane, sixty-five, had collapsed and died months earlier in the lobby of the Schubert Theater. On September 27, seventeen thousand fans came out to Fenway to pay tribute to him and to be entertained by baseball's elite players. The friendly, circuslike scrimmage, pitting the Red Sox against a team selected by Connie Mack, offered a sweet diversion from the somberness of world war.

Boxer John L. Sullivan coached first base. Fanny Brice sold scorecards. Will Rogers rode a horse across the field at full speed while whirling a fluid lasso above his head. In one demonstration, he snared Cobb as Ty trotted past on horseback. An infield of Stuffy McInnis, Ray Chapman, Rabbit Maranville, and Buck Weaver—with an average height of five-foot-nine—dazzled the crowd with a rapid-fire, fast-practice exhibition. Players competed in contests. Mike McNally proved quickest, running to first base in three and two-fifths seconds. Dutch Leonard won for accuracy, throwing a ball from home plate into a barrel at second base. Shoeless Joe Jackson took distance honors, hurling a ball 396 feet.

In the pregame introductions, Cobb and Walter Johnson got more applause than anyone but the hometown players. On the field, fans marveled at the sight of "the $100,000 Outfield" of Cobb, Jackson, and Tris Speaker. In a nod to each other's abilities, they rotated in right, center, and left every inning. Babe Ruth started on the mound for Boston and stymied the opposing lineup. He allowed only three hits, including a weak single by Cobb.

Over the 1916 and 1917 seasons combined, Ruth had pitched stunningly well, winning forty-seven games and allowing fewer than two runs per nine innings. But he also pounded out five home runs and hit for an average higher than most of his teammates. He had a lusty swing, and he liked to bat. "It must be great for a club to have a pitcher that can hit like Ruth," remarked one Detroit reporter. Ruth was coming to the conclusion that he no longer wanted to be just a pitcher.

At the Tim Murnane benefit, he and the Sox prevailed 2–0. It was a colorful afternoon filled with good fun. But the biggest single thrill for some at Fenway wasn't Boston's victory. It was the fungo contest, which Ruth won by pounding a ball farther than anyone else—402 feet. It was just a hint of what was to come.

7

How Much Longer?

Ty Cobb with son Ty Junior. ERNIE HARWELL COLLECTION,
DETROIT PUBLIC LIBRARY

F ANTASTICAL TRADE RUMORS SWIRLED AROUND TY COBB
almost every season. St. Louis reportedly offered George
Sisler in a one-for-one deal, and the Yankees were rumored to have
put up big money for the Peach. Another party lobbied to see
Tyrus dealt straight up for Walter Johnson. Cobb remained baseball's dominant figure. But for how many more years?

A version of that question got asked every spring and several
times throughout the season. In 1916, when Cobb started slowly, a
Detroit paper ran an illustration showing how Cobb had lost a
step. When he failed to capture a tenth straight batting title that

year, some saw it as an ominous sign—the beginning of the end. Cobb is slipping, they said. Though he reclaimed the title in 1917, besting runner-up Sisler by thirty points, the issue still surfaced the following spring. Cobb "cannot retain his best form and unquestionable supremacy very much longer," contended *The Sporting News*. Months later, the *St. Louis Post-Dispatch* figured, "It is a gamble from now on how much longer Ty will last as a major leaguer."

He was only thirty-one, but baseball writers were already impatiently searching for his successor, for a fresh face. Would it be Sisler in St. Louis? Or Rogers Hornsby? Or Edd Roush? Or maybe Ruth, who was lighting up the crowds in Boston every now and again? By season's end, some would have their answer.

Babe Ruth tagged three home runs in early May 1918 and got a load of attention for it. The quick start delighted many, but not Cobb. In a May 18 contest, as the Sox were pursuing a sweep of the Tigers, Cobb engaged the Boston fans behind the dugout in a critique of Ruth's hitting abilities. Cobb belittled Ruth, attributing his performance to mere luck. The words irritated Ruth. In the sixth inning, Ruth drove a ball past Cobb and off the wall in center. It should have been a triple, but Ruth cruised satisfyingly into second, which put him physically close to Cobb. As the play ended, Ruth turned to Cobb and laughed.

Ruth was enjoying his success at the plate, and now wanted to hit regularly. He pressed the issue with Ed Barrow, Boston's new manager, but Barrow resisted. A former bare-knuckled boxer, he was no pushover and could be as stubborn as Ruth, whom he needed on the mound. Besides, if he converted one of the game's best left-handers into an outfielder and the experiment failed, he would be marked forever, ridiculed for pulling a boner of mammoth proportions, probably laughed right out of the game.

Ruth asked teammate Harry Hooper to intervene on his behalf. Hooper, Everett Scott, and Heinie Wagner, who was assigned to room with and watch over the freewheeling Ruth, served Barrow as an informal advisory committee. "Play him in the outfield so he can hit every day," Hooper recommended. "You know they come out when Ruth pitches, but they come out to see him hit. Play him in the outfield and they can see him hit every day." With or without Hooper's influence, it was inevitable that Barrow would test the idea.

In an early June series against Detroit, Ruth gave everyone— Barrow, Cobb, teammates, fans—a glimpse of the possibilities. Cobb had injured his shoulder after a nasty tumble on a diving catch and was limited to pinch-hitting, heckling, and arguing with irritable Carl Mays. ("Yes, you'd better go over there," taunted Mays in the first game as Hughie Jennings called Cobb to the dugout and away from an altercation.) In the second contest, Ruth, who had struck out earlier on three voracious swings, swatted a long home run to right field. He hit another the day after, and the next afternoon recorded his third. Three home runs in three games.

But not everyone was impressed.

~

In an era dominated by Baseball Science—and by its finest practitioner, Ty Cobb—no one made heroes of home-run hitters. Critics viewed them as selfish and unproductive, pursuing their individual triumphs at the expense of the team's success. Up-and-coming players sought to emulate Cobb's methods. They aspired to slap, slash, and speed their way around the bases like he did. In the mid-1910s, books and magazines espoused Cobb's refined techniques. He was the authority, and he could talk for hours about how to read opponents, how to deceive and outthink them, how to draw players out of position and then take advantage through bunts and fake bunts and place hitting and base stealing. That was how the game was played: one run at a time.

Cobb advocated chopping at the ball. Take short, sharp swings, he said. Avoid the long cuts. "The only excuse for taking a big swing is to throw the infielders off their guard," he said.

No one had ever paid much attention to out-of-the-park home runs—a fact that riled power hitters like Gavvy Cravath of Philadelphia. From 1913 to 1917, Cravath topped the National League in home runs four out of five seasons. But neither fame nor money

accompanied the achievement. The handsome contracts went to
the men with towering batting averages, and those averages, Cravath pointed out, didn't treat singles any differently than doubles,
triples, or home runs.

Admitting that his suggestion might be dismissed as "the crab-
bing of an old fossil," Cravath, thirty-seven, proposed—while en
route to his fifth title—that baseball create a formula that would
give extra weight to extra-base hits. "For forty years," he complained, "the records have been all in favor of the scratch hitter.
Let's be fair about this thing and give credit to the man with the
wallop, the man who delivers the goods, the man who really bats
his innings."

Let's also give him the car, he was probably thinking. It peeved
Cravath that in 1913, when he topped the league in home runs,
hits, and runs driven in, Jake Daubert of sixth-place Brooklyn won
the Chalmers Award as most valuable player. Cravath knocked in
seventy-six more runs than Daubert, beat him in every offensive
category except batting average, where he trailed by nine points,
and still finished second in the balloting. Daubert got a snazzy new
Chalmers roadster; Cravath, maybe a wreath of flowers.

When Ruth crushed eight home runs in June, raising his total to
eleven, his reputation—and that of the home run—inflated faster
than a carnival balloon. Purists might not care for the long ball, but
almost everyone else enjoyed it. Ruth split his time between pitching and playing outfield (and occasionally first). Although performing acceptably in both capacities, he wanted desperately to retire
from the mound. Ed Barrow and Ruth clashed repeatedly on the
subject. The conflict festered into July until, finally, Ruth quit the
team in protest. His walkout lasted only a few days.

Upon returning, Ruth clobbered four doubles and five triples
during a seven-game stretch. Though he collected no more home
runs in the war-shortened season, he did, in just 317 at bats, tie
Tilly Walker of Philadelphia for the league title with eleven.

The Red Sox won the pennant and then the World Series, with
Ruth contributing on the mound and at the plate. Admirers proclaimed him the Sensation. The Babe was, admitted a Detroit paper,

"a star of the first magnitude." Said another scribe, "Ruth is just getting into the best of his stride."

~

America was consumed by a world war that was calling its sons overseas. By the autumn of 1918, ballplayers were fully involved in the effort. More than a hundred were serving. Eddie Collins was in the Marines, Tris Speaker was training to become a naval pilot, Branch Rickey and George Sisler were working in the army's Gas and Flame Division, and Pete Alexander, the future Hall of Famer and flea-circus performer, was near the front lines suffering bombardments that would leave him shell-shocked and partially deaf.

As Ty Cobb prepared to head off to France to serve beside Christy Mathewson in the Chemical War Service, he dropped several hints that he would not return to baseball. Reporters had grown accustomed to such talk. For several years, whether out of sincerity or merely as a bargaining ploy, Cobb had been mentioning that he might walk away from the game. He didn't need the money. He had invested wisely in cotton, real estate, and more than a dozen stocks. He was well on his way to becoming baseball's first millionaire player. Financially, Cobb would be fine without the game. But Cobb wasn't just about money.

Months later, at Hanlon Field in France, Cobb got a taste of mortality. He, Mathewson, and dozens of other soldiers were accidentally exposed to poisonous gas in a doomed training exercise. Cobb survived, but he saw several men die. Christy Mathewson would never fully recover. After the fighting ended in November, Cobb returned aboard the *Leviathan* and announced that he planned to retire. "I intend to break away from baseball," he said. "I'm tired of it. I've had fifteen years of it, and I want to quit while I am still good." With those words, Cobb headed home to Augusta to golf, hunt, and spend time with his wife, Charlie, and their three young children, Ty Junior, Shirley, and Herschel. Around Christmas, Ty and his offspring were featured on a porch swing in a holiday photo shoot for *Women's Home Companion.* The Rockefellers and the Roosevelts shared the center spread with the Cobbs.

Despite his stated intentions, Cobb could not walk away from the game. Something pulled him back. He believed that baseball was on the cusp of incomparable growth. "It's going to boom this season as it never has done before," Cobb said. An astute businessman, he realized that postwar pride and prosperity would drive expansion, and he was right. But another factor would contribute as well—one Cobb did not foresee and would not appreciate.

8

The Rise of Ruth

Female admirers with Ruth. NATIONAL BASEBALL HALL OF FAME
LIBRARY, COOPERSTOWN, N.Y.

~

ROM TY COBB'S PERSPECTIVE, THE ASSAULT ON THE GLORY
days of baseball began in 1919, the year Babe Ruth became
an almost-everyday player. As Cobb had predicted, Americans
turned to the national pastime in unprecedented numbers, flooding into ballparks and crushing attendance records. In some cities,
turnstiles registered two to three times as many spectators. The

country was going baseball crazy, and the press, titillated by Ruth's spring batting bombardment (a 508-foot blast in one game, four home runs in another), fed the frenzy with talk of the young slugger. What might he accomplish playing every day? How many home runs could he hit?

Ruth started slowly, juggling offensive and pitching duties. Through June, he had only seven home runs. But as the weather warmed, so did his bat. In early July, he stroked five home runs within seven days. In the middle of the month, he surpassed his 1918 total of eleven. Cobb had never hit that many in one season. He had never tried. You couldn't do it swinging properly, chopping down on a ball, after all.

Babe Ruth rarely sliced at the ball. His swing angled upward, toward the open sky and its endless possibilities. And it was a huge swing. He swung powerfully, and when he missed, everyone knew it. The momentum could twist him into the dirt.

By mid-August, Ruth had nineteen home runs, and crowds were streaming to see him. The Boston papers nicknamed him the Colossus, and everyone in baseball was talking about the phenomenon. Newsmen turned to authorities like Clark Griffith for historical perspective. Manager and part owner of the Washington club, Griffith came from pioneer stock. Born in a log cabin, he crossed paths with Jesse James as a boy and sung in saloons prior to becoming a fine pitcher for Chicago in the 1890s. Years earlier, he had faced Buck Freeman, holder of the American League season record of twenty-five home runs. "Ruth is far and away the hardest hitter of all time, in my opinion," said Griffith. "He is not so consistent a batter as many I have faced. But when he connects, the ball goes farther. I am pulling for him to beat Buck Freeman's old home-run record."

Babe's ways were so flamboyantly different that even opposing players—Ty's teammates, no less—were intrigued by his feats. Among the curious was Oscar Stanage, Detroit's iron-footed catcher. Ruth pitched against the Tigers on Monday, July 21. In the ninth inning, with Detroit comfortably ahead 6–1 and no one on base, Stanage got an idea.

"Give him this one and see how far he can bust it," he told pitcher Howard Ehmke, a blond twenty-three-year-old. Ehmke liked the suggestion, and Stanage let Ruth know that a sweet pitch would be coming. Ruth appreciated the notice and twisted his powerful torso into it, blasting it over the right-field wall, across Trumbull Avenue, and into Brooks Lumberyard. "I saw how far he could hit it," Ehmke said. "I was satisfied."

Cobb had placed three infield hits, driven in one run, instigated a second by forcing an error, and scored a third, going from first to home on a hit-and-run single. It was a grand demonstration of Baseball Science. But despite Cobb's game-winning efforts, Ruth stole the headline in the next day's paper: BABE RUTH SETS A NEW RECORD FOR LONG DISTANCE DRIVING. Ruth was the biggest story in baseball. Every fan was talking about him. On sandlot diamonds, boys were imitating Babe's robust swing. Suddenly, Cobb was looking old-fashioned.

The game's greatest rivalry was beginning to take shape.

~

It would be difficult to imagine two personalities more destined to dislike each other—or a set of circumstances more ideal for causing them to clash. It was almost as if the heavens blessed baseball fans with a Halley's Comet–like occurrence by placing Ty Cobb and Babe Ruth in the same time period, in the same sport, and on the same field, and by giving them spectacular, but wildly different, talents. There were, of course, the numerous differences in their familial, religious, educational, and economic backgrounds. But what really stoked their grudge was two seemingly minor traits that when combined with the other factors would lead to a volatile relationship: Cobb was caustic, Ruth was thin-skinned, and the two together were combustible.

A master at the art of "goat getting," Ty Cobb believed that by irritating, challenging, upsetting, embarrassing, or otherwise pricking an opponent he could distract him, intensify the pressure, and ultimately prevail. Cobb's techniques took various shapes. Sometimes, it was as simple as heckling and haranguing another player. Most teams had guys who lobbed verbal bombs, but few embraced the effort with the passion or precision of Cobb. He prided himself on being a student of behavior.

Once, frustrated by catcher Billy Sullivan's success in cutting him down stealing, Cobb alerted Sullivan in advance that he intended to swipe a base. He hoped to give Sullivan something to think about. At bat, he reportedly told him, "Bill, if I get on this time, I'm going down on the second pitch." Crouching behind the plate, Sullivan didn't respond. Cobb got on and took off for second as promised. Sullivan's throw went high. The next at bat, Cobb warned him again: "Third pitch this time." And again Cobb stole the base, Sullivan's throw going high and wide. "I never had any trouble with Sully after that," Cobb remembered.

Neither friends nor teammates were exempt.

In late August 1913, after a contest in Chicago against the White Sox, Cobb went for dinner with Ring Lardner, one of his admirers. Lardner clutched a list of the leading hitters in the American League. It showed Joe Jackson about ten points ahead of Cobb. "That means it's time for me to get busy," said Cobb. Days later, the Tigers faced the Indians. Jackson, like Cobb, grew up in the South, and they were buddies. When their teams played, the two usually renewed their friendship near the batting cage. But when this series opened on Thursday, September 4, Cobb ignored Jackson, walking past him as he extended his hand.

"Hey, Ty, where are you going?" Jackson called.

Cobb cast him a chilly glance and kept moving.

"I decided to high-hat him," Cobb recalled later. "I was pretty vain about that championship, and I wasn't going to give it up if I could help it."

Cobb credited the intentional snub with taking Jackson's mind off the game. Cobb outhit Jackson over the four games. As the series ended, Cobb said he shook hands with Jackson, who then saw that he was part of one of Ty's elaborate plots. The realization angered him and kept him off-kilter long enough for Cobb to surge ahead in the standings. Although Jackson denied any correlation, his average plummeted by nearly twenty points over several weeks. In the week after their series, Cobb got twice as many hits as Jackson. By mid-September, he was batting .379 and had displaced Jackson. By season's end, Cobb was tops at .390 to Jackson's .373.

No one was immune. Cobb once tried to set a fire beneath teammate Bobby Veach by instructing fellow outfielder Harry Heilmann to harass Veach from the on-deck circle. Veach did some fine hitting that season—and developed an aversion to Heilmann.

Cobb had been targeting Ruth since his early days in the American League. But as Ruth's popularity multiplied—and his home runs began to overshadow Cobb's achievements—Cobb doubled his efforts. He called Ruth names and disparaged his talents. "Nigger" was a potent favorite.

Racism was a particularly unseemly and undeniable force in Cobb's life. Born and raised in late-nineteenth-century Georgia, Cobb embraced the biases of his time. He believed that blacks should be subservient, and when they weren't, there could be trouble. Cobb had more than his share of fights with both blacks and whites, but those with a racial tinge were often the most brutal and indiscriminate. He assaulted a black groundskeeper for an alleged affront and then attacked the man's wife when she came to his defense. With a knife in hand, he sliced a black hotel watchman who had intervened in his dispute with a black elevator operator. He injured a black street worker who had sworn at him after he accidentally stepped into wet cement, and he rebuked a black hotel maid who objected to being called "nigger."

Though often depicted as the emperor of all baseball racists, Cobb wasn't radically different in his views from many other men in the major leagues—either in his time or after World War II, when Jackie Robinson debuted with Brooklyn. (Rogers Hornsby and Tris Speaker were admitted Klansmen, according to baseball writer Fred Lieb.) On a personal basis, Cobb grew close to several blacks.

In his autobiography, he would deny accusations of bigotry. "My true feeling was that of anyone who'd had a Negro 'mammy' as a child, which I did, and who had lived most peaceably with colored folk for years," he said. Over time, Cobb's beliefs—like those of much of his generation—would begin to change. In interviews, he would praise black players like Robinson, Roy Campanella, and Willie Mays. He admired their talents. One wonders how differently Cobb might be regarded today had he lived another two decades beyond 1961—and had his views continued to evolve. Would he have been like those reformed Southern congressmen who survived politically into the 1980s despite having supported segregation two decades earlier?

For his part, Babe Ruth hardly qualified as a paragon of enlightenment either, though he was considered more tolerant than Cobb. Some Negro league players, like Ted "Double Duty" Radcliffe, viewed Ruth as a friend and said they spent time with him. Ruth would be pictured intermittently in the papers with black fans—a rarity for Cobb.

With his broad facial features, Ruth battled rumors that he had a black ancestor. Fred Lieb reported that early in Ruth's career Cobb refused to room with him at a hunting lodge, contending he was black. Opposing players knew that the surest way to rile Ruth was to question his race. After one such occasion in a future World Series, he would storm into the New York Giants locker room to confront the culprit. "I don't mind being called a prick or a cock sucker or things like that. I expect that," Ruth would supposedly say. "But lay off the personal stuff."

In Cobb's mind—and Ruth's—there wasn't much worse you could call a white man than "nigger." Cobb didn't hesitate to use the derogatory term against Ruth. But it wasn't the only way he irritated Babe.

Whenever he and Ruth passed while heading to and from their outfield positions, Cobb would grunt, whistle, clear his throat, kick at the sand—anything to get Ruth's attention. In the 1920s, Charlie Gehringer would bear witness as Cobb called on one of his reliable standards, the dig about Ruth's hygiene. "Something smells around here," Cobb said as they neared Ruth. Babe chased the laughing Cobb into the outfield.

Having grown up around bars and in a reform school, Ruth was more vulgar than Cobb. In contrast to his image, he spiced his dialogue with creative profanities and stung Cobb liberally, often at the encouragement of teammates. Occasionally, Ruth would infuriate Cobb by saluting his neck, a gesture that implied Cobb was so full of shit that it was in his throat. Like Cobb, Ruth had a temper. But his flared brightly and dissipated quickly.

Cobb's opponents discovered that their attempts to needle him often backfired. "I noticed many times that anybody who made Cobb angry really had something on his hands," said White Sox manager Kid Gleason. Connie Mack agreed. He felt Cobb played best when under attack, so he directed his Athletics to steer clear of him. Said Cobb, "A guiding principle of mine is to always keep the other man anxious. Try to get on his nerves instead of letting him get on yours."

As Ruth closed in on Buck Freeman's home-run mark in late August, newspapers tracked his progress in special columns. The Red Sox were out of contention, playing below .500, when they pulled into Detroit on August 23. Ruth's arrival guaranteed heaps of publicity. Expecting huge crowds, Detroit erected circus seats in the outfield. Twenty thousand fans showed up on a Saturday hoping to witness one of Babe's "home-run tricks."

In the third, as Ruth strode to the plate with a bat on his left shoulder, Cobb drifted back toward the center-field fence. Veteran pitcher George Dauss had struck out Ruth earlier on a full count. But now the bases were full, and Detroit's two-run lead was in jeopardy. Dauss delivered a strike, and Ruth heaved himself into it. The ball soared high and deep to right-center. Cobb did not move. He did not turn to see how far it would go. He did not shake his head; he did not cast an admiring glance. He treated it like a pesky annoyance that would go away if ignored. Cobb knew the ball was a home run. It sailed over the bleachers onto Cherry Street, where a boy eventually chased it down. The cover was tattered. The ball had flown twenty-five feet farther than the one Ruth had hit in July.

It amounted to another new distance record. The thunder of the fans shook the stands, frightening birds from the upper-deck rafters. The buzz resonated for minutes.

The crowd had barely settled when Cobb got his turn. The famous Georgian led off with a bunt single. Bobby Veach and Harry Heilmann followed, both also bunting their way on. With all bases occupied, Cobb, prancing around third, signaled a triple steal. When the deliberate, inexperienced, nineteen-year-old Waite Hoyt went into his motion, Cobb, Veach, and Heilmann took off for the next base. The ball beat Cobb to the plate, but he slid safely around catcher Roxy Walters. (Cobb owed much of his base-stealing success to his deceptive, fade-away slide, which required he read the fielder's eyes and wait until the last possible minute before committing to his approach.) Veach and Heilmann advanced and scored on the next two plays. Two more runners followed them, and they also executed a double steal. The Tigers reclaimed the lead.

It was almost as if Cobb wanted to provide a lesson to Ruth and those who lusted for the gimmicky long ball: This is how you win ball games. Cobb and almost every other authority in the game believed you fought for runs one at a time. Home runs, critics contended, were more about luck than talent, more about brute force than intelligence.

The Sox looked ready to rally in the ninth. Everett Scott and Frank Gilhooley got on base in front of team captain Harry Hooper, the leadoff hitter. When Hooper popped a ball high between second and short in shallow center, Ty Cobb sped in and called off the infielders. The runners stayed close to their bases as Cobb, positioning himself for an easy catch, settled beneath the ball. At the last second, he allowed the ball to drop, trapped it on the rebound, and threw out Scott at third. Bob Jones relayed to second for a double play. It was another shining example of Cobb's brand of brainy baseball, and the Tigers won because of it. But it wasn't Cobb's name that traipsed off the tongues of fans as they emerged from the dark tunnels beneath the stands. It was Ruth's. . . . "Did you see how far the Babe hit that ball?"

On September 8, Ruth passed Buck Freeman, now a minor-league umpire, and finished with twenty-nine home runs. His record for the season amazed fans. He had knocked a ball out of the Polo Grounds. He had become the first player to hit a home run in every American League park in one season and the first to hit four grand slams in one year. No one had ever seen anything like him. Ruth was unquestionably the new star of baseball. And if there was a new star, there had to be an old one. Despite winning his twelfth batting title, Ty Cobb qualified. "Ruth is today the great drawing card in baseball," wrote *Washington Post* columnist J. V. Fitzgerald. "As a box-office attraction, he has put Ty Cobb in the class known in the theatrical circles as 'the chaser.' His home run stunts are the big act in baseball."

As if the reality of Ruth weren't enough, there was also the myth of him, and it was beginning to take root. One reporter noted that Ruth had blistered a ball "several hundred miles an hour." And Connie Mack, twenty-two years into a managerial career that would exceed a half century, exclaimed, "Why, that fellow could hit the ball harder with one hand than those old-timers could hit it with two hands! . . . Why, it's uncanny!" Grantland Rice was the nation's most-read sportswriter and a friend of Cobb. He had brought Tyrus his earliest significant publicity. When Cobb was playing in the minor leagues, Rice began receiving postcards alerting him to the fabulously talented Georgia boy. Unbeknownst to Rice, Cobb had mailed the cards, masquerading as various baseball fans. Rice responded by making note of the hype in print. As their fame grew, Cobb and Rice became close. But even Rice couldn't ignore Ruth. In words that invoked the Mighty Casey, Rice wrote: "And when he caught one on the beak, and wrecked a distant flat / Not a rooter in the place could doubt, was Babe Ruth at the bat."

Cobb disliked much about Ruth. But one of the things that irritated him most was Ruth's lifestyle. The Babe lived with wild abandon, ignoring curfews, staying out all hours, drinking, partying, overeating, and snaking through towns in search of sex. On top of that, he was loud, brash, and uncouth. Cobb was nearly fanatical about taking care of himself, about being prepared for games, and about making sacrifices for the long term. He felt confident that Ruth's nocturnal adventures would eventually undermine him.

Cobb's aversion to Ruth was building and becoming more apparent. Reporters knew about it, and enjoyed poking the Georgia Peach by describing the Babe's feats in peachy terms. Ruth had made "a peach of a record" . . . "a peach of a catch" . . . "a peach of a hit." Soon, he would sign "a peach of a contract."

~

In December 1919, Ruth headed to the West Coast to perform in exhibitions, explore film opportunities, savor his fame, cavort with celebrities like Charlie Chaplin, golf in the salted air, and frolic with women other than his wife. While there, he delivered a long-distance ultimatum to Harry Frazee, the financially strapped owner of the Red Sox. Ruth wanted a pay raise. Although two years remained on his contract, Ruth vowed he would not return to Boston for less than twenty thousand a year—twice his salary—and he insisted he wouldn't play anywhere else either.

Cobb found Ruth's stance audacious, and said so. It's unclear whether Cobb sought out a reporter or vice versa, but he minced no words. Ruth had signed a contract; he had a legal and moral obligation to honor it. Repudiating a pact was immoral, Cobb said. Underlying his objections—but unspoken—was the dollar figure Ruth attached to his demands. Twenty thousand dollars! That's what Cobb earned, and it had taken him fourteen years to reach that plateau. Ruth was hoping to get there in half the time. Cobb's condemnation had no impact on the situation itself, but it helped further erode the already-dismal relationship between the two players. Ruth, noting that he wouldn't have said anything against Cobb had he held out for more money, wanted to kick Cobb's ass. "I'll settle the question when I meet Cobb," he said.

Frazee negotiated privately with Yankee owners Jacob Ruppert and Tillinghast Huston. On the day after Christmas, he signed an agreement to sell Ruth to the Yankees for $25,000 in cash, $75,000 in notes, and a $300,000 loan. Before announcing the pact, the Yankee owners wanted to make sure Ruth wouldn't buck. So they dispatched manager Miller Huggins to Los Angeles. Huggins found Ruth on the Griffith Park municipal golf course. Ruth had been spending considerable time on the fairways amid the manzanita and sagebrush. Baseball wasn't the only sport ballooning in popularity. Golf officials expected a record year in 1920. In February, golf-ball factories would be working at full capacity. Demand would be so high that plants would institute second and third shifts, trying to avoid problems that had surfaced in 1919, when balls had to be rushed to market midsummer coated with an inferior, poorly adhering paint.

Ruth and Huggins came to terms on the golf course. The Yankees doubled Ruth's salary, putting him in Cobb's stratosphere. In return, Huggins demanded that Ruth be better behaved and more cognizant of curfews. Further, said Huggins, he didn't want the Babe to slide. "You're too valuable a piece of machinery to be taking such risks," he said. Leave that to guys like Ty Cobb. When the announcement came, fans greeted it with anger in Boston and with elation in New York. Ruth was a Yankee, and he would be hitting at the Polo Grounds, with a cozy right-field fence 265 feet down the line. The park would provide "an awful temptation to the Babe," said retired Christy Mathewson.

"I sold Ruth for the best interests of the Boston club," said Frazee. "The Babe was not an influence for good or for team play. He thought only of himself, whether the question was one of breaking contracts or making long hits."

Cobb couldn't have said it better.

~

At the Congress Hotel in Chicago on Monday, February 9, 1920, American League president Ban Johnson argued privately in the public lobby with Frazee and Ruppert. Observers speculated it was over the sale of Ruth and their efforts to give greater authority to Kenesaw Mountain Landis.

Throughout the first decades of the century, Byron Bancroft Johnson had been the most powerful figure in baseball. A straight-laced, no-nonsense individual, Johnson, as founder of the American League, had tamed the sport's wild reputation by curbing profane behavior and outlawing alcohol in ballparks. Johnson had wielded the greatest influence of any member of baseball's ruling commission, but his grip was loosening as new owners balked at his authoritarian ways. The gathering of baseball's magnates often inflamed divisions rather than healing them: American League versus National League, Johnson allies versus Johnson enemies, original owners versus new ones ("insurgents," some called them). Rival factions plotted behind closed doors. Power, pride, profit, and the direction of the game played central roles in their disputes.

During the day and into the evening, baseball leaders debated and adopted numerous rule changes. They gave umpires more rain-delay authority, depriving home managers of the ability to cancel games for tactical reasons. They barred freak and doctored pitches, but as a compromise allowed two spitball throwers per team. They raised the fine from five to twenty-five dollars for managers who neglected to inform umpires of lineup adjustments. They decided that a ball crossing the outfield fence in fair territory would be a home run even if it landed foul in the stands—a change that would bring about the marking of foul lines on all decks and the erection of tall foul poles. They updated the content of box scores and fine-tuned the counting of stolen bases, sacrifices, and errors, and on and on.

But one proposal, prompted by Babe Ruth's power, ignited a fierce argument between Clark Griffith of the Washington club and veteran umpire Hank O'Day. Griffith hated the intentional walk, and so did the ticket-buying fans, who hissed when pitchers employed it against Ruth. It evinced cowardliness and a lack of competitive spirit, and it deprived fans of their money's worth, critics said. Griffith wanted the intentional walk banned. He felt a catcher should be required to stay behind the plate until the pitcher released the ball. Failing that, every runner should be advanced one base.

O'Day, a pitcher in the 1880s and one of baseball's senior arbiters, envisioned a game in which all hell might break lose. What if a catcher called for a pitchout with runners on first and third and then moved from behind the plate too early? The umpire would be forced to order home the winning run. It would be pure pandemonium and downright dangerous. Umpires already had enough with which to contend. After games, fans typically exited ballparks by walking across the fields. If dissatisfied with the officiating, they hassled the umpires. Angry ballplayers occasionally fought umpires beneath the stands.

Ruth had been walked 101 times in 1919, second to Cleveland's Jack Graney, a Canadian leadoff hitter who had a meticulous sense of the strike zone and tried for free bases. Graney's walks were almost never intentional. It was different for Ruth, who walked about once every fourth appearance, much to the disappointment of stadium crowds. "There is no play which is so unpopular with baseball fans," said *The New York Times*.

Ruth despised the walks. "It's part of the game, I guess, but when I'm ready to give that ball a ride and that fellow out there passes me, I want to wring his goddamn neck. I'd rather take a punch in the nose than a base on balls."

At the Chicago meeting, baseball officials banned intentional walks. Catchers would have to remain behind the plate until the ball was pitched. It was a technicality. Intentional walks might be officially prohibited, but in practice there would be more than ever. No one could keep a pitcher from throwing wide when facing Babe Ruth.

9

A Baseball Revolution

Ruth takes a mighty cut. NATIONAL BASEBALL HALL OF FAME
LIBRARY, COOPERSTOWN, N.Y.

WHO'S BETTER, TY COBB OR BABE RUTH? THE *Reach Baseball Guide* asked the question prior to the 1920 season, but it was on many minds. The hype surrounding Babe Ruth—his groundbreaking performance, his monstrous pay raise, his record-setting sale price, his move to New York—left no doubt that Cobb's successor had been anointed and that the new year would bring a battle for dominance. In his syndicated "Sportlight" column, Grantland Rice approached the issue with humor, noting with false alarm that Cobb's advancing age threatened to lower his batting average to .370. But even Cobb's chum couldn't ignore Ruth's impact. "Babe Ruth has challenged the supremacy of Ty Cobb . . . ," wrote Rice, "and it will be interesting to see how Cobb responds. There was a day when Cobb might have met the challenge with an unstoppable rush."

The rise of Babe Ruth did not affect Ty Cobb's plans for spring training. As usual, he didn't report with the other players. He stayed in Augusta, close to his growing family. He and his wife, Charlie, had a newborn at home, their fourth child, daughter Beverly. Cobb also had a new business interest, Ty Cobb Tire Company. He could often be found in the Broad Street shop overseeing the enterprise. The place was a magnet for visitors, a hangout where friends came for conversation. Among those who dropped by was Al Monro Elias, a baseball buff who was becoming known as "the world's greatest statistician," and who was the founder of what would become Elias Sports Bureau.

Cobb had been reporting late to training camp for as long as his star status had allowed. Though teammates complained, Jennings and owner Frank Navin tolerated the situation. Cobb contended it wasn't a matter of preferential treatment but one of common sense. But no one else had the option. Cobb stayed in shape over the winter, he said, by going on vigorous hunting excursions. "Four to six weeks of training as it is carried out hurts rather than helps a ball player," he argued. "When the season opens, he may look good and start fast. But the long training period has taken its toll on his endurance and the season is not far along until he has lost some of his dash and speed and spirit as well."

Babe Ruth got to his camp in Jacksonville on time. He arrived ready to give it his all—on the field and away from it. Ruth's fame had multiplied over the winter, and every baseball fan, from the Black-Jack-gum-chewing boys in the bleachers to the titans in their vests and bow ties, had something to say about him.

Walter Johnson described Ruth as a freak. "Not a freak as a ballplayer," he said, "but a freak as a batter. He hits further than any batter I have ever faced, and he hits harder. I do not know that he has any particular batting weakness. Some days he misses the low ones and the next time out he drives them over the fences."

Dr. William Keane, the Tigers' team physician, labeled him a superman. "There are plenty of ballplayers who are as strong physically," he said. "But they cannot do the things Ruth does for the reason that their eyes and their muscles are not in such perfect accord. Ruth has tremendous hitting powers. His back muscles are marvelously developed, and his eyes are remarkably clear. I believe his vision is as nearly perfect as it is possible for a man's vision to be. Along with that, his brain works in perfect conjunction with the muscles of his back, his shoulders, his arms, and his eyes."

New York fans already had high expectations for the Babe, but Ruth inflated their hopes by pledging he would hit an unheard-of forty home runs. The season opened in mid-April, and two weeks passed before Ruth began to deliver. His first pair of home runs came, gratifyingly, against Frazee's Red Sox. He hit three more a week later against Chicago.

When Cobb and the Tigers arrived in New York on Monday, May 24, Ruth had six home runs—and momentum. The Yankees were in fourth place, losing as often as they won. But their record looked brilliant beside the Tigers' 7–21 mark. Expected to battle for first place, Detroit had started the season with thirteen straight losses. The Tigers were anchored in last place, and Cobb figured mightily in their downfall, struggling to top .200. The forecasts of his demise appeared to be coming true.

Manager Hughie Jennings was frazzled. The once-great Jennings acted tired all the time. He was sour, drank too much, and often seemed oblivious to what transpired on the field. He confessed his frustrations to Cobb in hotel rooms on the road. Sadly, he had fallen far since his heyday. A star with the same 1890s Baltimore team that had produced managers John McGraw and Wilbert Robinson, the redheaded Jennings had been a colorful character with an infectious smile. The ninth of twelve children born into a coal-mining family, Jennings became an attorney in the early 1900s, serving as a college baseball coach in exchange for his education. He became a widower in his first marriage, and was left to raise a young daughter. Throughout his baseball career, Jennings had a penchant for surviving serious accidents. Three times, he suffered skull injuries that left him near death: one from a ball-field beaning, another from a dive into an empty pool at Cornell University, and a third after his car plunged off a bridge in the Poconos. Now, his players were testing his survival skills.

As motivation, Jennings made his team an offer: If the Tigers took two out of three games from the Yankees, he would buy every player a straw hat. If only it were that easy. In New York, former French prime minister Georges Clemenceau, known as the Tiger for his fierce stances, tried to bestow good luck on the Detroiters. Clemenceau sent Jennings a "jinx-chaser"—the claw of a Bengal tiger. Jennings wasn't about to turn it down.

In the second inning, with the game scoreless, Ruth faced Howard Ehmke, the boyish right-hander. Cobb, Bobby Veach, and Ira Flagstead took several steps back toward the outfield fence. Ruth rocketed a warning shot past Cobb and off the wall in right-center. Cobb retrieved it as Ruth cruised into third base, He scored moments later on Del Pratt's infield out. Ruth had struck first, and the race was on.

Not all of the action was on the field. In the bleachers, Broadway composer Louis Hirsch created a scene over seating. Trying to escape a man smoking cigars beside him, Hirsch snuck into better seats. When an usher ordered him back to his own spot, Hirsch resisted and got ejected. (The composer of "Going Up" would file a futile $100,000 suit for "assault and brutal treatment and humiliation.")

During the third inning, heads turned to a conflict behind the visitors' dugout. Rehabilitated craps champion Charlie McManus, accompanying cops on a tour of the Polo Grounds, pointed out shady characters. Police discovered a hotbed of gambling. It's possible the gamblers were wagering on this curious new figure, this Tarzan of the Diamond, this Master of the Mace, this Batterin' Behemoth, this Sultan of Swat, or whatever else he was being called at the moment. When would Ruth get his next home run? Someone somewhere would have wanted to put money on it. But more likely they were merely gambling on the game. The problem was widespread. The crackdown in New York was part of a baseball-wide effort—a response to the rumored throwing of the 1919 World Series. Officers arrested forty-seven culprits in the bleachers at Wrigley Field on the same day.

Countering Ruth's triple, Cobb managed a single, made it to third on errors, and tagged on a fly to Duffy Lewis, beating his throw to home. Detroit won 3-1, and dreams of a crisp straw hat filled Cobb's head that night. Or didn't.

The next afternoon, Ruth belted a home run. The man who recovered the souvenir in the upper deck traded it to the Babe for another ball. Dutch Leonard pitched Ruth wide in his remaining at bats, disappointing the casual fans who came solely to witness the spectacle of Ruth. It seemed every baseball enthusiast had a friend or family member who was suddenly interested in the sport and wanted to watch Ruth plunk a home run. Some expected him to do it in every appearance.

Eighteen thousand turned out on Wednesday. It was a grand audience for a weekday game. Ruth jumped on the first pitch from George Dauss and sent it into the upper deck. A few innings later, a fog-horned fan yelled to Ruth as he prepared to bat.

"Get a home run!" he hollered.

"I got a home run," Ruth replied.

The Yankees took the final two games, and Hughie Jennings wasted no money on straw hats. But Cobb had bigger concerns; he had gotten only one hit in the series. His poor showing was not lost on the giants of the press box, who held great sway with the public. New York had more than a dozen daily newspapers, and they were coming down hard on Cobb. *The New York Times* offered a brutal appraisal of him, saying he was "in eclipse" and "a second fiddle." William Hanna of the *Sun* noted, "Ty is hitting like a man who hasn't had enough practice. His timing of pitched balls is poor. He is off balance when he hits and is meeting the ball thinly." If it had just been the New York reporters, it wouldn't have been so bad. But the Detroit contingent concurred that Cobb paled beside Ruth. "There is no use in arguing otherwise," wrote Harry Bullion of the *Detroit Free Press.*

Cobb did not take kindly to criticism, but there was no denying his pathetic batting average. He was pressing. And who could blame him? People were already writing their eulogies.

The Detroit series launched Babe Ruth on a hitting frenzy. He swatted three home runs against Boston in the next series, then four against Washington. Between May 25 and June 30, Ruth averaged a home run every other game. He had twenty-four before July arrived. The crowds defied comparison. The Yankees set attendance records at home and on the road. On May 31, the largest baseball audience in New York history—36,688—flooded through the gates to see Ruth drive a Walter Johnson pitch off the park's flag-lined ornamental crown in right. The ball ricocheted back onto the field. The men in the press box had never heard a player receive so deafening an ovation as they did when Ruth headed to his position.

On a mid-June trip to the baseball version of the West, New York drew larger crowds than ever. Attendance records fell in St. Louis. In Chicago, fans crowded onto the field behind ropes. When Ruth drove a deep fly into the overflow area at Comiskey Park, Joe Jackson disappeared into the throng and then reappeared with the ball. Umpires theorized that he had actually caught it. No one could tell for certain.

Ruth's comings and goings, often with a cigar in hand, occupied columns in the papers. Fans, celebrities, and civic groups clamored to meet him. In New York, the Knights of Columbus made him an honorary member and presented him with a diamond watch fob. Applause and presentations greeted him wherever he appeared. Tributes abounded. The lyrically minded also weighed in. Writers had long celebrated the national pastime in newsprint poetry. Ernest Thayer's "Casey at the Bat" appeared in the *San Francisco Examiner* in 1888. Nearly thirty years later, in New York's *Globe,* Franklin Adams immortalized a mediocre double-play combination as "the saddest of possible words, Tinker-to-Evers-to-Chance." In verse in 1920, one bard wrote of a wife who accompanied her husband to the ballpark to see Ruth. The final stanza: " 'They call that fellow Babe!' she cried. 'How can they, Jim? / And aren't you delighted that our babe don't look like him?' "

Kids could buy Babe Ruth shoes and gloves, could join Babe Ruth clubs, and soon would be able to read Babe Ruth books and see Babe Ruth movies. "The country is Babe Ruth mad," said *The Sporting News.* "Every day is a World Series day when the Yankees play." By the end of July, Ruth had dethroned Cobb almost everywhere. He was unmistakably the game's most dazzling star. Detroit stood as the solitary holdout, Cobb's last bastion. But it too was about to fall.

10

Coup in Detroit

Ruth watches a long drive, ERNIE HARWELL COLLECTION, DETROIT PUBLIC LIBRARY

I N JUNE, TY COBB COLLIDED WITH IRA FLAGSTEAD WHILE RAC-
ing for a fly ball. The collision tore ligaments in Cobb's left
knee. Although he tried to play through the injury, the pain was
too severe. Frustrated by his slow recovery—and his diminished
standing—Cobb confided to friends in Augusta that his career
might be over. But in July he returned, lifting his average into the

.310s. Far in front of him, all above .380, were Tris Speaker, George Sisler, Joe Jackson, and Babe Ruth.

Ruth and the Yankees rolled into Detroit on Thursday, August 5, 1920, for a four-game series. New York had dropped three in Chicago, where more people—38,823—had turned out for Ruth's Sunday appearance than for any of the White Sox championship games a year earlier. Ruth had satisfied them with his thirty-eighth home run. Each home run he hit set a new record.

Showers threatened throughout the day in Michigan, and the weather kept attendance to 5,000. Though modest in size, the crowd cheered every glimpse of Ruth. The affectionate welcome contradicted the words local reporters were using to describe him: *monster, elephant, demon, caveman*. Ruth treated his devotees to a second-inning home run. He drove another ball to such heights that thirty-seven-year-old catcher Oscar Stanage got dizzy staring skyward and dropped it in foul territory. Twice, Ruth walked, and each time the spectators booed pitcher Howard Ehmke. They seemed not to care that the Tigers were en route to a 7–1 victory thanks to Cobb's four runs and three hits. The cheers for Babe overwhelmed those for the forgotten Tyrus.

On Friday morning, sensing an epidemic of Ruth mania, *The Detroit News* dispatched female reporter Buda Stephens to the two-year-old Hotel Fort Shelby, just a few doors down West Lafayette. Her assignment, given amid the clacking typewriters of the newsroom: Interview Ruth from a woman's perspective. Answering the knock at his door in a silk shirt, Babe gruffly agreed to meet Stephens in the lobby.

Heads couldn't help but turn when he appeared. From a distance, Ruth looked polished. He wore a fancy shirt and a tailored brown suit. A diamond ring adorned his pinky, and a sapphire-and-diamond pin glittered on his lapel. His clothes advertised that he had money. But up close, even before he opened his mouth, one could see a lack of refinement in the details. Ruth was no beauty. Yesterday's grime remained under his fingernails, and his suit showed stains, probably from the late night before. Yet, there was something magnetic about him.

Ruth, who had reportedly spent eight hundred dollars on hats for his wife, Helen, complained to Stephens about the pricey tastes of women.

"If you want a pretty picture, you've got to pay for it," she remarked.

"Not fifteen or twenty times," he replied.

In the hotel coffee shop, Ruth ate cantaloupe with one hand and scooped eggs and ham with the other, few words passing between him and Stephens.

"Do you wear brown to match your eyes?" she asked.

"God, did you notice I got brown eyes already?"

God . . . hell . . . damn—Ruth used the words in the company of women, too.

Stephens, unimpressed by his demeanor, pronounced Ruth as lacking in sophistication. "He doesn't know the answer to anything if it's more than one syllable." . . . "He is not suave and intellectual." . . . And, finally, "Babe Ruth possesses none of the Ty Cobb charms." Her unflattering portrait, titled RUTH JUST BIG JUNGLE INFANT, played on page one. The piece might have been a gift to Cobb, a sweet effort to make up for the sports-section headline that stung him the day before: TY DETHRONED BY BABE RUTH. COBB, LONG IDOL OF FANS, SEES SWAT KING HAILED AS BALLDOM'S WONDER MAN. And in Detroit, of all places.

The weather improved on Friday, and fifteen thousand fans flocked to the park. It was another all-Ruth audience, and he crushed a solo shot to the peak of the single-decked, center-field bleachers. Three innings later, with Aaron Ward and Roger Peckinpaugh on base, Ruth swatted a second home run, number forty-one.

In the eighth, Detroiters rooted for a third. "Forty-two!" they chanted. "Forty-two!"

Dauss retired Ruth, and instantly hundreds of folks departed, escaping on streetcars, rightly figuring that Babe wouldn't get another swing. It was happening everywhere. "Can you imagine it?" Carl Mays had said at the Polo Grounds. "One man out in the eighth and they are through for the day? They know Babe will not come up again and they have seen what they paid to see. When Babe is through, they are through."

Afterward, in the locker room, Ruth posed shirtless, clenching his hands behind his head as photographers pointed their bulky box cameras at his bulky, boxy shoulders, their shutters clicking at his beefy backside.

The danger with Ruth, surmised reporter H. C. Walker, was that fans would come to expect every hitter to perform at his level. "He stands so much in a class by himself that he makes all other batters look cheap," he wrote. Other fine hitters would pale beside him due to their inability to hit for distance, he said. Therefore, Walker concluded in a masterful example of logical thinking, Ruth should be considered a "menace to baseball."

Manager Miller Huggins didn't see it that way. He acknowledged Cobb as the greatest player ever, but credited Ruth's enormous wallops with drawing crowds. "He makes the turnstiles click," Huggins said. "Cobb, brilliant as he is, appeals to only a portion of baseball followers. Cobb is the idol of students of baseball. But all those interested in the game are not students; most of them miss the fine points, the inner dope. Cobb cannot be fully appreciated unless you are a student of baseball. . . . But Ruth appeals to everybody."

Hughie Jennings, whose signs Cobb was allowed to embrace or ignore at will, sided with his star. "There is no comparison between Cobb and Ruth," said Jennings. "I'd rather have one Cobb than five Ruths. I don't mean to detract from Ruth's wonderful work, but I don't believe there is any question that Cobb tops all ball players of modern times."

Detroit denied Ruth on Saturday, but that didn't deter twenty-eight thousand people—the second-largest crowd ever at Navin—from showing up on Sunday. Throughout the series, Detroiters had been rooting for Babe as if he were one of their own. They applauded every time he emerged from the cement dugout, approached the plate, or headed to right field. The Peach, according to the beakish Harry Salsinger of *The Detroit News*, felt deeply "how fickle the adoration of the sport-going public is."

To the fans' disappointment, Ehmke pitched a three-hit shutout. The Tigers won 1–0, and Cobb got the lone run. He had collected nine hits in the series, scored four times, helped win two games, and batted .500. But few noticed. Ruth had conquered; his coup had succeeded. Even in Detroit, he rated as a bigger star than Ty Cobb. Rhapsodized George Phair, in an era when sports columnists often began or ended their stories with verse: "Forgotten are the ancient throbs we felt when Tyrus held his sway / We used to call 'em second Cobbs, we call 'em second Ruths today."

Ruth's successes mounted, along with his numbers. He was receiving between fifty and a hundred letters a day. MEET THE AMERICAN IDOL, suggested one magazine. On Monday, September 13—a day after the Tigers walked Ruth four times—he hit his forty-ninth home run before a sizeable weekday crowd in Detroit. Cobb wasn't a factor. "The shrinking violet of baseball is Ty Cobb when he and Babe Ruth are side by side on the ball field," reported *The New York Times.* The next day, Ruth scored twice. His 147th run of the season catapulted him into a tie with Cobb for the twentieth-century record for most runs scored in a season.

Every acclamation for Ruth seemed to carry an insult for Cobb. The public comparisons were endless, and Cobb now came up on the losing end. It wasn't enough for Ruth to be crowned; Cobb must be exiled. A lesser player might simply have conceded, exited the public arena for retirement, and left it to historians to sort out the rest. But Ruth's rise propelled Cobb. Ty batted better with Babe on the field. He hit for a higher average when Ruth was in the lineup—twenty-five points higher from 1917 through 1919. In the 1920 season, Cobb's batting average in games against Ruth would nearly top .420, far superior to his .334 season average against all opponents.

Leaving Detroit by train, Babe Ruth might have passed the newsstand at the depot and spotted the night blue cover of the current issue of *Physical Culture* magazine, featuring a back-and-shoulders portrait of a well-toned Samson. The monthly, feeding off the fitness fad, exploded with ads for whole-wheat breads, bran cereals, muscle-control courses, miracle milk diets, and violet-ray generators that harnessed the "curative forces of electricity" and that promised, among numerous other things, to ease runny noses when deployed to the nostrils. But what might have interested

Ruth most was the article teased on the cover: WHAT TY COBB THINKS OF BABE RUTH.

"Ruth is a freak hitter," said Cobb, "but, more than that, he is a freak hitter who will not last long." Cobb predicted that a severe batting slump would shake Ruth's confidence and lead to his downfall. "He is bound to go into a slump. Every player does. And when that happens, I do not believe he will have sufficient versatility to bring himself back." Cobb emphasized that his views were purely professional, not of a personal nature. Well, that almost went without saying.

Except that three months on, Cobb offered another strictly professional assessment in a different magazine, saying he feared that Ruth was going to get fat. "Ruth must be a well-conditioned athlete or his fame is going to be short-lived," Cobb said.

He could hope, anyway.

The New Commander

Cobb with three of his children. ERNIE HARWELL COLLECTION, DETROIT PUBLIC LIBRARY

O N A WINDY WINTER DAY IN DECEMBER 1920, TY COBB and team owner Frank Navin met privately for four hours in a suite at the Hotel Vanderbilt in New York. When they emerged, Cobb was player-manager of the Tigers, the successor to Hughie Jennings, who had resigned after the team's seventh-place finish. In the lobby, his voice rattled by a miserable cold, Cobb outlined his plans and philosophies before an audience of reporters.

"What I want is a hustling ball club," he said. "They don't all have to be perfect. Just let them be fellows who will go out on the ball field and fight for everything that will help to win." He pledged to "rub the boys the right way, not to do anything that would tend to discourage them."

Cobb had long contended that he didn't want to be a manager, once referring to the bench as "a hot bed of team bolshevism." But Navin's persistence and assurances helped convince him. Other factors played a role, too: Jennings's encouragement; friend Tris Speaker's triumphs as player-manager of the world-champion Cleveland team; and Cobb's concern that Pants Rowland, whose baseball credentials he viewed skeptically, would be hired if he refused. (Rowland had limited minor-league experience before being plucked from an Illinois grill to run the White Sox.) But perhaps the most enticing reason was the one left unspoken. As manager, Cobb could put his acclaimed baseball intelligence to the test. He would have an opportunity to show that the scientific style he championed could subdue the long-ball ways of that crude sensation who lived in a lavish eight-room suite at the Ansonia Hotel at Seventy-third and Broadway.

Oh, and there was one other important enticement: Cobb's $35,000 contract. It meant he was once again the best-paid player in baseball. But even news of his appointment—coming on his thirty-fourth birthday, no less—didn't allow Cobb to entirely escape Ruth. In announcing the hiring, one New York paper identified him in its lead graph as "the brightest luminary among the stars of baseball until Babe Ruth came on to usurp the throne."

~

The Tigers won their first game under Cobb on Thursday, April 14, and they played .500 ball through the early months of the 1921 season. The Yankees were slightly ahead of them at the end of May and just behind Speaker's first-place Indians.

Cobb became the most hands-on manager the club had seen. He was a flurry of activity, flitting about the diamond, darting from bench to batter with whispered advice, shouting directions from center field, trying the patience of umpires with his frequent confabs, and charging in to dictate the course of action to players. He flashed signs continuously to his pitchers and catchers. "That man makes me so nervous I don't know if I'm here or in Peking," one player complained—anonymously, of course. If a batter missed a sign, Cobb wouldn't hesitate to halt the game and trot in from the coaching box or from a base he occupied to clarify the matter. He also continued needling opponents. "Boot it! Boot it!" Cobb yelled as opposing players fielded ground balls.

Cobb had a talent for teaching hitting, and he shared his knowledge. To his credit, he ensured that the young guys received better treatment than he had as a rookie, when veterans hazed him unmercifully by breaking his bats, stealing his spikes and glove, and denying him swings in the cage. Cobb established a schedule that guaranteed prospects got practice cuts against established pitchers.

Umpires got no breaks from Cobb. They no longer had to deal with him only on the close plays that affected him. Now, they had to face him on every controversial call that went against his team. The sight of him storming in from the outfield to argue became a common, time-killing annoyance. In one game, attempting to prove an umpire wrong, Cobb sprinted to the bleachers to take testimony from eleven police officers and hundreds of fans who witnessed, and were closer to, the contested play than the ruling official. (The call stood, incidentally.)

The 1921 Tigers played the Cobbian way, slashing, fighting, battling until the end. Under Cobb, they would execute more sacrifices, steal more bases, and hit for a higher average—forty-six points higher—than their 1920 counterparts. Cobb was an acknowledged master of strategy. He knew the ins and outs of the game, the fine points, and the intricate details. But he did possess one glaring, pride-induced blind spot, and in it stood Babe Ruth. "Every long hit I made was a personal insult to him," Ruth would say later. With Ruth approaching the plate, Cobb frequently rushed to the mound to tell his pitchers how to handle him. For a while, he tried a shift on Ruth, swinging his fielders toward right. But when Ruth adjusted and punched the ball down the third-base line for a stand-up triple, Cobb abandoned the shift. The one thing Cobb refused to do was give Ruth a free pass.

Ruth had set a record by walking 148 times in 1920, and in the new season managers were every bit as inclined to pass him. Tris Speaker directed his staff to walk Ruth when there were runners on base or the score was close. It struck most as common sense: Don't give him anything to hit with the game on the line. But it was wisdom that Cobb did not—or could not—embrace. His pitchers challenged Ruth. Perhaps it was simply his competitive nature. Maybe he believed the intentional walk cheated fans of game action. Or maybe he disliked the idea of so publicly acknowledging the threat Ruth posed.

When the Yankees came to Detroit for a four-game series on May 10, 1921, the season was not a month old, and already Ruth had eight home runs. It didn't take him long to add another. Even with his wrist injured and taped, Ruth slammed one over Cobb's head in the first inning. It careened off the bleachers in deep center. Two runs scored—all the Yankees would need. Ruth hit his tenth home run two days later and also knocked in the tying run and scored the winning one. On the next day, he tripled off the center-field fence with the bases full. New York took three of four games, and Ruth played a key role in all of the victories. Before boarding the steamer to Cleveland, Babe predicted he would hit sixty home runs. "I'll get two in every five games," he projected.

~

The advocates of Baseball Science could be as serious as economists when espousing its merits. By 1921, many of them had begun mourning what had been lost. The changes Ruth brought disappointed traditionalists like Ring Lardner, who savored Cobb's play. Once the slugging started, Lardner never felt the same affection for baseball. He wrote less and less about the sport.

While Cobb could illuminate the reasons for everything he (and anyone else) did, Ruth struggled to analyze his play when questioned. "I pick out what looks good to me—the others I leave alone," he said. "There is no secret to my hitting. . . . I just stand up there and swat." Ruth's simple explanations did nothing to reverse the notion that Cobb's style was more intelligent. Fans might prefer Ruth's slugging, but those who really knew baseball appreciated the "inside game" of Cobb and his comrades. Or so the argument went. It was finesse and intellect versus luck and beastly strength. "Ty out-foxes rivals," Eddie Collins would explain. "The Babe overpowers them."

"It may be a triumph of brawn over brain," explained F. C. Lane of *Baseball Magazine*. "It may suggest the dominance of mere brute strength over intelligence. It may show a preference for the caveman over the finished artist. It may be what you will. But rest assured it's a fact. Babe Ruth is the uncrowned king of the diamond, the master figure of the baseball season, the big noise in the biggest game on earth."

It irked Cobb that Ruth's style was making his own methods passé. It frustrated him to watch someone he considered inferior challenge his standing in the game. Babe Ruth bristled, too—for a different reason. He was tired of the brains versus brawn characterization. Who wouldn't resent being portrayed as the lumbering oaf to Cobb's sharp-minded genius?

Ruth wanted to dispel the belief that he was a one-dimensional player on offense, so he set out to demonstrate that he could do a few things that were considered Cobb's domain, including stealing bases. In 1921, no teammate would top his seventeen thefts, and no one would get caught more often either.

In one contest, Ruth seemed intent on proving his adequate base-running talents. After doubling and advancing to third, he attempted the one feat that no one in baseball history had ever come close to doing as well as Cobb: He tried to steal home. (Cobb would do it an unparalleled fifty-four times.) Ruth took off as the pitcher went into his full windup. But Detroit catcher Eddie Ainsmith blocked the plate and tagged him out. Innings later, Ruth singled to center and tried to stretch it into a double. Cobb pegged him at second.

There was no hiding the distaste the two men felt for each other. It stood out like the Woolworth Building, Manhattan's tallest skyscraper. Fans saw it in the looks Cobb and Ruth cast. They detected it in their telling gestures and obvious slights. Their teammates heard it in the words they spoke—taunts so crude and profane that reporters could not print them. Cobb hated Ruth, and Ruth hated Cobb. They could barely tolerate the sight of one another, and their relationship wasn't getting better.

War of 1921

U NDETERRED BY GATHERING STORM CLOUDS, THIRTY
thousand fans turned out at the Polo Grounds on Saturday,
June 11, to see Cobb and Ruth face off in the first of a four-game series. The action opened quickly. With Donie Bush on first, Cobb
stroked Waite Hoyt's first pitch off the Piedmont Tobacco sign in
right field. Bush scored on the double. Ruth and the Yankees answered with three runs. The Tigers responded with two more, Cobb
slugging another double and scoring moments later. They added
three more runs to take the lead, Cobb driving in one on a single and
scoring a second on Bobby Veach's home run. Detroit was ahead 6–3.

In the seventh, Chicken Hawks and team captain Roger Peckinpaugh got on base. A buzz swept across the stands and grew
louder as Ruth strutted to the plate.

Cobb trotted in from center field for a conference near short with Bush, Amish catcher Johnny Bassler, and pitcher Jim Middleton— the umpteenth time he had delayed the game in such a fashion. The discussion, uninterrupted by umpires, lasted so long that Ruth retreated to the bench. Cobb and company glowered their disapproval at Ruth. It was an obvious attempt to exasperate him. All afternoon, the two had been butting heads. This was just one more in a string of standoffs.

After Ty and the others returned to their positions, Ruth lingered in the dugout. *Who the hell does Cobb think he is?* Ruth must have wondered. He was tired of Cobb's disrespect. He could play the waiting game, too. Finally, umpire Bill Dinneen ended the stalemate and ordered Babe to bat.

Middleton tossed a strike and then teased Ruth with two wide pitches. When the fourth floated off the plate, Ruth stretched for it and drove it against the wind down the right-field line and over the fence, tying the game. As he jubilantly circled the bases, Ruth doffed his cap at Cobb. The Yankees went on to win.

Before the next day's game, a press photographer found Cobb on the field and asked if he'd be willing to have a shot taken with Ruth. It was common for opponents to pose together prior to games. Scrapbooks from the early 1900s are filled with clippings of rival stars shaking hands and smiling at one another. Cobb agreed to the photo; he had taken dozens like it before. He and Ruth had even taken one at the Polo Grounds a year earlier, the two of them standing side by side, showing off their different batting stances. But this time, Ruth refused.

"Say, I wouldn't pose with that stiff for no sort of money—not me," responded Ruth in the censored version.

The slight pricked Cobb's ego. "If I had a beak like he's got, maybe I'd be a little sensitive about having it photographed, too," he was quoted as replying—though his actual words were likely much harsher.

The remark got back to Ruth, and he roared. And so began Sunday at the Polo Grounds.

Hostilities flared throughout the muggy afternoon. At one juncture, Cobb answered Yankee catcalls by strolling over to their dugout. He and Huggins argued chest to chin another time, heads bobbing and words flying furiously. Lu Blue and Wally Schang had to be separated once, and 140-pound Donie Bush got ejected after slugging umpire Dinneen in the stomach and chin and kicking him in the foot. Several players vowed to settle matters under the stands.

But the real feature was Cobb versus Ruth. They exchanged jibes throughout the game. Once, Cobb made ape gestures at him. After Ruth struck out in the fourth—missing on one of his ferocious swings—Cobb laughed as they passed on the field, flattening his nose with his index finger. Ruth stormed after him. They went face-to-face with fists clenched as umpires and teammates intervened. In the stands, one young female spectator fainted while worrying over her rosary beads.

An inning later, Ruth punched a 3-0 pitch into the upper deck in right. The cheers of thirty-four thousand fans thundered from the ballpark, echoing off Coogan's Bluff. Cobb was furious, and he took his anger out on his pitcher. He ran in from center and publicly chastised Suds Sutherland, a rookie who had spent eight years in the minors waiting for his chance. Sutherland would not start another game for Cobb—or anyone else. (He played only one year, accumulating a 6-2 record and batting .407.) Ruth added two doubles, and the Yankees won. But Cobb's pestering had gotten to him, and he wanted to retaliate.

The next day, Monday, June 13, Ruth insisted Miller Huggins let him pitch. When the Tigers saw Ruth warming up, they could hardly contain themselves, especially coach Dan Howley, who had roomed with Ruth for a short time with the Red Sox in 1919. Howley served not only as Cobb's assistant manager but also as his prime mouth. He heckled with the best of them, going at it so furiously that when he got laryngitis in the heat of a later pennant race, the ailment cost Detroit the flag, according to Cobb.

"What! You going to pitch?" yelled Howley, all smiles. Ruth ignored him and continued loosening his arm. Although he had shown himself a gifted pitcher with Boston, he had seen little action with New York. He had pitched in only one game in 1920, and was now preparing for his only start of 1921. Despite his rustiness, Ruth held the Tigers scoreless through four innings, allowing just one single.

Tiring quickly and drenched in sweat, Ruth surrendered a double to Pep Young to open the fifth. Young scored on an error. Ruth was weakening and turning wild. It had been a draw so far with Cobb, who had walked once and flown to center. He ached to paste Ruth, and Babe wanted as badly to disgrace Cobb. He had insisted on pitching, after all, just to quiet the Peach. Ruth knew it would be his last chance to subdue him.

As Cobb stepped up, Ruth corralled his remaining energy. Revenge was on his mind, and he delivered it deliciously, fanning Cobb. It was the only strikeout Ruth would record that day, and it was one of only nineteen that Cobb would surrender all season. "The Polo Ground galleries were tossed into a state of hysteria," said one witness. Ruth spent his last good pitches against his hated enemy. Instantly, he gave up two triples and walked a batter. When Huggins removed him, Ruth went cheerfully into the outfield as Cobb stewed on the bench. Ruth had completed his mission. He had embarrassed the great Ty Cobb in a very public showdown. The Peach's defenders said that Cobb had been overeager because "Ruth looked easy to wallop." Regardless, Ruth had won.

He wasn't finished, though. Babe drove two home runs into the stands, the last one screaming over Cobb's head into the bleachers in center—a drive of 450 feet. No ball had ever been hit there before. A pack of boys chased it as it ricocheted beneath the wooden benches. Ruth bowed and tipped his cap as he jogged around the diamond. He followed with two more home runs the next day, one estimated at 475 feet. Each time Ruth headed to the plate, he stared at Cobb and smiled. He knew he had gotten the best of him.

Ruth hit six home runs in four days, and only once did Cobb grant him an intentional pass. It was another first for Babe: his first six-home-run series. Tellingly, his first three-home-run series and his first four-home-run series had also come against Cobb and the

Tigers, in 1918 and 1919. The Yankees swept Detroit, and for the first time the usually loyal Detroit press began questioning Cobb's managerial methods. "No other club," noted Harry Salsinger, "has lost seven out of eight games to New York, simply because no other club would show the same policy in pitching to Ruth." Doing so in crucial moments, added the *Detroit Free Press,* "is like touching a match to a fuse in a bomb."

Ruth had twenty-three home runs, and eight of them had come against Detroit. Clearly, Cobb's approach was failing. Even *The Sporting News,* billed (and recognized) as "the baseball paper of the world," questioned Cobb's wisdom: "It has been, it seems, rather a personal issue between Cobb and Ruth. . . . Will Cobb yield, swallow his pride, and have his pitchers throw wide to Ruth?"

Not that anybody was doing terribly well against Babe. Shy of not pitching to him, there appeared to be no way of stopping him. Everywhere he played, he seemed not only to hit home runs but also to set distance records. There were the two long home runs in New York, but in May, in both Washington's Griffith Stadium and Cleveland's League Park, he had belted balls farther than anyone had ever done before. On July 18, with Cobb on the bench, Ruth powered a ball out of Navin Field, striking pavement an estimated 560 feet from home plate, out where Francis Ouimet had deposited a few golf balls in that 1915 exhibition. The home run catapulted Ruth past nineteenth-century star Roger Connor. Ruth had 139 career home runs. No one had hit more, and Ruth was only twenty-six.

"If this crashing Titan truly is human," wrote Dan Daniel, "we have arrived at the physical superman, and Ruth is writing a remarkable postscript to Genesis. . . . Before Ruth came along it was Cobb the Magnificent. Now the Babe monopolizes the limelight. The great Tyrus is an 'also ran' in the race for the wild hurrahs of the crowd."

Among Ruth's admirers was Chick Shorten, who had played with him in Boston and now played against him in Detroit. It seemed almost sacrilegious when Shorten publicly praised Ruth while in Cobb's clubhouse. "Ruth is the greatest natural ball player that ever stepped on a ball field," Shorten said. "He just does the right thing because he can't do anything the wrong way in base-ball." Coincidentally perhaps, Shorten was waived after the season.

~

Ruth's feats were so extraordinary that they begged explanation. Af-ter one summer game, a friend convinced Ruth to be tested at Co-lumbia University. Still in his dirty Yankee uniform, Ruth arrived at the university's psychological research lab, where two bespectacled grad-student scientists put him through a three-hour examination.

They gave him a fifty-four-ounce bat, strapped a hoselike appara-tus around his chest, stationed him in front of a field of charged wires, and had him swing at a suspended ball so they could measure the speed and strength of his stroke. They tested his eyes by seating him before a darkened cabinet and having him tap a Morse-like device every time he detected one of their flashes of light. They gauged his hand-eye coordination by registering the number of times he could repeatedly poke a stylus into the three holes at the points of a triangle. They flashed letters and words at him; they had him rap an electric pen on a charged surface; they ran him up and down a staircase five times. The goal of all this effort: to uncover the secret to his superiority. They concluded that under stress Ruth re-mained more composed than 499 out of 500 people, that his eyes and ears reacted more quickly than the average person's, that he op-erated at 90 percent physical efficiency (compared to 60 percent for mere mortals), that he swung a bat at 110 feet per second, and that he could touch a stylus to a flat surface at a rate of 193 times per minute. Oh, and they—these two scientists who admitted knowing little about baseball—determined one other thing: that Ruth could perform even better if he didn't hold his breath as he swung.

Others offered different explanations for Ruth's achievements. In Pittsburgh, Professor Hans Kestler, a healer with feral eyes and long black hair, cornered manager George Gibson at the team ho-tel, promising great things.

"Behold in me the wonderful instrument whereby Babe Ruth has become the most amazing batsman in the world," he said.

Gibson was amused. "How did you do it?" he asked.

"By the laying on of hands," the stranger replied, thrusting his gaunt fingers at Gibson. "I shall lay my hands on Herr Carey of your club and he shall run like the frightened deer."

Gibson declined.

Ty Cobb didn't credit Ruth's home runs to anything mystical. He blamed them on the "lively ball." Though officials and ball manufacturers disputed the claim, most baseball observers of the era, including Cobb, believed that the baseball had been changed to encourage home runs. It had a different cover or a more tightly wound core, they contended. Something physical had to explain the change in the game, they reasoned. After all, the number of home runs in the American League had jumped from 96 in 1918 to 369 in 1920. HOME-RUNNING! EVERYBODY'S DOING IT, heralded one headline.

As a fielder, Cobb could tell balls were traveling greater distances. "Over in Washington there is a drain out in center field and this drain has a rubber covering," he said. "Before this year, I played behind the rubber for only one player on the Washington club. . . . In the series that we closed there yesterday, I played behind this rubber for every batter on the Washington team. . . . I was not too far out on any of them."

Cobb himself was hitting home runs at a pace he had never before approached. In 1919, he had recorded just one. Now, he was on his way to a career-high twelve. Was it because of the "rabbit ball" or the recent banning of trick pitches like the spitball or the fact that umpires were putting fresh, clean balls into play more frequently? Was Cobb trying to show that he too could clear the fences? The latter wasn't out of the question.

～

In late September 1921, when the Yankees were struggling with the Indians for first, Cobb tried frantically to upset New York's pennant hopes. Cobb's disrespect for Ruth was palpable, and his desire to deprive New York of the title flowed from it. So long as Ruth's individual success didn't translate into a championship,

Cobb could use it as evidence that home runs weren't the route to victory. As he would point out, regardless of Ruth's records, neither the Red Sox of 1919 nor the Yankees of 1920 had captured the American League flag. Baseball Science, as practiced by the White Sox and Indians, had prevailed in those two seasons, and Cobb was pulling for it again.

In that final series, Cobb played with an intensity uncommon for a player on a team far out of the race and with little hope of a share of the World Series money. (Clubs in the top half of the standings got a portion of the championship payday.) Cobb was trying almost too hard at the end, taking unnecessary risks, making unusual decisions. In one game against New York, he got picked off third base. In another, he changed hitters in the middle of the count, sending Shorten to bat for Dutch Leonard with one strike remaining. It was all to no avail. The Yankees were bound for the World Series.

The Tigers had improved to 71–82 under Cobb, but the team remained out of contention, twenty-seven games back. Cobb batted .389, second-best in the league, just behind protégé Harry Heilmann and ahead of Ruth. But Ruth dominated all of baseball. His fifty-nine home runs more than doubled the number hit by his closest challenger, and his 171 runs batted in and 177 runs scored set twentieth-century records. While Cobb's boosters in the press argued his case—*The Sporting News* ruling that "there is none greater" and James Isaminger of *The Philadelphia Inquirer* reminding all that Cobb was the best "without exception" and the respected John Sheridan fawning continually over "the greatest of them all"—no one could deny Babe Ruth's towering presence. Not even Grantland Rice. In a column titled "Ty Cobb vs. Babe Ruth," he admitted that Ruth's hits were "the more spectacular," but he urged the baseball world to delay judgment until both men had concluded their careers. And that seemed a fair request. Cobb had been playing brilliantly for more than fifteen years. Ruth had been a full-time hitter for only three seasons—three remarkable seasons. He had a long way to go. But it was looking as if the only person who could derail Babe Ruth was Babe Ruth.

The Other Babe

Ruth and Cobb pose with businessmen. GEORGE BRACE
PHOTOGRAPHY

~

O VER THE NEXT TWO SEASONS, COBB AND RUTH'S RELA-
tionship festered. They would, according to one mutual
friend, go three years without exchanging a cordial word. It wasn't

just a matter of Cobb being jealous of Ruth for seizing his station. It was Ruth, too. He was becoming intolerable.

Ruth in person differed from the public image of him as a rambunctious man-child. Fame and money were changing him. Waite Hoyt, who had played with Ruth in Boston, detected the difference immediately upon joining New York. "In Boston, he had been a surprised young man, hardly able to assimilate the extravagance of success," Hoyt recalled. But in New York, Ruth demanded deference. He flaunted his success and not so gently put others in their presumed place—behind him. Ruth could be gentle and generous, but as his ego bloated he became more difficult. He sought special treatment, made demands, and not so delicately reminded others who he was. Reporters outside his protective New York circle often found him "big and bluff," unhelpful, impatient, and prickly. Cullen Cain, a *Philadelphia Public Ledger* writer, had encountered him at training camp one spring. "Once is enough for me," he said.

After the Yankees had fallen to the Giants in the 1921 World Series, Ruth defied Commissioner Landis and went on a postseason barnstorming tour—a clear violation of baseball rules, which prohibited players on championship teams from appearing in such exhibitions. Landis ordered Ruth to abandon his plans. "You can tell him to go to hell," Ruth said. "If Landis wants to pick on me and put me out of baseball, he can do it. I'm going on with the tour." Ruth's rebellion lasted about a week before team owner Col. T. L. Huston convinced him to repent.

Ruth's brusque side continued to emerge publicly in 1922. As a result of his autumn revolt, he started the season on suspension. Upon returning, he resumed his contemptuous ways. In May, after a close call went against him, Ruth hurled a handful of dirt in anger. It found the face of umpire George Hildebrand, earning Ruth an ejection and a fine. In the same game, he charged into the stands in pursuit of a heckling fan. The outburst cost him the title of Yankees captain. In June, he was suspended again, for brawling off the field with umpire Bill Dinneen.

American League president Ban Johnson was livid. He blazed a letter to Ruth at the Brunswick Hotel in Boston. He said the league had indulged Ruth while he struggled to regain his prestige. He called his behavior reprehensible, accused him of betraying his team, and said he was no longer valuable to his club. "The American League cares nothing for Ruth," he wrote. ". . . A man of your stamp bodes no good in the profession. . . . You should allow some intelligence to creep into a mind that has plainly been warped."

Johnson wasn't the only person who thought Ruth needed to be brought down. So did Cobb and other American League veterans. Cobb pounced on Ruth's difficulties. By midseason, the Tigers held an 8–1 series advantage over the Yankees. "You fellows ought to be ten games in front today," Cobb yelled toward the New York dugout one day. "If you were on my club, I'd hit you over the head with a bat." He might well have been directing his comments at one slugger in particular. Ruth didn't just respond to Cobb's relentless attacks. He instigated his own. Prior to another game, Ruth heaved vulgarities at Cobb from the bench, trying to incite him as he stood near the batting cage within earshot of fans.

Ruth's troubles did not mute his brashness. On June 16 at Navin Field, he put on a brazen show as he prepared to bat. Ruth theatrically yanked a handkerchief from his pocket, dusted his spikes with it, looked out to Cobb in center field, and waved the tissue at Cobb. Ty responded with a wave of his own. After Ruth missed the first pitch, Cobb gestured more excitedly. When Ruth fouled off the second pitch, Cobb flailed his arms at Babe. He also did so after the third pitch, a ball. On the fourth, Ruth whiffed, prompting Cobb to remove his cap and fan it above his head as Ruth stalked back to the bench.

Cobb's pitchers thought they had figured out Ruth. They boasted of having developed a secret system to defeat the Bambino. Through July, they had surrendered no home runs to Ruth. He had only five singles in twenty-seven official at bats. But in August, before the largest crowd yet at Navin Field, Ruth ended the streak. With thirty thousand jammed into the park, police locked the gates to repel the crowds, leaving thousands of fans milling outside the stadium. Some found spots in trees and on telegraph poles. Ruth entertained them with a home run and a double. He got two doubles the next day and hit a home run in the fourth game—after

Cobb had robbed him of another. Harry Salsinger of *The Detroit News* described Cobb's catch as one of the greatest ever made at the park. Cobb climbed over collapsed bleachers and leaped at the fence to deprive Ruth of glory. Cobb and Ruth often played their best baseball against one another.

Cobb glowed in 1922. He topped .400 for the first time in a decade. At age thirty-five, he had gotten five hits in four separate games, establishing a league record. He outperformed Ruth. Though Ruth had overshadowed him in the previous three seasons, Cobb had remained a powerful force. His name still appeared among the league leaders. "When you get a man of high ability who also has ambition and energy then you have a Cobb, a towering genius," said John Sheridan of *The Sporting News*.

While Cobb prospered, Ruth suffered an off year. His thirty-five home runs were not enough to attain the crown. In the World Series against the Giants, he managed just two hits in seventeen at bats, and the Yankees lost again. Ruth had tumbled from his pedestal, and Cobb seized the moment. He salted Ruth's wounds by reminding several reporters that he had predicted Ruth's downfall.

In dreamy moments, Cobb must have imagined that Ruth was on his way out of baseball, that his current problems were just the start of a long spiral downward, that Ruth would drift out of fashion, out of favor, out of the sport, and into obscurity, a deserving victim of his own foolishness. And then Cobb could retire, his standing secure, his stature solidified, his immortality certain, his brilliance appreciated more than ever. And wouldn't that be sweet?

But Ruth roared back in 1923. By the end of May, the Babe had eleven home runs, and the Yankees were locked in first place, where they would remain. During one mid-August series, American League president Ban Johnson shocked Ruth by restricting his choice of bats. Johnson ordered Ruth to stop using a bat that Sam Crawford had crafted for him from four pieces of hardened wood. Johnson said he was acting on a formal complaint. Johnson declined to name the petitioner, but it may have been more than coincidence that his directive came midway through a New York homestand against Cobb's Tigers. Without his prized bat, Ruth still hit two home runs in the series. Over the season, Ruth drove in 131 runs, batted a career-high .393, and captured the American League's Most Valuable Player Award. The Yankees took the pennant, outdistancing Cobb's second-place Detroiters. They stormed into the World Series, and trounced the Giants to win their first world championship. This time, Ruth had outshone Cobb in every area. His average was fifty-three points higher than Cobb's. He had bested him in hits, runs, doubles, triples, runs batted in, walks, and, naturally, home runs. He had even stolen more bases—seventeen to Cobb's pitiful nine.

By the spring of 1924, sportswriters were deriding Cobb as "decrepit" and an "old war horse." They were beginning to treat him as a museum piece. He was surely on his way out now. Damon Runyon urged fathers to take their sons to see Cobb perform. "It will mean something for him to be able to say 'I saw Cobb' when he is older." But Cobb wasn't ready to become a relic. He had more to prove, and he knew he didn't have long to prove it. It was almost as if Cobb were staying around to foil Ruth and safeguard his own legacy. Cobb burned with a sense of purpose at spring training.

~

It didn't matter how big or small the issue. Cobb and Ruth always seemed to end up on opposite sides. They were rivals in every conceivable way. They couldn't even agree on whether golf was good or bad for ballplayers.

With great seriousness, team managers deliberated over that issue at training camp in 1924. A host of them, including Cobb, decided golf harmed ballplayers. With no advance warning, Cobb banned his men from playing golf. In the team clubhouse, he seized their mashies, midirons, spoons, and niblicks. "Some say they can get into condition by playing golf, but they can get into condition just as well out on the ball field," he said. "All we ask is that they be at their best two hours a day on the field and they can't give their best if they're playing golf." It was an almost-unbearable punishment for the Tigers, who were holding camp in Augusta.

What made it worse was that the players had their Sundays free because baseball—unlike golf—was prohibited in Georgia on the
Sabbath.

Cobb was not alone. Bucky Harris, first-year manager of the
Washington Senators, issued an edict against golf, and so did John
McGraw of the New York Giants. "Golf is too good," said McGraw,
"for it sometimes grips a ball player so tightly that he gives more attention to perfecting his midiron shots than he does to polishing
off his batting style. The first-class baseball player must think, talk,
and eat baseball in addition to playing it, and I don't want any of
my players sitting around and talking nothing but golf in the heat
of a pennant race. There isn't any question about it: the baseball
stroke and the golf stroke are vastly different, and the mastering of
one spoils the other."

Meanwhile, in Hot Springs, Arkansas, the world-champion Yankees had no qualms about their players hitting the greens. As Cobb
was instituting his prohibition, Ruth, a husky 233 pounds, was
stroking an 89 in a country club tournament—good enough to put
him in medal contention. Ruth was convinced that hours on the
course prepared him for the baseball season.

Sometime during his pitching tenure with Boston—possibly as
early as 1914 but absolutely by the summer of 1919—Ruth had discovered golf and become enamored with it. His relationship with
the game was quite different from Cobb's. Golf provided Ruth with
a joyous pastime that would span his adult life—from the moment
he discovered it to his final, cancer-ridden years when it would provide a welcome diversion. It would be a long love affair, docu-
mented on the nation's sports pages. When Ruth hammered a golf
ball 280 yards, he would make headlines. Ruth always included a
few weeks of golf as part of his training regimen. He would play
during the season, too, his fondness for the game even figuring into
a public scandal when Delores Dixon filed a $50,000 paternity suit
against him. He called her "my little golf girl," she said.

"A ball player doesn't get as much work during a season as people
think," Ruth said. "Half the time during a game, he is on the bench. In
the mornings and at night, he does nothing but sit around the

hotels. [His roommates must have laughed at that one.] I believe ball players do more sitting than any other outdoor men. For that reason, their legs stay in shape for speed but not for endurance. When we loaf in the winter, it is a tough job to get back in shape and I figure that golf in a warm climate should make me just right."

That spring, a grizzled goat named Tin-Can Nanny turned up at Cobb's training camp in rainy Augusta. She was Detroit's new mascot. "The Yankees' goat," the Tigers called her, as in "we've got their goat." Cobb promised reporters that his team would be among the top two in the American League, a contender for the crown. Regardless of whether or not they won the title, the Tigers would best the Yankees, he told Grantland Rice. "We'll beat them oftener than they will beat us," he said. That was Cobb's goal. He wanted to stop the Yankees. Of course, by stopping the Yankees he would also be stopping Babe Ruth.

With Ruth coming off a superb world-championship season, Cobb intended to do everything he could to distract, upset, and fluster his rival in 1924. For Cobb, it was merely part of the game. For Ruth, who had been a target for years, the routine was stale and unbearable. He had long ago tired of Cobb's shenanigans.

Riot at Navin Field

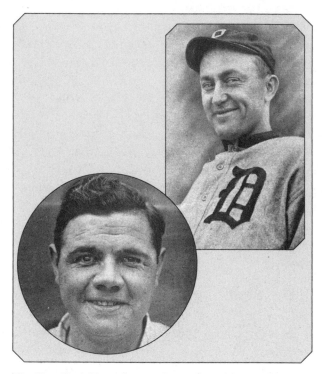

The New York Times hypes the Yankees-Tigers rivalry in a photo layout.

∽

Y EAR-OLD YANKEE STADIUM, THE MOST MAGNIFICENT ballpark in the major leagues, resembled a palace. Decorated in flags and bunting and crowned with a copper frieze that gave it a royal air, it was "The House That Ruth Built," proclaimed reporter Fred Lieb. It might also have been called "The House

Built for Ruth," for its right-field wall stood that cozy 295 feet down the line.

The Tigers chugged into New York on May 23 for their first series against the defending World Champions. Over the past three seasons combined, ever since Cobb had become manager, the Tigers and the Yankees had been the top-drawing teams in the American League. The bad blood between them—comparable to the animus between the Yankees and Red Sox of more recent times—flowed from the tainted relationship of the game's two giants, and it guaranteed crushing weekend crowds.

The opening series threatened to set a caustic tone for the season.

The Tigers led through most of the first game and were looking to pad their lead in the sixth. With the bases loaded and the count full, Harry Heilmann, the defending batting champion, got called out on a pitch near the edge of the plate. Fuming, he spun around to challenge Pants Rowland, now an umpire. In doing so, he slammed his bat—accidentally, he claimed—into the shins of catcher Fred "Bootnose" Hofmann. Rowland ejected Heilmann despite Cobb's protests. Until that point, it had been a good day for Cobb. He had been nearly perfect at the bat. But fortunes turned. In the eighth, irked by an earlier misplay by second baseman Del Pratt, Cobb charged in from center field to commandeer what should have been an easy pop to Pratt. Cobb passionately called off all others, insisted the fly was his, and then lost sight of the ball. It dropped safely, setting up the tying run. The Yankees and their fans howled at Cobb. Ruth, who had homered earlier, rubbed it in by singling and scoring the winning run.

Detroit took the next game and in the third contest rallied before forty-five thousand fans, with Cobb hitting a home run and scoring twice. Midway through the affair, animosities sparked when Yankee Mike McNally interfered with Lu Blue on a play at first. Blue challenged McNally, and the field erupted. Wally Pipp tried to intervene, and soon five-foot-six Fred Haney had him by the neck. The near brawl emptied both benches and got Blue and McNally ejected. Somewhere amid the commotion were Ruth and

Cobb. Nerves remained frazzled and raw for the remainder of the game. The dissension would carry over to the next series.

~

A smallpox epidemic engulfed Detroit in 1924. By mid-June, 1,450 residents had contracted the disease, and about one in ten of them had died. On a grim Tuesday, an army of 153 policemen, fifty-three doctors, and fifty assistants stormed into a fifteen-block area a mile from Navin Field and quarantined the neighborhood. In a four-hour period they vaccinated eight thousand people. Fearful that the epidemic might stall the city's growth—it had become the nation's fourth-largest city—Detroit officials assured newcomers that all hotel, restaurant, and store workers had been immunized.

The Tigers hadn't escaped the needle either, and it cost them. Heilmann reacted badly to the vaccination. By the next day, with the Yankees having arrived in town, his arm had swollen to twice its normal size. He missed the first game. A Detroit official suggested the Yankees should be vaccinated, too. It sounded like something Cobb might have instigated. One couldn't be blamed for wondering. This was Cobb's town, after all, and his team was in second place. And he had always been willing to go to extreme lengths to win.

Already, players throughout the league questioned the erratic use of "circus seats" at Navin Field. Clubs often anticipated overflow crowds by erecting temporary bleachers in the outfield. But in Detroit the tiers appeared and disappeared like a Houdini prop. Demand for tickets factored less into the decision than the hitting abilities of the visiting team, critics contended. Because portable bleachers altered ground rules, a ball that might ordinarily be a single would become a double or a triple when it bounced into the shallow seats—a fact that Cobb used to tactical advantage. Of course, demand for tickets often placed fans on the edges of the field, which in itself could impact a visiting team. Hometown children raced enemy players for balls hit into the outfield. If they reached them first, they could turn a Detroit single into a double.

In one 1924 contest, Yankee Earle Combs complained that a Detroit fan stole a pack of tobacco from his back pocket when he pursued a ball into the crowd. In another game, Babe Ruth objected vehemently when the pro-Tiger crowd cleared a path for Cobb, allowing him to encroach into the overflow area to catch a fly ball that would otherwise have been a triple.

And then there was the matter of the infield grass. Detroit had speed; New York didn't. Cobb and his groundskeeper conspired to create a minefield between home plate and third base. When completed, it resembled the work of a drunken barber. The shaggy turf in front of home stood inches higher than the close-clipped grass near the base. Depending on where the third baseman played, Cobb's speedsters could either drop a bunt on the stifling sod—which had been soaked, by the way—or send a ball skidding past the fielder. A bunt along the line often stayed fair, for Cobb and company had created a slight ridge to persuade it.

In Wednesday's opener, the interaction between opposing players was pronounced. Pitcher Joe Bush laughed at Cobb when he swung at and missed a curveball. After singling, Cobb chortled at Bush from first base. Insults and slights filled the game. Yankees manager Miller Huggins knew enough to be leery of Cobb's sly ways. In the sixth inning, Cobb ran in from center field to consult with his pitcher, Earl Whitehill. Ruth had just walked, and Whitehill had fallen behind on Bob Meusel. It might be that Cobb simply wanted to settle Whitehill's nerves—a challenging task given that Cobb's presence often had the opposite effect. But Huggins suspected something else. He believed that Cobb was trying to get close enough to needle Ruth or Meusel. Huggins took no chances. He called both sluggers to the bench and didn't let them return to the field until Cobb was back in center field.

The game belonged to Cobb. He led Detroit with two triples, three runs, and dazzling defense. Through his daring, he stretched a double and turned a force-out into a run. It was, in the words of one smitten observer, "another of those brilliant days of his that are becoming like gems in a cluster ring." Pal Harry Salsinger of *The Detroit News* was nearly delirious in his praise of the old master (though Cobb might have preferred he make the point without painting him as a cane-clutching geezer):

> Never has there flashed across the baseball horizon a man that came through as often as Cobb when coming through meant everything in the final result. Some of his speed is gone. He cannot get the number of hits that he used to get. . . . He cannot cover the ground that he once defended in the outfield and his throwing arm is even weaker than it was but the spirit of Cobb and the fire of him have not been dimmed by age. The surge of battle is as strong as ever, the ambition just as keen.

Even New York reporters couldn't keep from complimenting the Peach. "The Yankees lost—lost not to the Tigers, but to an unbeatable Ty Cobb," noted Ford Frick, the future baseball commissioner.

Tiger fans enjoyed the victory almost as much as they enjoyed hooting at Babe Ruth when he struck out on a cyclonic swing. But when Ruth connected the next day, the crowd loved him for that, too. His fifteenth home run fluttered high over the right-field wall and dropped onto brick-paved Trumbull Avenue. It put his team well ahead, 8–0. Cobb could bunt and steal all he wanted, but he wouldn't be able to erase that difference. The game was out of reach, which made what happened an inning later suspect: Syd Johnson drove a fastball into Ruth's ribs. Still later, another Tiger pitcher, Herm Pillette, nailed Ernie Johnson after he had tripled. Johnson had bitter words for Pillette while taking first.

The Yankees were furious. They believed that Cobb ordered his men to peg batters, and the statistics offered some evidence. In the previous three years, Detroit pitchers had pelted batters 192 times—40 times more than any other staff.

Ruth was in his eleventh season in the American League. He was twenty-nine, and no longer the greenhorn to Cobb's bull moose. He hated the way Cobb treated him, and he was tired of

Cobb's digs, his mind games, his disrespect, and the beanballs. Ruth knew that he—not Cobb—was now the best player in baseball, and he was in no mood to tolerate Cobb's crap any longer.

Cobb had been in charge of Detroit since 1921, and in each season the Yankees had captured the pennant and competed in the World Series. It burned Cobb. He didn't play the game for fun. It wasn't Parchesi, he once said: "Baseball is a red-blooded sport for red-blooded men. It's no pink tea, and mollycoddles had better stay out. It's a contest and everything that implies, a struggle for supremacy, a survival of the fittest."

Ruth and the Yankees surely celebrated that night. Detroit offered abundant options. Boxing champ Jack Dempsey was in town doing a vaudeville show. Onstage at the Orpheum, eighteen-year-old Eugenie Davis, "the psychic marvel," shared her forecasts. Burlesque strippers shimmied in and out of spangles in a dozen dives. For the romantic and more sedate, the Boblo Island steamer, its deck glowing with lights, glided on the Detroit River, the moon's reflection shimmering on the water.

It was Prohibition, but there was no shortage of liquor. The proximity to the Canadian border assured a plentiful supply. By some estimates, Detroit played host to more than twenty thousand speakeasies, blind pigs, and illegal basement bars. Ruth visited more than a few of them. He loved to drink and to eat, and he savored the single life—though officially married. A parade of flappers and free-spirited young women generously made themselves available, and Ruth took full advantage. Once, a Detroit officer responding to a complaint reportedly found Ruth frolicking inside a judge's home with a naked co-ed perched atop his shoulders.

The nightlife did not belong to Ruth alone. He had the company of teammates like Meusel and even Tiger opponents like Heilmann and Heinie Manush, whose proclivities would get him labeled a "home buster" in one couple's divorce proceedings. (The husband had discovered his wife's love notes in Manush's hotel room: "Oh, Heinie, how I love your kisses," she wrote. "I sleep with your picture under my pillow.")

Ruth rated as a notorious curfew breaker. He stayed out late, missed bed checks, and lived the wild life. Roommates contended he spent little time in his bed, which made his endorsement of Simmons mattresses all the more incredulous. In advertisements appearing in the Detroit papers, Ruth credited plenty of "restful, sound sleep" for his performance. "Whoever it was that said 'early to bed makes a man healthy and wise' knew what he was talking about," declared Ruth with the straightest of faces.

Cobb's late nights—tame by comparison—were mostly behind him. A Shriner, he often spent his evenings at the Masonic Temple in Detroit, just blocks from the ballpark. He frequently asked pitcher Eddie Wells to come along. Wells usually accepted. How do you turn down your manager? Cobb tried to set an example for his players, some of whom—like ace George Dauss—were inclined to drink too much. Baseball came first for Cobb, and he thought it should come first for every player.

~

It was Friday the 13th. Worse, Wally Pipp's dad was at the park. Known affectionately as Uncle Bill, the older Pipp had come from Grand Rapids to see his son's team play. An accepted member of the pinstripe fraternity, Bill Pipp was a gregarious fellow, one of the nicest chaps around—and a known jinx.

Superstition flourished in baseball. Teams hired black children, hunchbacks, and misfits as good-luck charms. The 1911 World Series had seen the clash of two of the most famous mascots, Charles "Victory" Faust, described by some as a lunatic, and Louis Van Zelst, a dwarf. (Faust's Giants lost; within three years, he was in an insane asylum.) The Tigers had a six-toed batboy in 1919. They adopted a mutt, nicknamed Victory, in 1923—a year after experimenting with a live tiger cub. The St. Louis Browns even toured with a monkey—until the team started losing.

Cobb himself had the exuberant Alex Rivers, who since 1908 had acted as his personal assistant and number-one devotee. Rivers, a five-foot-two black man from New Orleans, was a familiar sight at

Navin Field, bounding from the dugout to retrieve bats, flashing his toothy smile. "I want Alex around," Cobb said during a Detroit winning streak. "I realize that the work of our players wins games, but just the same I wouldn't like to start one without Alex here. Superstitious? Well, maybe." Cobb's feelings for Rivers, though tinged by Cobb's bigoted, paternalistic beliefs, were genuine. After Rivers had failed to show for one ball game, Cobb, learning he had been in trouble with the law, rushed to the county jail to intercede on his behalf.

The Yankees employed the prize of all mascots. The much-sought Eddie Bennett had joined the team as a grinning, seventeen-year-old batboy in 1921. Before games, Ruth and Bennett sometimes entertained with a game of catch in which Ruth would continually hurl a ball just above Bennett's reach. Ruth wanted only Bennett to handle his bats. Believers credited the stunted, crippled orphan with helping the White Sox, Dodgers, and Yankees win pennants from 1919 to 1923. But even the presence of Bennett and Rivers might not be enough to ward off trouble at a game doubly doomed by the cursed Friday the 13th date and the attendance of Bill Pipp.

It was the first truly pretty afternoon of the season, the kind that tickled children with the promise of a summer of sandlot games and swimming excursions. Outside the ballpark, at the congested intersection of Michigan and Trumbull avenues, police officers waved thin-tired vehicles through the intersection and past the bars and cigar shops that hugged the brick-paved roads. Fans in caps and hats and fine clothes poured from trolleys that clacked to a halt beneath a web of wires strung above the streets. In the distance, locomotives rumbled into Detroit's Central Station, their whistles heavy on the air. The city hummed with noise. Nearly identical boxish, black Model Ts packed the small parking lot beside Navin Field, their bumpers touching. But most of the eighteen thousand fans who poured into the park for the three o'clock contest came by streetcar or on foot, streaming up the cool, dank concrete ramps and into the tobacco-sweetened grandstands.

It didn't take long for the scoring to begin. Second baseman Del Pratt, playing in what would be his last year, flubbed a double-play ball in the second inning, which triggered a three-run Yankee rally.

Detroit responded with two runs, and the Yankees answered an inning later. With men on second and third and no one out, pitcher Lil Stoner intentionally walked Babe Ruth. (Cobb had since abandoned his no-pass policy.) Bob Meusel followed with a two-run double, and Ruth scored on a sacrifice fly.

Detroit fought back. Willowy Bert Cole, who had relieved Stoner, shut down the Yankees. The Tigers scored twice in the fifth and sixth innings. The momentum had shifted. The game stood at 6–6. Cole, however, collapsed in the seventh, allowing four runs. In a close play at first, Ruth straight-armed the pitcher. The already ill feelings between the teams were growing more poisonous.

In the ninth inning, when Ruth ambled to the plate looking for his first hit, Cole greeted him by sizzling a pitch at his head. And then another. Players did not wear helmets, and an errant fastball could be deadly. Four years prior, Carl Mays had killed Cleveland's Ray Chapman on a pitch that fractured his skull. When a third ball zoomed toward Ruth's skull, Babe—remembering that he had been pelted a day earlier—concluded that Cobb had ordered the beanballs. After fouling out, a wrathful Ruth shot Cobb a look in center.

Bob Meusel batted next. He had been bulleting the ball recently, raising his average to .355. Detroit catcher Johnny Bassler, whom one observer said would be pressed to "beat another fat man up a hill," tried to lighten the mood by teasing Meusel, who was a friend. He had been bantering with Yankee players all afternoon. Bassler asked Meusel where he'd like to be plunked.

"Come on, now," Bassler called to Cole. "Don't be afraid to get it too close to his head." But any sense of frivolity evaporated when Cole blistered the first pitch into Meusel's back. Instantly, the Yankees exploded with rage. Meusel threw his bat aside and stormed the mound, umpire Billy Evans chasing after him.

"No, Bob," yelled Huggins, the scrawny, pinch-faced manager, racing from the third-base line. "No, Bob."

Meusel swung at Cole and missed. Evans grabbed him from behind as umpire Red Ormsby pushed between Cole and Meusel. Players were swarming the field, some locking onto Meusel's muscled arms.

Babe Ruth barreled toward the disturbance, challenging every-one along the way. Ty Cobb charged in from center. Ruth spotted Cobb and rumbled toward him with bent elbows and clenched fists. Umpires Evans and Ormsby raced to the new hot spot.

After five years of their rancid rivalry, it had come to this—again. Each man had sufficient reasons to want to pummel the other, to want to finish the matter right then. Shouting over a tangle of bod-ies, Ruth rabidly accused Cobb of ordering his pitchers to target Yankee batters. When Cobb denied it, Ruth challenged him to fight. Cobb cackled as Ruth's teammates grabbed Babe's arms and pulled him away. By now, police officers had joined the commotion.

Perhaps it was telling that Cobb did not respond with his fists. Though he had long resented Ruth, viewing him early on as a fluke who had undeservedly stumbled into success, Cobb qualified as an astute student of the sport and was begrudgingly beginning to real-ize that Ruth possessed real talent. He wasn't a circus freak, after all.

For a few years, mutual friends had been trying to bring Cobb and Ruth together, trying to help each man see that the other wasn't so terrible. Christy Walsh, who owned a newspaper syndicate, was working on them. So was John Roesink, a Detroit haberdasher and well-known sportsman. Grantland Rice also likely aimed to have a similar, positive influence. None of it meant, however, that Cobb wouldn't continue to heckle and razz Ruth if it worked to his advan-tage. As the Joe Jackson incident showed, he did it to friends as well as enemies. On the ball diamond all was fair in pursuit of victory.

Cobb could separate actions taken on the field from his friend-ships away from it. He could battle Walter Johnson for nine innings and still play cards with him later. He could throw out Tris Speaker, or be thrown out by him, and still enjoy hunting with him in the off-season. Cobb could compartmentalize his life in that way, and he didn't understand why others couldn't. Cobb could, for exam-ple, be brutally honest with friends and then dumbfounded when his words resulted in hurt feelings. "I get into a lot of trouble by speaking too plainly," he had once said. "I have made enemies by it, I suppose. . . . [But] a man's friends won't mind what he says when they know his way."

In the bedlam at Navin Field, Billy Evans ejected Cole and Meusel. But as Meusel was being ushered through the Tigers dugout and into the clubhouse tunnel, someone let into him with more insults, and the fists flailed again. As the players turned toward the tumult, hundreds of fans leaped onto the field for a closer look, and there the real fighting began.

Police fought spectators, spectators fought police. Fans battled fans. One officer who had been punched to the ground pulled his gun and prepared to fire but relented when ex-Tiger Davy Jones seized his arm. By the time riot police arrived, a thousand people occupied the diamond. The game could not be resumed; the Tigers forfeited. An hour later, mobs still waited in the park and outside, shouting for blood. Ruth, Meusel, and the other Yankees were smuggled out a back entrance and escorted to their hotel by officers.

The Yankees fingered Cobb for the fracas. "The players on our club do not blame the Tigers for their quarrelsome attitude as much as they blame their manager," said Huggins.

Cobb denied directing brushback pitches and accused Ruth of agitating. "Babe rushed on the field challenging me and several of the other Detroit players to fight him then and there," said Cobb. "He kept shouting these challenges and inflaming the crowd even when struggling with the police who were trying to get him away."

In his earlier days, Cobb would have taken a swing at Ruth.

"I could not afford to get into the fight," he said.

American League president Ban Johnson described the riot as "one of the most disgraceful incidents in all baseball history." He suspended Meusel and Cole for ten days and fined Ruth fifty dollars—the same amount, incidentally, that Ruth offered for the return of his ball glove, which like most bats and balls had been stolen in the melee. (Ruth's glove was never returned, though a few imposters were offered.) The Yankees won the game, but the victory did not absolve the cursed Uncle Bill Pipp. Without Meusel, the team went into a tailspin that started the day after the suspension. The Yankees fell from first to fourth place in less than two weeks, but they would recover.

15

The Making of a Delicate Peace

George Sisler, Babe Ruth, and Ty Cobb at the 1924 World Series. ERNIE HARWELL COLLECTION, DETROIT PUBLIC LIBRARY

T HE LONG 1924 SUMMER BEGAN TO WEAR ON TY COBB. IN pursuit of a record ninth two-hundred-hit season, as well as a pennant that was looking surprisingly possible, Cobb kept a frenzied pace. Aside from managing the team, he was playing in every game and batting more than ever. By season's end, he would have 625 official at bats, his all-time high. But his average, though among the best in the league, would drop and his play on the field become less invincible. He was running the bases like a man chasing his past. Against the Yankees in mid-July, he cost the Tigers a game by trying to score from second on a shallow, one-out single. Meusel's throw beat him by a couple horse lengths. Two innings later, with the bases loaded, Cobb took too big a lead at second, and Bob Shawkey picked him off. "In the Kitty League, they would call this bush baseball," chided one reporter.

Some of the swagger was vanishing from Cobb's voice. In Boston, he talked about retiring. "The strain is beginning to tell, and it would be foolish for me to try to prolong my playing days beyond my strength," he said. In Toronto, he dreamed of what might have been: "If I had my time over again, I would probably be a surgeon instead of a baseball player." And in Detroit, where bleacher bums harangued him over managerial decisions, he sounded especially deflated. "If they keep on razzing me for no reason at all, I'll surely quit," he said. "If that's what they aim to do, then they can have their wish."

As Cobb's fortunes fell, Ruth's soared. His average rose, along with his home-run total. Ruth clouted his twenty-ninth on July 23 against the Tigers. The home run came in the eleventh inning and won the game, putting the Yankees back in first place. The imposing walls of Yankee Stadium could not contain the joy. The cheers spilled onto the streets and across the Harlem River. Hundreds of fans swarmed around Ruth as he bobbed around the bases, pushing through the crowd toward home plate like some heroic figure in a silent, sprocket-skipping Hollywood melodrama. If Ruth had sat out the remaining months, he would still have led both leagues at season's end. By early August, he had thirty-three home runs. He swatted three more on consecutive days in Detroit.

~

On September 19, the Yankees returned to Navin Field, flush with confidence after winning nine of their last ten. New York shared first place with the Washington Senators. Ten games remained, and the Yankees needed a solid showing to capture their fourth consecutive pennant. The Tigers had faltered and fallen seven games out of first. Though their hopes for a league title were exhausted, they could still impact the race, and Cobb planned to see that they did. He had one goal to achieve: Beat the Yankees more often than they beat him. Going into the final series, the two teams had a split, each having won nine games.

Given the hostilities between the squads, no one should have been surprised that Cobb and the Tigers wanted the Senators—not the Yankees—to capture the pennant. The lingering bitterness between New York and Detroit was enough to account for that preference. But there were other factors. The Senators played Cobb's brand of small ball. Their offense relied on singles, speed, and stolen bases. In Cobb's mind, a final verdict had yet to be rendered on home runs as a route to victory. He might yet influence that discussion. And then there was the matter of Walter Johnson. The brilliant and much-loved pitcher had toiled for Washington his entire career and had never appeared in a World Series game. He and Cobb were friends. If Cobb couldn't be in the championship himself, he preferred Johnson be there.

The taunting began immediately. Harsh words flew from both benches. The drama reenergized Cobb, who always seemed to have something to prove. Batting in the ninth inning of the first game with the score knotted at 5–5, Cobb slapped a soft grounder between Waite Hoyt and third baseman Jumping Joe Dugan. As Cobb tore down the path on his spike-scarred legs, Dugan charged the ball, fielded it, and flung it past Wally Pipp. Cobb kept running. When the play finished, he was standing on third base. The Yankees loaded the bases intentionally to set up a double play, but Fred Haney lined a single, and Cobb scored the winning run.

It rained hard the next morning. The seats were wet and the field was slippery when the game began. Cobb drove in the first run with his two-hundredth hit and then promptly stole second and third. Innings later, he belted a double and scored the second run. In the fourth, he crashed into the scoreboard, robbing Pipp of extra bases on a sharp defensive play. The Yankees finally answered with two runs of their own in the eighth. Again, the game was tied in the ninth. And, again, the Tigers won, with Cobb chirping from second

112 THE BASEBALL YEARS

base as pitcher Bob Shawkey unleashed a wild pitch that allowed Heinie Manush to score.

The Yankees were in a miserable mood Sunday and desperately needed a victory to salvage their hopes. Forty thousand Detroit fans turned out to root against them. The New Yorkers decided to try to beat Cobb at his own game by needling him. Among the most fervent hecklers was a twenty-nine-year-old rookie, smiley Shags Horan, who some thought might be a right-handed Ruth. Before pursuing baseball, the oxlike Horan had been a soccer player with a championship team from St. Louis. Horan tried to goad Cobb into a fight. Walking past the Tigers dugout, Horan flung a handful of dirt in Cobb's eyes. Cobb was livid, but refused to allow the inexperienced hack to draw him into battle. "I'll get you, Horan, next season," he threatened. "I'll get you on waivers and send you to Toronto, where they'll make you play ball." (In thirty-one official at bats, Horan failed to hit a home run; the Yankees waived him after the season.)

New York scored first on Sunday, but Detroit took the lead with four runs in the sixth. Cobb contributed a bunt single, raced to third on a hit by Heilmann, and scored the go-ahead run on a squeeze play when a flustered Yankee pitcher flung the ball into Cobb's back as Cobb plowed into catcher Fred Hofmann.

But the Yankees fought back. With the bases full, Columbia Lou Gehrig punched a single to right, driving in two runs. He headed for second, thinking the runner on third would break for the plate. Instead, Gehrig got snagged in a rundown—an embarrassing, rally-killing oversight that inspired an insult-laced diatribe from Cobb. Afterward, Cobb took his coaching spot along the foul line and continued to jab Gehrig verbally. It worked. Gehrig and Everett Scott thundered out of the dugout to confront him, and both got ejected. "If I live to be one hundred, I will never see a more fascinating picture than he made," Scott later said of Cobb. "He was a cyclone, a tornado, a typhoon, all rolled into one." The Tigers took the third game, too.

Although player-managers are now extinct—Joe Torre and Frank Robinson in the 1970s and Pete Rose in the 1980s being among the last of the species—they were common during Cobb's career. In the 1924 season, five of eight American League teams were managed by significant everyday players: Cobb, Tris Speaker in Cleveland, Eddie Collins in Chicago, George Sisler in St. Louis, and twenty-seven-year-old Bucky Harris in Washington. With the exception of Harris, all were stars. It was no wonder Ruth thought he might eventually get a shot at managing.

Team identities were strongly linked to the men who led the clubs. Connie Mack's name was synonymous with the Philadelphia Athletics, John McGraw's with the New York Giants. Miller Huggins's Yankees were frequently called the Hugmen and sometimes the Hugginsians, and the Brooklyn players were known as the Robins in honor of Wilbert Robinson. During Cobb's tenure, reporters liked to call his charges the Tygers. His very presence offered a definite statement of what they stood for and how they played the game.

The Detroit sweep left the New Yorkers two games behind Washington, a gap that would hold in the final standings, which meant that Cobb had achieved at least one of his goals. He had deprived Ruth and the Yankees of the pennant and a return to the World Series. Just as Cobb had pledged to Grantland Rice in spring training, the Tigers had beaten the champions more often than not. Detroit was 13–9 against New York. It had been a remarkable battle. Eight of the games had been decided by a single run. The rivalries—Cobb versus Ruth, the Tigers versus the Yankees—fueled a box-office bonanza. Both clubs drew more than one million fans. No other teams came close. Of course, no other teams had Ruth or Cobb.

~

Although deprived of another World Series appearance, Babe Ruth had a superb year in 1924, winning the home-run crown. But he wasn't the only player hitting home runs. In 1918, major leaguers totaled 235 home runs; in 1923, they hit 980—and stole about four hundred fewer bases. By 1925, the number would rise to 1,169. Home runs were becoming as common as cars in Detroit. In

Philadelphia, Cy Williams hit 41 in 1923, up from 15 a few seasons earlier. Ken Williams hit 10 in 1920, 24 in 1921, and 39 the year after. Jack Fournier, who used to get a handful a year, also joined the twenty-plus ranks with Brooklyn and later led the Nationals. Hack Miller punched out 20. Rogers Hornsby jumped from 9 to 42 in two seasons.

Cobb realized the game had changed. At Yankee Stadium one afternoon, the Tigers watched from the dugout as Babe Ruth lifted balls into the right-field stands during batting practice. Cobb stood beside Grantland Rice and stared out at the big slugger.

"Well, the old game is gone," Cobb said. "We have another game, a newer game now. In this game, power has replaced speed and skill. Base running is about dead. They've all just about quit stealing. . . . Ruth has changed baseball. I guess more people would rather see Babe hit one over the fence than see me steal second. I feel bad about it because it isn't the game I like to see or play. The old game was one of skill—skill and speed and quick thinking. This game is all power. . . . A lot of these kids, in place of learning the true science of hitting or base running, are trying to knock every pitch over the fence."

But Ruth did more than hit home runs in 1924. He scored more runs than anyone else, and, more significant from Cobb's perspective, Ruth took the batting title. As the holder of twelve of them, Cobb could appreciate that feat. Ruth had nearly done it the year before, as well. Even if Cobb didn't like the long ball, he would have had to admire Ruth's average—and the fact that Babe had collected two hundred hits in each of his last two seasons. By the autumn of 1924, Cobb recognized that he couldn't dismiss Ruth as a strange spectacle, a curious anomaly, a freak, a fad, or an oddity. Ruth qualified as something more.

It was significant that during the riot at Navin Field, Cobb hadn't swung at Ruth. He had the opportunity; he had an invitation. Babe had challenged him, but Ty hadn't accepted. Throughout his career, Cobb had seldom backed down from an altercation. Could it be that beneath the brutal heckling, the name-calling, and his razor-sharp zeal, Ty Cobb had come to admire and even like some things about Babe Ruth? No longer was Ruth simply a power hitter. He had won the batting title. He had excelled in the one category that Cobb valued most. How could that not have changed Cobb's feelings about Ruth as a ballplayer?

~

As the 1924 World Series approached, Christy Walsh, Ruth's personal manager, hatched a plan. He wanted to thaw the icy relationship between Ruth and Cobb. "All my life," he said, "I have derived a great kick out of bringing so-called adversaries together." So in October he gave it a try with two of his celebrated clients.

Walsh, an attorney by degree and a cartoonist by trade, made a fortune syndicating stories bylined by famous individuals, usually ballplayers. He found his initial success selling the first-person tales of fighter pilot Eddie Rickenbacker, but eventually he went after the star who would make him wealthy, Babe Ruth. Convincing a nearby grocer to allow him to handle a beer delivery to Ruth's suite at the Ansonia, Walsh enticed Ruth with the promise of big money. Ruth agreed to put his name on twice-weekly articles that Walsh would syndicate to newspapers. The "signed stories," as editors called them, would be ghostwritten by New York journalists. Walsh expanded rapidly, selling players' life stories in serial format. By 1924, the italicized tagline of the Christy Walsh Syndicate was a familiar sight on sports pages nationwide.

The October classics, in particular, provided rich opportunities For the Washington–New York series, Walsh had six stars under contract: Walter Johnson and Nick Altrock of the Senators, John McGraw of the Giants, George Sisler of St. Louis, and Ruth and Cobb. Walsh had snagged Johnson in a Pullman restroom after Washington had lost to Boston on September 30. It amounted to a coup. Johnson, a fan favorite, would be making his first series appearance after seventeen seasons. Walsh lured him with a thousand-dollar advance. Johnson's reports would bring in seven thousand dollars over seven games.

Although some journalists objected to the ghostwritten stories, feeling that the lucrative contracts made star players less likely to share their thoughts free of charge, many baseball writers appreciated the arrangement because they profited from it. John Kieran, Bugs Baer, Bill Corum, Joe Williams, Boseman Bulger, Harry Salsinger, Bill Cunningham, Ford Frick—over time, all of them ghosted stories for Christy Walsh. Some players, like Cobb, insisted on playing an active role in the articles attributed to them. Most, like Ruth, were content to let their writers worry about it.

With both Cobb and Ruth coming to Griffith Stadium on his behalf, Christy Walsh schemed to get the two together. Giving neither advance notice, he arranged for the three of them to share a ride. "I managed to get them to the ballpark in Washington in the same taxicab," he said.

Cobb and Ruth teased each other, getting in a few digs. Cobb relished reminding Ruth that if not for the Tigers, Ruth would be playing—not watching—the series. On the field prior to the game, Ruth, Cobb, and George Sisler posed for shots. Eventually, Christy Walsh assembled his army of star reporters for his annual photograph. Ruth and Cobb stood beside one another, both in dress suits, Ruth's wide face set off by a tiny bow tie.

At the second game, on Sunday, they sat a seat apart in the expanded press booth above home plate in the second deck. Midway through the seventh inning, fans stood when the Senators came to bat. Washington boosters bordering the press area noticed that neither Ty nor Babe was on his feet. They began heckling both of them. Cobb and Ruth argued that standing for the Senators would show favoritism, but one loudmouthed fan, interpreting their action as disrespectful, persisted. Ty and Babe grew angry and called for a police officer to handle the matter, lest they handle it themselves.

In the ninth inning, both forecast the ending of the game, projecting that if Jack Bentley tossed Roger Peckinpaugh an inside curve, the contest would be over. He did, and Peckinpaugh socked it for a double, knocking in the winning run. Cobb was coming to appreciate that Ruth's knowledge of baseball was deeper and more sophisticated than he initially perceived. Ruth understood the game. On the ball field, Cobb had seen that Ruth could adjust his play. He could defy a shift. He could place the ball. He could hit for high average. He could bunt if necessary. He would even choke up on the bat if necessary. Ruth wasn't one-dimensional. His experience beside Ruth in the press box confirmed that insight.

Over the series, which Washington would win, writers sprinkled their game reports with notes about Ruth, Cobb, and their warming relationship. Though most of the interaction took place out of sight of the vast throngs, one very public encounter occurred before the fourth game at the Polo Grounds. Many couldn't believe what they were seeing. Cobb and Ruth were sharing a spot near the Senators' dugout, autographing ticket stubs and scorecards—together.

It was a start.

16

Reversal of Fortunes

~

I N EARLY FEBRUARY 1925, WEEKS BEFORE HEADING TO TRAIN-
ing camp in St. Petersburg, Babe Ruth ventured down to Hot
Springs, Arkansas, for the publicly stated purpose of getting in
shape. Though he had reportedly been in Sudbury, Massachusetts,
for two months, allegedly working hard while tending to his crumbling marriage and his expansive farm, Ruth had added thirty five
pounds—a gain that contradicted stories about his vigorous tree cutting and snow shoveling. "Just how the Home Run King managed to
run up his weight to 245 pounds during such strenuous exercise is
hard to understand," snipped Joe Villa of *The New York Sun*.

Hot Springs was known for its therapeutic mineral baths, as well
as its gambling, golf, and good times. Celebrities and businessmen

went there to "boil out." Ruth had discovered the town while with the Red Sox, who trained there. It was now a regular stop for him. Annually, it seemed, Ruth would be stricken with influenza or some other ailment while in the Ouachita Mountain valley. This time, while running along a mountain road, Ruth collapsed with excruciating pain.

Reports filtered out of Arkansas that Ruth was dallying with a woman who wasn't his wife. Maybe even two women. And he was devouring large amounts of food and, as usual, gulping bubbling glasses of bicarbonate soda to fight off the resulting discomfort. He was dropping piles of money, too—fifty dollars a day in a local shooting gallery, for one example. Hundreds on wagers. And maybe even partaking in the latest dance rage, the Charleston, which shook floors so forcefully that one overly cautious police chief banned the dance in wood-beamed buildings.

By late March, Ruth was battling "lame legs" in exhibition games. "He was going day and night, broads and booze," Joe Dugan would tell author Robert Creamer. In April, his face beaded with sweat and his body in pain, Ruth became violently ill. The ailment, gently described as "the bellyache heard around the world," put Ruth in the hospital. Amazingly, though Ruth was reported to be "fighting off a coma," his ghostwritten column continued to appear. What ailed Ruth? A hernia? An abscess? Venereal disease? No one seemed quite sure.

Ty Cobb took no public pleasure in Ruth's fall. For years, Cobb, Miller Huggins, and others had been muttering that Ruth's wild ways would catch up to him. Now, apparently, they had. But Cobb didn't publicly rejoice. Something had changed.

Cobb still took care of himself—and still enjoyed preaching that others should. At thirty-eight, he was the oldest everyday player in either league. He was beginning his twenty-first season, and he felt it in his ravaged legs. His enemy was his age, not bad habits. As Cobb's years increased, so did forecasts of his decline and demise. He hadn't won a batting title since 1919, and despite a career-best 625 at bats in 1924, his average had fallen for the second straight year. Dangerous as he might still be, no one was forecasting great things for Cobb when the 1925 season opened.

~

On May 5, a strong wind swept across the St. Louis ball field toward right field, kicking up infield dirt and sending trash wrappers waltzing atop the turf. The gusts got Cobb plotting ways to break the run of bad luck that had left his team at 4–14. He directed his Tigers to swing for distance and height. Hit the ball high and toward right field, he ordered. Let the wind carry it.

The Detroiters followed his orders, and it worked. Lu Blue got a double and a triple, Frank O'Rourke three doubles, Heinie Manush a home run, Harry Heilmann two hits. The Tigers got seventeen hits in all. But, phenomenally, more than a third of them belonged to Cobb himself. He crushed home runs in the first and second innings, doubled in the fourth, dropped a bunt single in the sixth, and in the eighth hit his longest yet, a third home run, which tied the modern-day record of three in one game. Cobb was five-for-five when the ninth inning arrived.

"Hit another!" a Browns fan called out.

"We're with you!" cried a second man.

As Cobb twirled his three bats, the crowd rose in respect. The applause and whistling intensified as Cobb started for the plate. The recognition affected the Peach, and he turned to the audience behind home plate, tipped his hat, and then spoke without the aid of a megaphone. The crowd quieted, straining to hear him. "Ladies and gentlemen," he bellowed. "I have been coming to this ballpark for twenty-one seasons, and this is the first time in my long experience that a St. Louis crowd has ever applauded me. I sincerely thank you." They cheered him more.

Although the fans hoped for a fourth home run, Cobb could only manage another single. But with six hits and sixteen total bases, it marked his finest single-game batting performance. BIGGEST DAY WITH BAT COMES AFTER 20 YEARS, crowed one headline. TY WAITS 20 YEARS FOR GREATEST FEAT, said another. The next day, as the still-sick

Babe Ruth got a wheelchair ride on the second floor of St. Vincent's Hospital, Cobb added two more home runs. The triumph prompted *The Sporting News* to anoint him as the "effervescent old man of baseball." Cobb's five home runs on back-to-back days toppled the modern record of four, held by Ruth and two other men.

Legend says that Cobb predicted the five home runs, reportedly telling sports writers Harry Salsinger and Sid Keener that he was going to show the world how easy it was to hit the long ball. But that story appears to be more apocryphal than factual. Neither Salsinger, Keener, nor any of the other beat writers covering the games noted Cobb's forecast at the time, and they would surely have spotlighted it had it occurred. The tale of his prognostication only surfaced in print decades after the fact.

Babe Ruth insisted on returning to the Yankees lineup in June. He had a six-inch scar on his gullet, a confirmation that doctors had performed an unspecified surgery, but he was not his former self athletically. He stumbled in his first weeks back, collecting just three home runs during the entire month. Although he did better in July, he was still performing poorly, and the Yankees were near the bottom of the standings.

Ruth no longer had patience for the rules and restrictions of manager Miller Huggins, and Huggins had reached the point where he could no longer tolerate Ruth's arrogance and insolence. Ruth flaunted his disregard for Huggins and regularly belittled him in front of teammates. The two made for an odd couple. Standing beside each other, they looked like a comedy team, Ruth the big-bellied bully and Huggins the skinny sidekick. A good hundred pounds lighter, Huggins came up to Ruth's thick shoulders. His pants were cinched tight around his bony waist, his arms often crossed beneath his chest, his feet splayed apart like Charlie Chaplin's.

Ruth hit bottom on a Saturday in late August. Coming in late for batting practice after having disregarded curfew several nights straight, Ruth found Huggins in the nearly vacated clubhouse.

"You don't have to dress today, Babe," Huggins began. He told Ruth he was suspending him and fining him five thousand dollars, an astounding amount in an era when most players barely made that much in a year. Even for Ruth, it amounted to a substantial fine. Outraged, Ruth hurled profanities at Huggins and threatened to punch his ears off (if only he were his size). Ruth vowed that the punishment would not stand, that he would exact revenge, that Huggins would be fired. Over the next day and a half, Ruth scathed Huggins to any reporter who would listen. He promised that he would never again play for that little prick.

"If Huggins is manager, I am through with the Yankees," Ruth ranted. "Either he quits or I quit. . . . Can you imagine a fellow who hit about .240 when he was playing ball trying to tell players who have .350 averages how to hit the ball?"

Given the adulation he enjoyed, given what he had done for the sport, given the fact that he had pretty much been allowed to do as he pleased in recent years, Ruth expected that Commissioner Landis and team owner Jacob Ruppert would side with him and put Huggins in his place. But they didn't. Ruppert backed Huggins, scolded Ruth as if he were a mess-making pup, and left him at Huggins's mercy.

On the very day of Ruth's suspension in St. Louis, Detroit celebrated Cobb's two decades in baseball. At the ball field, as the opposing Athletics took batting practice, hundreds of fans lined up to meet him. Sporty boys, their hair slicked back for the occasion, beamed as they shook his hand. Businessmen in suits, matronly mothers in church hats, seasoned old men, and toddlers too tiny to remember waited to say thank you, to get autographs, and to have pictures taken with Cobb. Five bands, scattered about the park, flavored the festivities. In the first inning, thirty thousand fans stood and cheered after Cobb doubled and scored. Dozens showered him with straw hats.

That evening, a dignitary-filled audience of six hundred feted Cobb with a grand banquet at the Book Cadillac Hotel. Cobb entered the ballroom to the sounds of "Dixie" and the sight of a standing ovation. Connie Mack and umpire Billy Evans praised him. Movie clips flickered on a large screen: Cobb on the ball field, Cobb in Augusta, Cobb hunting with his dogs. Bugs Baer remembered the two of them laughing until dawn when stranded on a rowboat in Lake Oskiwana.

Tom Brown's Minstrel Band from the Masonic Temple performed, as did the Blossom Heath Orchestra. The mayor gave him a thousand-dollar grandfather clock, and Ban Johnson, president of the American League, knighted Cobb as "the greatest ball player of all time." Hours later, he would condemn Ruth's actions. "Ruth has the mind of a fifteen-year-old boy and must be made to understand where he belongs," said Johnson. "The American League is no place for a player who dissipates and misbehaves."

The conspicuous contrast between the two stars struck the New York press as too flagrant to overlook. "Cobb's wonderful record as a player never has been tarnished by fines or suspensions for violating the rules against dissipation," wrote Joe Villa. *The Evening Telegram*, noting that Cobb was "known in every hamlet," praised him in an editorial: "The story of Cobb and his baseball life is the story of a determination to succeed, to be first in the chosen endeavor of life. . . . He has contributed to the youth of the country a mark to shoot at, on the diamond or in business life." *The New York Times*, in an editorial titled simply TWO HEROES, drew distinctions: "Where most of them fail is in remaining modest, in properly judging the fleeting nature of their fame, in seeing the necessity of keeping in good bodily trim, and of saving something for the rainy days certain to come after the fair weather." The national *Literary Digest* described Ruth as "baseball's baby" and Cobb as its paragon and its "Admirable Crichton."

Fans, teammates, and reporters turned against Ruth in big numbers. Left with no choice and seeming remorseful, Ruth tried to apologize, but Huggins made him wait more than a week. Friends and advisers urged Ruth to be contrite. Finally, he returned to the lineup on September 8 and promptly hit his three-hundredth home run. But he continued to pay his penance. In a piece for *Collier's* magazine headlined I HAVE BEEN A BABE AND A BOOB, Ruth pledged to change his ways and confessed to having wasted $500,000—$250,000 on "high living," $125,000 on gambling (including $35,000 on one race), $100,000 on failed business ventures, and $25,000 on lawyers and would-be litigants like creditors, wronged women, and accident victims.

When the 1925 season ended, there was peculiar look to the leader boards. Bob Meusel led the American League in home runs and runs driven in, Harry Heilmann in batting average, Johnny Mostil in runs scored and stolen bases, Al Simmons in hits, Ken Williams in slugging average, Marty McManus in doubles, and Goose Goslin in triples. For the first time in two decades, there was neither a Cobb nor a Ruth listed atop any major offensive category.

For Cobb, it wasn't unexpected or reason for embarrassment. He had performed strongly, batting .378 and driving in 102 runs in only 415 at bats. But Ruth had fallen below .300 and recorded his lowest home-run total since becoming an outfielder.

~

The 1925 World Series opened in Pittsburgh on October 7. This time, feisty manager John McGraw and Pirate legend Honus Wagner joined Ty and Babe in the press box. The conversations and the camaraderie would allow Cobb and Ruth to take another step toward friendship. "These baseball men had been just as fiery and belligerent as I had been," Cobb recalled months later, "but that day we shook hands and spent a pleasant afternoon discussing the technical points of the game being played. Not a word of the past was brought up. That was because neither of us feared the other mentally or physically, and we respected each other's knowledge and ability in our profession."

In addition to Christy Walsh, John Roesink, and Grantland Rice, another of Ruth's confidants—the most important of them all— was likely encouraging Ruth to make peace with Cobb. Her name: Claire Hodgson.

Ruth had met her in May 1923 at a ball game in Washington. An impeccable dresser, Hodgson was fussing over her stylish blue outfit. She and a roommate had gone to Griffith Stadium as guests of actor Jim Barton, the star of a stage production, *Dew Drop Inn,* in which Hodgson had a part. Barton, a song-and-dance man in the same company as Eddie Cantor and Al Jolson, was among Ruth's legion of friends. During batting practice, he called Ruth to the box seats and introduced him to Hodgson. She was unimpressed. He sounded gruff and acted preoccupied. They talked briefly. After he left, Hodgson remarked to her roommate, "He's just a big kid." Later, she claimed, "I certainly had no girlish tremors that suggested I would ever be his wife. In fact, I had no reason to even expect I'd ever see him again. And I couldn't have cared less."

There was also the matter of his marriage. Ruth was one of the most famous men in America, and everybody knew he had a wife—even if that fact didn't quell his pursuits. Ruth and Helen Woodford had married when she was sixteen. But their wedded bliss hadn't lasted long. She struggled with her husband's philandering, one result of which was daughter Dorothy. The Ruths often lived separately, and if religion had not been an issue, they would have divorced. Instead, they would remain married until Helen perished in a 1929 fire at the home of her lover, a Massachusetts dentist. Her death would allow Ruth and Hodgson to wed and adopt each other's daughters.

Hodgson was a curvaceous, creamy-complexioned widow. At fifteen, she had married a man twice her age in Georgia. When the relationship faltered, she escaped to New York with daughter Julia and Marie Martin, a black maid. Hodgson worked as an artist's model and picked up small parts in shows. Her husband died in 1922 and then her father a year later, prompting her mother and brothers to move in with her in New York. Soon after meeting Ruth in Washington, she became first in his harem of gals. By 1925, newspapers were reporting on their affair. It was no secret.

Hodgson held sway with Ruth, and had a calming effect on him. Their association brought a glimmer to Cobb's face. Years earlier—back when her father, Southern attorney Col. James Monroe Merritt, represented him—Claire Hodgson had come to know Ty Cobb. She went to a few of his games in Georgia, and they dated seriously, according to Jimmy Cobb, Ty's youngest child. "For a while, it got interesting," Cobb told his biographer, Al Stump. While Hodgson never publicly admitted to a romance with Cobb, she did acknowledge a relationship. "In Georgia," she said, "I had known Ty Cobb very well."

Her relationship with Cobb would have helped Ruth to see another side of his ball-field rival. Likewise, Ruth's affection for a Georgia woman—this particular woman, especially—would have won him points with Cobb.

That winter, the Peach complimented Ruth in print. "There's no denying that Babe has made a deep impression on the game," he said. "There's a certain amount of magnetism about Babe." Cobb noted that Ruth had benefited from friendly New York writers who hyped his achievements while downplaying his troubles. "What I say about him isn't criticism," he said. "Perhaps it's envy."

The caustic sharpness of the Cobb-Ruth rivalry was dissipating as both men matured and began to see one another in more-human terms. A mutual respect was developing between them, but would it be able to survive the heated action on the ball field?

Scandal

Cobb—master of the bunt. ERNIE HARWELL COLLECTION,
DETROIT PUBLIC LIBRARY

~

BABE RUTH WORKED THROUGH THE WINTER AND INTO THE
spring to get in shape for the 1926 season. At training camp
in St. Petersburg, he dropped weight by wearing a sweat-inducing
rubber shirt—a look he accented with the latest fad, a tinted eye-

shade visor like a bookkeeper might wear. Ruth was below 215 pounds—thinner than at any point since his days in Boston—and friends noticed something else, too. He had toned down his behavior. Ruth acted with greater restraint and was becoming a more positive influence in the clubhouse. He was growing as a person.

The new season found Cobb, who had undergone eye surgery at Johns Hopkins in Baltimore to alleviate fuzzy vision, in a philosophical mood. "In my youthful enthusiasm, very likely I was carried too far many times and did things I should not have done," he said. "Everybody has. . . . Once he gets in the limelight, the ball player, you understand, is considered as a mature public character when, as a matter of fact, he is but a boy. He has just reached the age of mental poise and balance when he has to retire from the game."

Cobb and Ruth's encounters were becoming more playful and less frequent. In one game, after clobbering a home run, Ruth looked toward the Detroit dugout as he rounded third base.

"Cobb, you want to tell me how to hit a baseball now?" he yelled.

"No, George, but I'll show you," Cobb responded.

On occasion, however, the old embers would spark, as they did on May 8, 1926, a Saturday afternoon at Yankee Stadium. Thirty thousand fans had come to see the first-place Yankees face the Tigers.

In the final inning, with two outs, Earl Whitehill, a handsome left-hander who married the California Raisins model, delivered a two-strike pitch that clipped Lou Gehrig's hand. Whitehill thought the ball hit Gehrig's bat and protested umpire Bill McGowan's call in awarding Gehrig first base.

"Let's see that hand," Whitehill demanded.

Gehrig took offense and charged the mound. Yankees and Tigers stampeded from all points. Cobb and Heilmann rushed in from the outfield, Ruth dashed from the on-deck circle. As the umpires separated them, Gehrig and Whitehill vowed to meet under the stands.

Moments later, after the Tigers' 7–5 victory, both were in the same shadowy tunnel. What precisely happened there no one seemed to know for certain. But Gehrig was knocked unconscious—either purposely by Whitehill or Cobb, accidentally by Ruth, or coincidentally by contact with a concrete wall. Afterward, Ruth, who ended up on top of Gehrig, stormed into the Tigers' locker room and accused Cobb of kicking him while he was sprawled on the floor.

"They tell me you took a kick at me out there in the tunnel, and if you did we can settle things right now," Ruth challenged.

Cobb told Ruth he was wrong, and other Tigers shoved the big man out the door.

The fight drew fifty-five thousand spectators to the Bronx for the next day's game—the biggest crowd in two years. What they saw were Cobb and Ruth jabbering back and forth, teasing each other, and laughing at one another's misfortunes. Most of the laughing belonged to Cobb. He got four hits, drove in a pile of runs, and launched two home runs over Ruth's head into the right-field bleachers. Cobb trotted the bases as if he had never been so happy, waving to the crowd, baring his balding dome, chattering at the pitcher, grinning at Ruth, and commenting to the infielders as he passed. Ruth went hitless, and glared at Cobb when his pitchers walked him repeatedly.

The New York writers gushed about Cobb's performance. They affectionately called him the Old Sinner, the Old Sport, and the Old Cripple. (Cobb was feeling the passing of the years. Besides his eye troubles, he endured constant pain in his back and legs.) Old Fellow, Old Bean—the reporters couched those loving words in heaps of praise. "He is a county fair, a three-ring circus, and a perpetual motion machine combined," remarked Will Wedge. Sid Mercer described him as the last "of a fast-fading school of diamond swashbucklers." Added Ford Frick, "If Mr. Cobb is through as a ball player, then John D. Rockefeller is a hobo and Henry Ford hasn't a nickel." *The New York Times* was downright playful, teasing that "as soon as the young fellow gets the hand of things, they will let him play every day."

Despite Cobb's performance, the year belonged to Ruth. He redeemed himself, and the crowds returned to Yankee Stadium. During Ruth's troubled 1925 season, attendance had fallen below 700,000, with six teams outdrawing the Yankees. But with Ruth having regained his form, the numbers rocketed. Ruth was again smashing home runs. In a May home stand, he crushed ten and the Yankees strung together sixteen victories and claimed first place for good.

Cobb surrendered before June, admitting his team had no chance. "All of us have been underestimating the ability of the Yankees," he said, uncharacteristically predicting they would win the pennant. And they did, with Ruth hitting forty-seven home runs—twenty-six more than any other major-leaguer. Five times, Ruth hit two or more home runs on one day. In the fourth game of the World Series, he set a record by sending three into the stands. The Cardinals won, but Ruth's comeback was a triumph. In the off-season, he reaped the financial rewards, starring in a traveling production and leading a barnstorming tour. (Baseball rules had been changed to allow pennant winners to tour.) In all, Ruth made roughly $250,000.

Cobb played in just seventy-nine games. He batted only 233 times. His average fell forty points, and his team, though better than .500, dropped to sixth place. At season's end, he resigned and seemed destined to head off quietly into the record books, his brilliant career behind him. "The majors have lost the greatest human asset they ever possessed," said *The Sporting News*.

Detroit boosters viewed Cobb's managerial tenure with mixed emotions. Although he had only one losing season, Cobb's teams never won more than eighty-six games and never delivered a pennant. Meanwhile, New York had captured four crowns and Washington, two. In six seasons, the Tigers had finished second, third (twice), fourth and sixth (also twice). During that time, the Yankees, Senators, and Indians had recorded better winning percentages. But—and this is the most telling of facts—no division rival performed better against the Yankees than Cobb's Tigers. From 1921 through 1926, Detroit beat New York sixty-three times. No other team topped the sixty plateau. Excluding Cobb's rookie season as manager, the Tigers had a 58–50 record against Ruth and the dominant Yankees.

With Cobb retiring, the game's richest rivalry appeared finished.

Then scandal broke. Word leaked that Cobb and Tris Speaker had been forced out of baseball in a backroom deal after pitcher Dutch Leonard had accused them of betting on a game and produced letters that offered some substantiation. Several hellish weeks of national controversy rained down upon Cobb.

Ruth was on the West Coast golfing, playing in exhibitions, visiting orphanages, and headlining in Alexander Pantages's vaudeville shows, when a San Diego reporter asked him about the Cobb scandal. "Plain bunk!" Ruth exclaimed. He described Cobb and Speaker as "the finest names that baseball has ever known. . . . They never can hurt Cobb or Speaker or any of the men they have named. It is all a lot of talk." All along the coast—in San Francisco, before shooting in a left-handed foursome at the Presidio; in Los Angeles, while filming a movie—Ruth defended Cobb and Speaker. "I can't believe they did anything wrong," he said.

Public sentiment also favored Cobb. Fans refused to believe that the hard-playing Tiger would throw a game. The evidence— Leonard's letters—was ambiguous as related to Cobb. But at the very least, it indicated that Cobb may have helped Leonard and Joe Wood place a bet on a 1919 game—not an extraordinary act at the time. Given Cobb's wealth and his performance in the contest in question—he performed poorly in the game he was supposed to win—it seemed highly unlikely that he had participated in the bet.

When in January Dutch Leonard refused to face Cobb and Speaker and testify against them, Commissioner Landis responded by exonerating the two stars. By then, Cobb was angry at Landis for tainting his reputation. As part of a power struggle with American League president Ban Johnson, Landis had left Cobb and Speaker dangling from a rope for weeks before freeing them of the charges. Cobb would never forget it. He also would not forget that Ruth had defended him in his darkest professional hour.

Still, Cobb wanted vindication on the field. "I could not and would not leave the game with the slightest cloud over my name," he would say. Organized baseball apologized with a flurry of contract offers, and Cobb chose to play for Connie Mack in Philadelphia. The deal, reported at $70,000–75,000 a year, made him the highest-paid player in the game.

Cobb's new pact came at the wrong time for the Yankees, who had yet to sign Ruth for the 1927 season. If the fading forty-year-old Cobb could get $70,000, what figure might the thirty-two-year-old Babe Ruth demand? The Yankees had paid him $52,000 the previous season, but Ruth had just turned in a terrific performance. He wouldn't take less than Cobb, friends said. Ruth insisted he wouldn't sign for fewer than six figures. Cobb's contract "is likely to put bad ideas in Ruth's head," reported Bill Corum. Instead, it put big dollars in his pocket. The Yankees signed Ruth to a three-year $210,000 pact.

18

The Kindly Years

Ruth playfully inspects Cobb's bat. NATIONAL BASEBALL HALL OF FAME LIBRARY, COOPERSTOWN, N.Y.

I T WAS CHAOS NEAR THE BALLPARK ON TUESDAY, APRIL 12, 1927. Fifteen thousand ticketless fans were pressing around the imposing walls of Yankee Stadium, with still more flooding from subway trains into the gray afternoon. They pushed, jostled, nudged, and climbed over one another trying to get to the gates. Police with billy clubs strained to keep order. Inside the park, seventy thousand fans jammed into the stands, swarming seats, elbowing in the aisles, and struggling to stake out a spot with a view.

They chomped their stogies and clutched their scorecards and crushed peanuts from their shells. It was opening day, and baseball had never seen such a crowd.

The new mayor, showgirl-caressing Jimmy Walker, held court in the bunting-bedecked front row, debonair as always with his black bowler and dark brows and a stylish kerchief poking from the pocket of his overcoat. Beside him stood team owner Col. Jacob Ruppert. Nearby were philanthropist and tea-bag entrepreneur Sir Thomas Lipton, former German chancellor Wilhelm Cuno, war hero Adm. Charles Plunkett, and Broadway dandy George M. Cohan.

The Yankees and the Athletics occupied the field, loosening up for the contest. They represented an amazing array of talent, including possibly the largest ensemble of future Hall of Famers ever suited and assembled for a regular-season game: Lou Gehrig, Tony Lazzeri, Earle Combs, Waite Hoyt, Herb Pennock, managers Miller Huggins and Connie Mack, Mickey Cochrane, nineteen-year-old Jimmie Foxx, Al Simmons, Lefty Grove, Eddie Collins, Zack Wheat, and, of course, Babe Ruth and Ty Cobb—the latter in his new Philadelphia uniform, with a white elephant stitched over his heart.

More than twenty photographers and newsreel cameramen roamed the field capturing images until someone thought to get Cobb and Ruth together, and then they flooded toward the two stars. Ty and Babe had posed in uniform sporadically over the years, first in the 1920 season and then again around 1923. Those shots left little doubt about how they felt toward each other. Their mutual disdain was apparent. In one, Ruth stood straight with arms folded tight across his chest, not a hint of joy on his perturbed face, while Cobb, next to him but not touching, stared with suspicion at the photographer. The shot had the feel of a command performance for both men, with a line of suited businessmen curtained behind them.

But this time it was different. Ruth and Cobb were enjoying the moment. They hammed it up for the cameras. Cobb showed Ruth one of his bats and pretended to lecture him as Ruth patiently absorbed the lesson.

Before the game, Mayor Walker honored both legends. He handed Ruth an inscribed silver bowl; Cobb got a horseshoe-shaped wreath of flowers. The record-setting crowd provided a taste of vindication for Cobb. The New Yorkers responded to the gambling accusations by greeting him enthusiastically when he appeared at home plate and in right field. For Cobb, it was the beginning of a pleasurable two-year run with Connie Mack's aging Athletics—"MacGuillicuddy's Antiques," one observer called them. Free of the managerial albatross, Cobb played his brand of ball fiercely, dropping bunts, place-hitting, even stealing home. "He was," Joe Williams reported after one such display, "the Cobb your Dad knew—a vibrant, impetuous base runner, asking no quarter and giving none, a forty-year-oldster thumbing a mature nose at the unskilled robustness of youth."

So long as he was playing, Cobb wouldn't be forgotten.

$\sim$

The game had changed. There was no arguing that. The place-hitters of Cobb's generation were disappearing faster than ice-boxes. They were being replaced by stronger, taller players who could pop the ball. Back in 1919, when Cobb had topped the majors with a .384 average, six batters hit ten or more home runs. In 1927, led by Ruth with a career-high sixty, twenty-two batters would reach the ten-or-more mark. One year later, in Cobb's final season, thirty-eight would accomplish it.

But the changes weren't limited to style of play. "Twenty years ago, the boys didn't know or talk about anything but baseball," said Kid Gleason, whose professional days traced to the 1880s. "Nowadays, when you travel around with a ball club you're apt to hear them discussing anything from politics to the Einstein theory. And they know what they're talking about, too."

Connie Mack noticed that the new breed of players enjoyed reading and indulged in such tame, trendy pastimes as Mah Jong and crossword puzzles. Other observers credited tougher rules and steeper fines for keeping the men in line.

The number of college-educated players in the major leagues swelled in the 1920s with the addition of guys like Mickey Cochrane of Boston University, Ted Lyons of Baylor, Bibb Falk of Texas, Ownie Carroll of Holy Cross, Eddie Wells of Bethany College, Joe Sewell of Alabama, and Moe Berg, a magna cum laude graduate of Princeton. At Yankee Stadium, a pair of soft-talking, well-behaved kids—Lou Gehrig of Columbia and Earle Combs of Eastern Kentucky—had cracked the lineup in 1925.

"The ball player of today is more of a young businessman," said Cobb. "He enters the game with everybody reaching out to help him. His success makes him a business asset to owners and players. He is not heckled and roughly treated by his teammates. The new player of today comes in at a good salary, plays his game, and can enjoy it like any other successful young fellow."

It wasn't that way when Cobb had begun fighting his way to prominence. If it had been—if it had been easier—there might not have been a Ty Cobb.

In his final two seasons, the Georgia Peach, though feeling his age, continued to work hard and to do the things he had always done well. He did not glide gently toward retirement. He still argued with umpires and occasionally got ejected; he still managed to steal bases (twenty-five in one of the seasons) and to slap singles and to leg out triples (eleven of them) and to drive in runs (133 over two years) and to score and to contribute. And he still wanted to win more than anyone else on the diamond. In 1927, he batted .357, fifth-best in the league. In 1928, his average, .323, remained impressive. He could also still play mind games.

Decades later, Cobb would recall a trick he executed against Ruth and the Yankees while with the Athletics. "Babe came to bat, swaggering, and waved his handkerchief at our outfielders to move back," he said. "He took three swings powerful enough to cause a windstorm and struck out. When I came up next, I pulled the same stunt with a handkerchief. I waved the boys back. Then I bunted, beat it out, and stole second and third."

On a couple of occasions during Cobb's last years, Babe Ruth invited him to his apartment when Philadelphia came to town. The two shared drinks and memories—something that once would have been unimaginable.

Even if Cobb had retired after his tenure with the Tigers, even if he hadn't played an additional two years for Connie Mack, he would have left baseball with a spectacular record of achievement. In the end, when Cobb finally stepped out of his uniform, he needn't have worried about whether he would be remembered. Cobb retired as the all-time leader in hits, batting average, runs scored, runs driven in, stolen bases, games, and at bats. The only other man of his time who would come close was still adding to his achievements.

Ty Cobb's last at bat came on September 11, 1928. Pinch-hitting in the ninth, Cobb ended his career with a pop-up to the shortstop. It seemed only fitting that Babe Ruth was there to witness it. He just happened to be in the same ballpark, playing right field for the Yankees.

The Babe would perform for seven more seasons before stepping down in 1935 with 714 home runs—hundreds more than his closest challengers. He also would hold a bundle of other records, including some he had pried from Cobb.

Over the decades, there had been no scarcity of great rivalries in baseball. But none could compare to that of Ty Cobb and Babe Ruth. Fate or destiny or coincidence had overlapped their careers, placing on the same field of combat the two men who would vie for title of greatest player ever. But their battles rose above a simple struggle for superiority. They signified more than the tug-and-pull passing of a princely prize from one star to another. Ty Cobb and Babe Ruth represented different epochs in their sport's history. Cobb came out of the Deadball Era, and was the crowning figure of that time. Ruth launched the era that supplanted it, that of the Lively Ball, and dominated his age as no player has dominated any period since. And to make it all the more interesting, they were as different as two people could be, having little in common save for the early loss of their fathers and a mutual love for sport and competition. For a span of fourteen years, they played in the same games and put on a show that has never been replicated in baseball.

Was it any wonder that they wanted to give it one more try? Could it have surprised anyone that in retirement—despite their baseball legacies, despite the marks they left on the national pastime, despite their elite status—both men would turn their passions toward another sport and, once more, toward each other?

Babe Ruth - Ty Cobb

CHARITY GOLF MATCH

●

Commonwealth Country Club

CHESTNUT HILL, MASSACHUSETTS

Wednesday, June 25 1941

2:30 p. m.

●

Match arranged by Bill Cunningham

and sponsored by

New England Association of

LEFT-HANDED GOLFERS

for benefit of

The Golden Rule Farm

New England's Boys' Town, Franklin, N.H.

Admission $1.00

Please observe all the obviously necessary ground rules.

●

Part III

The Golf Match

19

With Bobby in Augusta

The pride of Georgia: Ty Cobb and Bobby Jones.

DURING THE SPRING OF 1941, AMERICANS WERE LAUGHING at the misadventures of Abbott and Costello in *Buck Privates*, bopping to the Andrews Sisters' "Boogie Woogie Bugle Boy," and coming to the conclusion that they would eventually be fighting a war overseas against Adolf Hitler. Much had changed in America since September 1928, when Ty Cobb had last played in the major leagues. Prohibition had disappeared, the worst of the Great Depression had come and gone, and the reign of Franklin Roosevelt had entered an unprecedented third term. Talking movies ruled at the box office, with Hollywood having recently produced such grand Technicolor films as *Gone with the Wind* and *The Wizard of Oz*. Radio, meanwhile, had popularized superheroes like the Green Hornet and the Lone Ranger and brought monstrous audiences to the swing music of Glenn Miller and his contemporaries. Sports still played an integral part in American life, though populated by a fresh generation of stars, like Joe Louis and Joe DiMaggio. Though the daily spotlight had long since faded on Ty Cobb, he remained a dominant name in the world of athletics.

In late March 1941, days before the start of the Masters tournament, Cobb returned home to Augusta, Georgia, for the first time in nearly a decade. While he enjoyed life near San Francisco and relished the climate on the Pacific coast, he missed his native state and the folks who lived there. "Georgia people, man, are just the finest in the world," he said. At his heart, Cobb still viewed himself as a small-town boy who had made good.

In most ways, Augusta was the same as when he had left. The business district still stretched along the aptly named, unusually wide Broad Street, and the Savannah River still flowed north of it. The graceful Bon Air Hotel, rebuilt after a 1921 fire, remained an elegant testament to the city's standing as a winter resort for the wealthy, as did the Partridge Inn, with its sweeping terrace and magnificent parlor, a home to glorious black-tie ballroom dances. Not far away, in the affluent Summerville neighborhood, the former Cobb residence stood yet on Williams Street, a reminder of pleasant times. This was the same Augusta that Cobb had cherished, its landscape graced by the beautiful courses of Augusta Country Club and Forest Hills; Cobb belonged to both.

But Augusta had changed in one stunning way since Cobb had lived there. When he had left for California in 1932 to escape the sweltering Southern summers, Cobb had not seen the fruition of friend Bobby Jones's idyllic dream, Augusta National. Cobb departed before the course made its debut in January 1933, and, despite his passion for golf, he hadn't been back yet to see it.

For years, his friend, Grantland Rice, had been telling anyone who would listen about the magic of the place. He championed it in his syndicated column, and he raved about it on his national radio show. When chatting with pals like Cobb, he nearly glowed about the course's challenging holes and its landscape, speckled with flowering dogwood and crabapple trees. (The par-three twelfth was particularly breathtaking, with its green nestled between a hilly slope, sand traps, and a placid pond.)

Ty Cobb finally got his first look at Augusta National prior to the 1941 Masters, and it impressed him. In the days before the tournament, Cobb took to the airwaves to help promote the event. In the remodeled, columned manor house—the second floor freshly designated for men only—Cobb, chairman Cliff Roberts, and defending champion Jimmy Demaret assembled around the microphones of the Dixie Radio Network and tempted listeners of twenty-four member stations with the excitement that awaited. "They have a mighty pretty course in Pebble Beach," said Cobb, "but the Augusta National is right there with it."

The world's top golfers were converging on the breezy, rolling landscape of Augusta. Five of the six men who had won the first seven Masters—Horton Smith, Gene Sarazen, Byron Nelson, Ralph Guldahl, and Demaret—were in town. Francis Ouimet, the gardener's son who had fueled the golf craze with an upset victory in the 1913 U.S. Open, and Walter Hagen, the debonair, free-spending pro who had transformed the sport, had arrived, too, along with Ben Hogan, Ed Dudley, Craig Wood (a runner-up twice), and dozens more. Plus, there were the press and radio guys, the stars

like Rice, O.B. "Pop" Keeler, and Henry McLemore of United Press
and the rookies like Ernie Harwell of WSB Atlanta, who would be
filing his reports from a tower above the eighteenth hole.

And, of course, there was Bobby Jones, the gracious host. This
was unquestionably his show and his party. The fact that Cobb,
Georgia's other favorite sports son, had returned just made the
tournament even sweeter. The sight of the two of them together
tickled fans and swelled state pride.

Cobb and Jones had known each other for almost two decades.
It was inevitable, perhaps, that they would become friends. They
had so much in common. They were two of the most celebrated
athletes in the world, and they had sprung from the same region.
Jones knew Cobb's children and even went to the Georgia Field
Trials one year to root for his bird dogs. They broke bread in each
other's homes. They golfed occasional rounds together.

One beautiful Sunday in March 1930, Cobb and Jones hit the
fairways at Forest Hills with the argyle-socked Rice and Johnny Farrell, winner of the 1928 U.S. Open. It was a chummy, good-natured
affair, and Cobb couldn't help but admire the play of the twenty-
eight-year-old prince of the sport. But two days after their match,
as he and Rice followed Jones's march toward the Southeastern
Open title, Cobb witnessed a bit of loafing that pricked his competitive spirit and made for one famously audacious incident. Jones
arrived at the sixteenth hole of the final round to find a backlog of
golfers and a twenty-minute wait. He was five under par, well in
front of the field, and en route to a course record. Exhausted, he
stretched out on the grass for a rest. Cobb was stunned and let
Jones know it. He chastised him. When play resumed, Jones hooked
his ball into the trees, creating a mess that cost him. It took him six
shots to make the hole.

"Did you see what that boy did? He lay down on the grass," Cobb
complained. "Right when he was hot and keyed up. Why do they
warm up a horse before they put him over the jumps? Why does a
pitcher put on a sweater between innings? How can a man expect
to hold his poise and his fitness when he lies down on the ground

and rests twenty minutes? If a ball player of mine did something corresponding to that in a tight place, I'd fine him."

Jones finished roughly—by his standards—recording a 71 on the final eighteen. But he easily won the seventy-two-hole tournament, thirteen strokes ahead of runner-up Horton Smith and even further ahead of Billy Burke, Gene Sarazen, and Farrell. At night, Cobb hosted the golfers at a party in his home. Perhaps regretting his early criticism, he shared his admiration for Jones. "I've seen enough of this game of golf," he said, "to know that baseball is, after all, only a hit-or-miss proposition compared with it. In golf, you have to apply control a couple of hundred yards away. . . . There is no way to estimate the genius of Bobby Jones. I am simply abashed watching him play. I want to play golf so much—and it is so impossible ever to graze his artistry. He is the greatest competitive athlete I have ever seen." That year, Jones would win what would become known as the Grand Slam and retire from formal competition.

After baseball, Cobb had focused on golf and promptly developed strong feelings about what was right and wrong with the sport, telling Rice that there was too much bad theory on the links and not enough education from observation. Cobb believed that the best golfers started as caddies and learned by studying and imitating the experts—a benefit he never enjoyed early in life but had certainly capitalized on in the years since.

Cobb had prevailed in a few amateur tournaments over the years. Nothing on par with the U.S. Open, of course. He had taken the Bon Air–Vanderbilt Cup in Augusta and, a few seasons later, a charity crown in Del Monte, California. One winter, he nearly qualified for medal play at the Bing Crosby Invitational. But until 1941, Cobb may have been best known to golf fans for an embarrassing loss he incurred in 1939, when a twelve-year-old eliminated him in the first flight of the club championship at San Francisco's Olympic Club. Witnesses chortled about the ribbing Cobb took and how angry it made him. "He was a fierce competitor," the victor recalled, "and I remember him getting mad at himself for not playing better. But he was nice to me. He shook my hand." Cobb may have found some consolation in his defeat when, two decades on, his young conqueror, Bob Rosburg, became a PGA champion.

~

Whether on hunting trips or at Masonic meetings or on golf courses, Cobb reveled in the camaraderie and company of other men. At the 1941 Masters, he soaked up the atmosphere by partaking fully in pretournament festivities. On March 31, he played in a foursome with three Southerners who would be vying for honors: Atlanta resident and British Amateur champ Charlie Yates; Sam Snead, the bookmaker's favorite to battle Byron Nelson for the title; and Sam Byrd, whose very presence must have gotten Cobb thinking about Babe Ruth.

Byrd had first tasted athletic fame as a member of the Yankees. As a baseball player, he had faced a formidable task—breaking into a New York outfield that featured Ruth, Earle Combs, Bob Meusel, and later Ben Chapman. Byrd was an adequate hitter but a marvelous golfer, as his teammates discovered in 1929 at his first spring training. It was there that Byrd mustered the courage to ask veterans Tony Lazzeri, Mark Koenig, and Mike Gazella if he could join them for a round at the celebrated Jungle Club in St. Petersburg. The three frequently played for lunch. After shooting an 8 on the first hole, Byrd settled his nerves and beat the veterans by carding a 72. Many more victories would follow.

Despite flashes of success on the diamond—he hit two home runs in one season opener—Byrd became best known as a late-inning replacement for Ruth. When ready to be relieved, Ruth would bring his glove in from the outfield, rather than leave it on the turf as was customary. That was Byrd's sign to get loose. Reporters referred to him as Babe's Legs, Ruth's Second Wind, Ruth's Stand-In, or Ruth's Caddy. On the golf course, however, Byrd didn't play second to Ruth or any other ball player. He and Babe became frequent golfing companions, and Byrd astonished Ruth with his long drives. "How does the little runt do it?" he asked. Grantland Rice once saw Ruth drive a ball 280 yards on the 550-yard sixteenth hole at the original Deepdale club on Long Island, only to see Byrd blast his ball forty yards farther.

Byrd quickly earned a reputation as the best golfer in the major leagues. While on the road with the Yankees, he often sought advice from club professionals. In the off-season, he practiced religiously, experimenting with grips and stances. "I saw Sammy put in nearly three hours one afternoon with the number seven iron alone," said Rice. One day in Philadelphia, Byrd played Llanerch, a private club, for the first time and came within a stroke of tying the record set by course pro Denny Shute, the defending British Open champion. "When I was a kid, I was never quite sure whether I wanted to be a professional ball player or a professional golfer," Byrd said.

By 1934, word of his abilities had reached Bobby Jones. When the Yankees came to Atlanta for a scrimmage, Jones invited Byrd to play nine holes. They were joined by Ruth and a fourth golfer. On the East Lake course—where Jones took his earliest swings—Byrd, using borrowed clubs, finished one over par and a stroke behind Jones. It was Byrd's introduction to the course. "He's the best man off a tee I ever saw," said Jones.

Later that year, the Yankees released Byrd. It was also Ruth's last season with the team. Byrd struggled to stay in the major leagues for two more years. "I wasn't getting any better," he said. "But all this time, I kept up my golf and found out that, even playing only now and then, I could still break 70 occasionally." Byrd rejected an $8,000 no-cut contract from Branch Rickey and instead accepted a position as assistant pro to Ed Dudley at the Philadelphia Country Club. It turned out to be a wise decision.

As Cobb, Byrd, Snead, and Yates made their way around Augusta National, the conversation inevitably would have turned to baseball, and from there it would have been a short step to Babe Ruth. And that would have sparked Cobb, and soon he would have been probing Byrd and Snead for details about Ruth's golf game, gathering info that might someday be useful. The challenge was still out there, after all, and Cobb was hungry for it. Four years after the match had first been suggested by PGA tour manager Fred Corcoran and two years after Cobb had slipped Ruth the note in

Cooperstown and one year after Joe Williams of the *New York World-Telegram* had promised that Cobb would be coming east to settle the matter, Ty Cobb and Babe Ruth still had not met on a golf course. The two greatest baseball players had yet to decide who was the better golfer. In a world consumed by the threat of war, it may have seemed a trivial matter. But to at least one of the two men, it was anything but.

~

The Bon Air Hotel served as headquarters for the Masters, and it bustled in the days before the opening round. Among the most raucous highlights was the annual Calcutta, a gambling sweepstakes party. Though officials would later frown on such enterprises, the Calcutta of 1941 drew dignitaries and golfers alike. Participants showed support for their favorites by bidding on the golfers they believed would win.

Odds-makers were giving the nod to the regally mannered "Lord" Byron Nelson. The Texas gentleman had won the Masters in 1937 and had finished in the top seven in the three years that followed. Observers were predicting good things for him. At the Calcutta, his ticket drew the highest bid. Cobb, based on his earlier round with Sam Snead, thought Snead stood the best chance, so he and his consortium answered the calls of the singing auctioneer and offered $1,125 for the rights to Snead. If Snead, a fellow country boy, were to take first, second, or third, Cobb and company would be in for some money.

Cobb had a grand time at the party, but something about the closeness of the golfers didn't settle well with his disposition. In a few days, they would be battling for one of golf's grandest honors, but here they were socializing together, sharing drinks and stories, slapping backs, and laughing. They were supposed to be opponents, enemies, and rivals, but they were partying together—not at some off-season banquet, but on the eve of a grand battle. Cobb didn't get it. He hadn't gone out on the town with Honus Wagner before the World Series of 1909. He hadn't even talked to his friend

Joe Jackson when the batting title was on the line. And there's no way he would have been hanging around with Babe Ruth when the Yankees and Tigers were clawing for the American League pennant in 1924. "Why, if I were competing in one of these things, do you think I'd even eat in the same dining room with the guy I was going to play?" he asked. "I wouldn't even speak to him. I'd give him the absent treatment, even on the course, until I ran him nuts. That's the way to beat somebody. Get his goat."

Cobb still felt the tug of competition. Everyone could sense it, including the PGA's Fred Corcoran, who had idolized Cobb as a boy. "He had the killer instinct in spades," he said.

Corcoran, who once hawked peanuts at Fenway Park, was a teller of tales, a cheery fellow inclined to exaggerate, and a promoter with—to use the words of the day—a nose for news. Under his guidance, the PGA tour would multiply in size and fortune. Corcoran also helped make Sam Snead famous, encouraging his headline-grabbing reputation as a hillbilly who played golf barefoot. In time, he would expand into baseball and become business manager for Ted Williams and Stan Musial.

In Augusta, Corcoran smelled opportunity.

On the morning of April 1, Cobb was at the first hole, getting ready to shoot a round with Yates, George Dawson, and Willie Goggin, who a year earlier had recorded a hole in one on the sixteenth. Corcoran spotted Cobb, and started plotting with Henry McLemore, a wire-service feature columnist. Both knew Cobb well. McLemore had visited him in January in California and had played golf with him. "He is the only golfer I have ever seen who even if he is three down and there are only two holes to play still figures he has a chance to win," he said. "He plays each shot as if his life depended on the outcome of it, and his behavior after a bad shot is about the same as it was when a pitcher dusted him off in the old days."

McLemore needed a story, and Corcoran had a rich one. Corcoran recalled how years earlier he had asked Cobb whether he could beat Ruth on the fairways and how emphatically Cobb had responded. McLemore decided to broach the topic again.

After Cobb drove his ball 220-plus yards down the lane, McLemore asked him about Ruth. Did Cobb think he could beat him at golf? Would he be willing to play him? McLemore didn't need to do much prodding. Cobb snapped up the bait.

"Anywhere, anytime," he said. "I have been hankering to take a shot at the Babe ever since I started playing golf."

It quickly became apparent that Cobb had given the matter more than a little thought since slipping the note to Ruth two years prior in Cooperstown. He was full of ideas. He said it might be fun to put on a baseball exhibition as part of the match. Run the bases, catch a few flies, show off the hook slide—at age fifty-four, he imagined he could still do all those things. (And he probably could.) Recalling the massive crowds that had packed ballparks in their playing days, Cobb said he hoped fans would come out and create a clamor. "After all, we are a couple of ballplayers and can stand a little noise," he said. "Let the gallery yell and boo and do anything it pleases. As a matter of fact, I would probably play a little better with an occasional boo from the customers. I heard quite a bit of that in the old days, you know."

Ruth hadn't even accepted the challenge, and already Cobb was making plans.

Ever the promoter, Corcoran did his part. He wired Ruth the invitation, and quickly began to crank up the hype. "I don't believe there are two other men who would draw as much as Cobb and Ruth," he said. "There have been ten thousand arguments as to which of the two was the better baseball player and that question never will be definitely settled. And in recent years, since they quit baseball, there have been arguments concerning their golfing skills. Now, we have a chance to settle that one."

Given their difference in handicaps—Ruth was a five, Cobb a nine—Cobb conceded that Ruth might be the better golfer. "But he won't beat me," he said. "I can talk him out of the match."

∾

The Masters opened at one o'clock on Thursday, April 3. Francis Ouimet and Walter Hagen were given the honor of teeing off first. It was Ouimet's first appearance at Augusta National. By day's end, both men would withdraw with scores in the 80s. Sam Byrd, Byron Nelson, and Ben Hogan had early time slots, and all shot well. But the most stunning performance came from Craig Wood, who had never won a major tournament. Wood bolted to a five-stroke lead on the opening day, shooting an astounding 66. On the second day, rival Byron Nelson, who had deprived Wood of the U.S. Open in a 1939 play-off, whittled his advantage to three strokes. Wood fought back on Saturday. On the fourth and final day, Nelson closed the gap after the first nine. The turning point came on the thirteenth hole, when Wood cleared Rae's Creek on his second shot, finding the rim of the green. Two shots later, he birdied the hole. Nelson took six shots. Wood won the title by three strokes, becoming the first wire-to-wire champion. Sam Byrd captured third place, topping Hogan, Dudley, and Snead.

The Masters was Grantland Rice's favorite annual event. Rice loved golf more than any other sport, and he treasured Augusta National—not only for its many qualities but also because it was Bobby Jones's creation. He admired Jones as he admired few others. Rice and Bob Jones Sr., a respected Atlanta attorney, had played college baseball against one another and had renewed their acquaintance in the early 1900s when Rice was making a name for himself at *The Atlanta Journal.* They became good friends. Rice watched Bobby Jones as a boy. He was there when the youth began claiming regional attention and developing a reputation as a fiery competitor. One day in 1915, Rice saw the thirteen-year-old miss a shot and launch into one of his hickory-tossing tirades. "He's a fighting cock, a hot head," Rice told Alex Smith, the former U.S. Open champion. "That one fault could prove his biggest hazard. If he can't learn to control it, he'll never play the kind of golf he'll be capable of shooting." Rice, like Jones Senior, and Pop Keeler, tried to get Bobby to tame his temper. Eventually, he did.

So close were the Joneses and Rices that when Bobby was fifteen, he stayed with Grantland and his wife, Kit, at their Riverside

Drive apartment while playing benefit matches around New York. "It was during [his] stay that Bob and I became acquainted in a way few persons with a gap of twenty-odd years between them ever do," wrote Rice in his memoirs. The relationship would carry through their lives.

A genial gentleman who enjoyed gin with his Coca-Cola, Rice—affectionately nicknamed Granny by his admirers—had been covering sports for forty years. He had seen everything there was to see, and at age sixty could be forgiven for the nostalgia that was seeping more frequently into his writing. It wasn't Wood's performance that most stirred Rice's lyrical muse at the 1941 Masters. It was the sight of his old friend Ty Cobb in the gallery on the first day watching Bobby Jones on the eighteenth hole. After Jones shot a forgettable 76, Rice ambled to the media tent and hammered out a sentimental poem on his clunky typewriter. It began with this verse:

> *The low, lost winds come whispering*
> *Over the red clay hills;*
> *They sing to me through Georgia pines*
> *The song of remembered thrills;*
> *They bring back ghosts from a vanished year*
> *Phantoms beyond all reach,*
> *When Bobby Jones was the king of golf*
> *And Ty Cobb was the Georgia Peach.*

20

The Babe Accepts

Ruth, who studied to be a tailor, models the latest in golf fashions. NATIONAL BASEBALL HALL OF FAME LIBRARY, COOPERSTOWN, N.Y.

B ABE RUTH RECEIVED TY COBB'S CHALLENGE IN NEW YORK. Formally and finally out of baseball—the talk of his someday becoming a manager had turned wistful—Ruth had been occupying his hours for the past several years by happily playing golf. His affection for the game had been constant and uninterrupted since he first picked up the clubs as a young player with the Red Sox. While Cobb and others had fretted during their playing days about the impact of golf on their baseball performance, Ruth had never given the matter two thoughts. He golfed before, during, and after the season—always for fun, frequently for money. Though golf sometimes frustrated him, inciting him to admonish himself with streams of obscenities, Ruth cherished the game.

In the mid-1930s, while still in the major leagues, he competed in an informal, round-robin winter league in Florida with fellow ballplayers. One week, they'd play at Dizzy Dean's home course in Bradenton, another week at Mickey Cochrane's in Lakeland or Paul Waner's in Sarasota. Gee Walker, Tommy Bridges, Wes Farrell, Goose Goslin, and Jo-Jo White were among the regulars. Contrary to his long-ball exploits on the baseball field—and despite the exaggerative sports-page reports and his heavy, 17.5-ounce club—Ruth didn't regularly drive the golf ball any farther than his peers and often not as far, according to submarine pitcher Elden Auker, who usually outdistanced Ruth by twenty or more yards. "He had a controlled swing and was seldom in trouble," said Auker. "He was a steady player, kept the ball in the middle of the fairway. But his drives weren't out of the ordinary." Everyone enjoyed golfing with the Babe, said Auker. It wasn't that they cherished his abilities; they cherished him. "He was just a big kid. He laughed and joked all the time."

In retirement, Ruth took refuge on the course. On the eve of one birthday, he entertained a pack of friends at his New York apartment. After wife Claire presented him with a rose-decorated cake that the hired help had prepared, Ruth was asked how much he missed baseball. "Boys, if it wasn't for golf, I think I'd die." Ruth estimated that he had played more than three hundred rounds the previous year.

He was arguably the most famous recreational golfer in the nation. His exploits, no matter how trivial, made headlines: BABE RUTH CLOWNS AND BAND PLAYS AT CHARITY GOLF MATCH . . . BABE RUTH TAKES DRIVING CONTEST . . . BABE RUTH MAKES DRIVE OF 352 YARDS. Every year, golf photos of Ruth appeared in newspapers and magazines. There's Ruth at St. Albans singing in the locker room with fellow members, and there he is perusing a copy of *Golf* magazine in the club's sitting room. There's Ruth driving a ball while clamping a cigar in his teeth, and there he is in a silk smoking jacket, practicing his putting on a Persian rug in his apartment. And there he is pictured on a course in New York or Cleveland or St. Petersburg or Boston with Tommy Armour or Grantland Rice or Paul Runyan or Rube Marquard or Gov. Al Smith or one of hundreds of others over the years. His affection for the sport was so well-known that when Brooklyn hired him as a coach in 1938, manager Burleigh Grimes addressed the issue. "The Babe doesn't belong out on any golf links," said Grimes, the grizzled spitball pitcher. "He is an institution in baseball, and that's where he ought to spend every day of his life."

But even while coaching, Ruth immersed himself in the golf lifestyle. One five-week stretch in 1940 provided a glimpse of how he spent a typical spring, with each event catalogued by the press. He golfed nearly every day, recorded a hole in one on April 11 (on St. Albans's 220-yard fifteenth), was feted by two hundred club members at a dinner a week later, and attended a day in his honor at Leewood Club, where he received a silver bowl inscribed TO BABE RUTH—A GREAT FELLOW. He had a talent for entertaining crowds. He chatted with galleries, placed hexes on opponents' balls, and sprawled out on the greens to shoot billiards-style with the end of his putter. Ruth was always willing to ham it up for spectators and photographers, which made him a natural for charity matches like the one held in November 1937 at Fresh Meadow in New York.

Promoters wanted to introduce a mysterious Hollywood wonder, John Montague, to the masses on the East Coast, and asked Babe Ruth, Babe Didrikson, and regional women's champ Sylva Annenberg to round out the foursome in a benefit for Mayor LaGuardia's camp for boys.

Montague and Didrikson were major sports figures. Didrikson was regarded as the top female athlete of her era—maybe of all time. She was fond of Ruth, from whom she drew her nickname while she was growing up in Texas. Before focusing on golf, Didrikson had parlayed her medal-winning track-and-field performance at the 1932 Olympics into a multisport career as a barnstorming entertainer. She played basketball and billiards and baseball. She swam and dove. She even tried in 1933 to get Ruth to face her in a boxing exhibition; he refused. She referred admiringly to Babe Ruth as "the Big Babe" and to herself as "the Little Babe."

The legend of Montague had been building for years. Those who had seen him golf, including Grantland Rice, vowed that if he would enter competition, he would dominate the sport. But Montague was an enigmatic and secretive fellow who avoided photographers and official events but put on fabulous, private displays of his prowess for the likes of Bing Crosby. Montague was a master of trick shots with rakes and shovels. He was a hustler who could launch monstrous drives with startling accuracy. Once, he reportedly plucked a bird off a telephone line with a shot. Montague was gregarious and liked to drink and found himself the toast of a circle of celebrities that included Crosby, comedian Oliver Hardy, and Johnny "Tarzan" Weissmuller. Part of Montague's allure centered around his seeming reluctance to become famous. As it turned out, there was a reason. When a photographer finally captured and published pictures of him, Montague was revealed to be La Verne Moore, a criminal wanted for seven years in a six-hundred-dollar robbery. With the backing of his California pals, Moore weathered the charges and was eventually acquitted. His outlaw status only added to his reputation.

New York papers were awash with stories of Montague's past as the November 1937 match approached. On the day of the event, twelve thousand fans stormed onto the Fresh Meadow course, catching officials unprepared. These weren't your typical golf spectators. They crowded the foursome, dangerously narrowing the driving lanes to ten feet in spots. It was chaos, and it took one hour for Ruth, Montague, and company to complete just three holes. The throngs flustered Montague, who had shot a 65 days earlier at North Hempstead in Port Washington. Out of safety concerns, officials called the match prematurely, with Ruth and Didrikson ahead.

The PGA's Fred Corcoran thought a Cobb-Ruth pairing would

draw even bigger crowds than Ruth, Montague, and Didrikson. Ty and Babe, after all, had been baseball's biggest stars and celebrated rivals. They were still household names. With Cobb having agreed to go east to meet up with Ruth, the only question was whether Ruth would be willing.

Cobb's challenge lingered for three, four days, then five and six, until a week had passed. One can only speculate why Ruth waited to respond. Maybe he didn't want the hassle of traveling around the region to play exhibition golf. Maybe he thought Cobb would cancel, as he had in 1939. Ten days after Cobb's invitation, Ruth responded by telegram: IF YOU WANT TO COME HERE AND GET YOUR BRAINS KNOCKED OUT, COME AHEAD. After their earlier failed attempts to get together, Ruth and Cobb were finally going to meet on the course. The match was on—this time for real.

Initially, the tournament was going to be a fund-raiser for Bundles for Britain, a war-relief charity. Matches were being planned for late May in two cities: Boston and New York. Philadelphia was also lobbying for consideration. Corcoran was trying to work out the details, going between Ruth and Cobb and various clubs. "I won't give you any trouble on any point," Ruth promised. "It's that Cobb who'll give you headaches about arrangements. I see he's already saying he hopes he gets me on a golf course with narrow fairways and tight greens, so that I'll be in the rough all day. Let him talk. I'll do my talking after the match is over." Ruth continued his daily regimen of a round of golf preceded by a few drinks and a steak breakfast.

But he was right about Cobb. When Corcoran called him and proposed they open the challenge at Commonwealth Country Club in Newton, Massachusetts, Cobb was suspicious, and proceeded to interrogate him.

"Is that where Ruth plays when he's in Boston?"

"I don't think so," Corcoran said. "In fact, I don't know that he ever played the course."

Cobb wasn't convinced: "You'll be telling me next that he's never been in Boston."

Ruth, in fact, had never seen the Commonwealth course. But how was Cobb to know that?

~

News of the war overseas dominated front pages throughout the spring and into summer. Despite the fierce battles being waged in Europe, Americans overwhelmingly opposed entering the conflict. Dr. George Gallup of the American Institute of Public Opinion found that nearly eight out of ten Americans wanted to avoid the fight. Even Germany's invasion of Russia wouldn't radically alter that viewpoint.

Baseball provided a diversion from the dour realities of war. By late May, Joe DiMaggio—once proclaimed as the next Babe Ruth—had strung together hits in sixteen straight games, and was putting on a home-run parade with teammates Charlie Keller, Tommy Henrich, and Joe Gordon. Over in Boston, Teddy Williams was keeping his batting average above .400 and in the realm of Cobb. But overshadowing the game on the field was the fate of Lou Gehrig, one of baseball's legends. Gehrig had not played ball since 1939, but he remained in the spotlight and dear to baseball fans. As late as April 1941, with Gehrig fading from amyotrophic lateral sclerosis, reporters kept alive the prospect that he might return to the Yankees. "Get back in the game?" asked Gehrig, parroting a reporter's question. "Well, let's not talk about it now. When you haven't your health, you can't plan too many things ahead."

Gehrig died on the evening of Monday, June 2. The next night, baseball's premier stars gathered in radio stations in New York, Cleveland, and Detroit to pay tribute to him.

"The days I spent with Lou Gehrig are the most pleasant I've spent," said Bill Dickey, his former roommate.

"I'm deeply grieved," noted Jimmie Foxx. "I had the pleasure of playing against Lou throughout his entire career. Lou Gehrig is a man baseball players will never forget."

"I lost a very fine friend," said DiMaggio. "Lou helped me more—as much as—anyone connected with baseball."

Bobby Feller called him "one of the toughest competitors I ever pitched against," and Mel Ott said he was "a wonderful man on the field and off."

Although estranged through much of the 1930s—most accounts blame a dispute between Ruth's wife and Gehrig's mother—Babe and Lou had reconciled in 1939 at Lou Gehrig Day in Yankee Stadium.

"I could talk here for an hour about Lou," said Babe Ruth on radio. "I really feel sorry."

~

The upcoming match sparked Cobb's competitive fire and filled him with a sense of purpose, something family members felt he desperately needed. Ty had been out of baseball for thirteen years, much longer than Babe, and he seemed to have far too many empty hours on his hands.

At home in California, Cobb worked at losing weight and getting in shape for the match. He was hitting the courses nearly every day, methodically honing his skills. Word leaked that he was concentrating on his approaches and developing a pressure shot. "My friends tell me I can take the Babe," he said, "but I know from our experiences on the ball field he is the kind of an athlete to break up the game on a minute's notice." Cobb sounded like a man who was either lowering expectations or playing mind games. You could never be sure, but the smart money was on mind games. Reinforcing that feeling was an incident in early May. Cobb, after shooting 88 in a left-handers' tournament at Pasadena's Annandale Country Club, complained of an injury to his side. The extent of his ailment—or whether it even existed—was a matter of speculation. Regardless, Corcoran pushed the dates of the matches into June.

As the pain eased, Cobb resumed golfing daily and seeking insights into Ruth's game. On a trip back to Michigan, he visited Oakland Hills, site of the 1937 Open. Cobb, showing off a new set of custom-made clubs, played with Oakland pro Al Watrous and close friend and former Athletics teammate Mickey Cochrane. Both men had golfed with Ruth, and Cobb mined them for information.

"Say, Al," said Cobb. "What kind of a game does the Babe play?"

"He's pretty good at times," said Watrous. "He hits a long ball but isn't so good on his short game."

"Does he hit them straight?"

"Some days he does, and some days he doesn't."

Cobb downplayed his own abilities, saying he had only recently begun practicing regularly. "My game is pretty rusty," he said.

"Peach," said Cochrane, "you'll beat the Babe. . . . The way he sprays them, you ought to take him easy."

Cobb told everyone he wasn't so sure. He confessed to being concerned about his shoulder, which hadn't fully recovered from a hunting accident. He said he was afraid he might lose to Ruth. "I want to give a good account of myself against the Babe," he said.

For his part, Babe was making no public statements about his chances against Cobb. But he felt confident he could handle him.

~

Fred Corcoran loved to stir excitement. He excelled in generating publicity, and had no qualms about pricking golf's staid reputation—if it meant a bigger crowd. In 1940, Corcoran had organized a charity exhibition at Shorehaven in Norwalk, Connecticut. He enlisted Ruth, Gene Sarazen, Jimmy Demaret, and boxer Gene Tunney for a hospital benefit, and came up with a madcap angle. Rattling golf tradition, Corcoran invited spectators to make noise while watching the match. He encouraged them to yelp and howl and heckle and whistle, and the result was like something out of a future Adam Sandler film, *Happy Gilmore*. Corcoran hired Fred Waring and the Pennsylvanians and radio comedian Colonel Stoopnagle to enliven the event. Waring's band performed songs like "Are You Having Any Fun?" and "Take Me Out to the Ball Game" while golfers took their shots. Meanwhile, Stoopnagle followed Ruth and company in a speaker-equipped truck, providing silly commentary and sound effects. The raucous fund-raiser drew about five thousand people. But Corcoran had crossed some lines in the view of USGA officials. The group's president called him the next day and told him, "I hope you never do it again." It was more an order than a request.

Cobb and Ruth agreed to a best-of-three series with contests near Boston, New York, and Detroit. The choice of cities was obvious. Ruth had spent his career in the first two, Cobb had made his name in the third, and all three had borne witness to their rivalry. The East Coast matches were set for June, to be followed by a final Michigan contest, if needed, in July.

Corcoran wasted no time feeding the publicity mill. He reminded everyone of the tense nature of Ruth and Cobb's battles. He announced that Arthur Donovan would be refereeing the New York match. Every respectable sports fan, especially in the Big Apple, knew of Donovan. He had been a prominent boxing figure, and he had been in the ring for many of Joe Louis's title fights. Presumably, he would be needed should Ty's or Babe's tempers flare.

It didn't take long for the stories to begin appearing in print. A *Washington Post* columnist declared that the battle—"in the making for at least fifteen years"—would be "big and historical." Added *The New York Times,* "There will be fireworks."

Through Corcoran's efforts, the buzz had begun. His focus on Cobb and Ruth's historic rivalry may have been designed as hype, but he must have known that there was more than a splinter of truth in his words. Both men were competitors, and, friendship or not, neither cared to lose. By mid-June, Ty Cobb was on his way east.

A Peach in New York

Jimmy Demaret, Cobb, and Arthur Donovan meet in
New York. NATIONAL BASEBALL HALL OF FAME LIBRARY,
COOPERSTOWN, N.Y.

~

Y COBB'S SUITE AT THE TWENTY-FIVE-STORY, RED-
awninged Hotel McAlpin was swarming with New York
sports reporters on Monday morning, June 23. Cobb had arrived
hours earlier at Penn Station, a block from the hotel, and was now
listening aghast as the scribes regaled him with tales of Babe
Ruth's feats on the golf course. Ruth regularly scored 69 and 70,

could drive the ball three hundred yards, and had mastered the short game, they said. Cobb looked crushed under the weight of the news. He was humbled. Had he been conned? Would Ruth blow him off the course? Cobb had already bet at least a thousand dollars that he would win. But it was more a matter of pride than money.

"Good Lord! If I'd known all this, I would have stayed home," he said. "Ruth will murder me. I'm just a fair amateur player, you know." Taken aback, Cobb declined to predict victory. "I wouldn't like to go out on a limb and find someone ready to chop it off right under me," he said.

The reporters were conning Cobb. They had conspired to fool him by hyping Ruth's abilities, and it was working. When they finally admitted their ruse, Cobb sighed. He was visibly relieved. "You had me pretty scared," he said.

The opening match was set for Wednesday outside of Boston. Cobb had come to New York to generate publicity and to practice at the local course. He had also hoped to get under Ruth's skin. Cobb had planned to come out swinging before the reporters, but they had gotten to him first with their false stories about Ruth's game.

With encouragement from Fred Corcoran and Bob Harlow, Corcoran's predecessor (and future founder of *Golf World* magazine), Cobb regained his composure and did his best to build up the competition. "I'll show that Ruth how to play left-handed golf," he pledged. He tried to reach Ruth by phone to get in a few public taunts, but Ruth had already left for Boston.

Cobb had carded his best game a few months earlier on St. Patrick's Day, scoring a one-over-par 71 on the ocean course at San Francisco's Lakeside Country Club. "Two days later, same course, same clubs, same player, I went around in 84," he said. "That should give you an idea of my game."

Among the spectators in the suite were referee Arthur Donovan and golfer Jimmy Demaret, who a year earlier had shot a record 30 on the second nine at Augusta National. Cobb admitted he was a bit uneasy about facing Ruth.

"I never worried before a ball game," said Cobb. "I would just get up there and swing. But golf is different. I think it is a tougher game, especially on the nerves. Look at Jimmy Demaret and some of the other young pros. They play themselves dry. One bad shot and a tournament is gone. In baseball, your average might dip but you have plenty of time to snap back again. And the paycheck comes in regularly in baseball."

The writers played along for a while, but when the golf conversation lagged, they led Cobb to the subject he knew best, and instantly they could sense the passion surging in his veins. Endorsing the use of helmets in baseball, Cobb grabbed a bat and demonstrated in cuffed sleeves and tie the proper way to dodge a beanball, springing back on the balls of one's feet. He launched into a monologue, pacing the room as he spoke.

Fingering a brown-papered cigarette that he had rolled himself—not to save money, but to help him reduce his tobacco habit—Cobb reeled off his all-time baseball team. In a polite display of respect in the wake of Gehrig's death, Cobb for the first time included Lou on his team of greats. (He would return George Sisler to the spot in the years ahead.) Cobb put Eddie Collins at second, Buck Weaver at third, Honus Wagner at short, and Joe Jackson, Tris Speaker, and Ruth in the outfield, with catcher Mickey Cochrane leading a staff that included Walter Johnson, Christy Mathewson, Grover Cleveland Alexander, Ed Walsh, and Eddie Plank. (He forgot Cy Young, but would correct that oversight a month later.) Of course, Cobb excluded himself from the list, knowing full well that no one else would.

"Whom would you rather have on your club, DiMaggio or Bob Feller?" someone asked.

"That is much too tough a question to reply to offhand," said Cobb. "Feller certainly is the pitcher of the day, DiMaggio the number-one outfielder, though I will admit I have seen this new sensation, Ted Williams, play only one game of ball. I would hate to be placed in the predicament of deciding to give up one for the other."

He praised Feller's curveball, but judged Walter Johnson as the faster pitcher. "Do you know, back in the days when Johnson and Big Ed Walsh were the pitching kings, they stopped rallies merely by coming out of the dugout and warming up? Psychology is terrific."

Cobb confessed that his own sense of vulnerability prompted him to retire at age forty-one. "I've never told this before," he said. "I suddenly was afraid of getting hit by a pitched ball. . . . I realized my reflexes weren't as sharp as they used to be and it would be my own fault if I were hit. I got to thinking about poor Ray Chapman, and when I caught myself dwelling on that, I knew it was time to get out."

When Cobb turned critical about the glory days of the long ball, a reporter wondered if he was taking a veiled slap at Ruth.

"I didn't mean it that way," Cobb clarified. "Ruth was wonderful. I admired that big baboon although I needled him all the time. If Babe just went after base hits, as I did, his percentage would've been tremendous. He was good enough to adjust himself to any type of game he wanted to play."

While Cobb relished the thought of defeating Ruth in golf, he expressed genuine affection for the man. After his baseball days, Cobb had often struggled to balance his innate competitiveness with his desire for closer friendships with fellow athletes. He had regrets. Years earlier, he was outside a ballpark with friend Fred Haney when they spotted a few players roughhousing after a game, all in good fun. Cobb stopped and watched from a distance. "I wish I could have done that," he said. Cobb yearned for such camaraderie. Yet that craving often clashed with his competitive disposition. With the golf match, the overriding question for Cobb was whether, while trying to beat Ruth, he would be able to check his zealous nature so that he could keep him as a friend.

~

As Cobb was entertaining reporters in Manhattan on Monday morning, Babe and wife Claire, a poof of flowers pinned atop her hat, arrived at East Boston Airport. Bob Worden, president of the Commonwealth Club, site of the first match, greeted them on the rain-dampened tarmac as they deplaned from their American flight. It was drizzling.

"Let's get out to Commonwealth," said Ruth. "If this rain stops, I want to hit a few. I don't want that son of a gun to beat me."

The Commonwealth Country Club was in the Chestnut Hill neighborhood of Newton Corner, one of the collage of thirteen villages that made up Newton, an old-moneyed suburb west of Boston. The city was home to Boston College. Newton traced its roots to the late 1600s, and over time had hosted writers, scholars, athletes, and celebrities as varied as Katharine Lee Bates, who penned the words to "America the Beautiful," and actress Bette Davis, who attended high school there. (A future star, actor Jack Lemmon, had been born in the elevator of a Newton hospital in 1925.) The town also inspired the name for the Fig Newton cookie, which was manufactured by the nearby Kennedy Biscuit Works.

Fred Corcoran, who had grown up in the Boston area caddying at the affluent Belmont Springs Country Club (once for Francis Ouimet), became acquainted with Commonwealth while working for the Massachusetts Golf Association, first as state handicapper, then as secretary. The course had begun in 1897 as an affiliate of Allston Golf Club, which would be replaced by Braves Field in 1915. In 1920, the nine-hole Commonwealth was transformed into a short, though not easy, eighteen-hole course by a well-known resident of nearby Newton Centre, golf architect Donald Ross. In the years since, it had been refurbished and lengthened to 6,240 yards. Still, in 1941 at least six holes measured 325 yards or fewer.

Ruth arrived at Commonwealth around noon, and word spread quickly, particularly among the caddies. In the clubhouse, Babe clipped his wavy hair back with a metal barrette, slipped out of his sports coat and into Irish green golf slacks and a white shirt, and headed to the first tee, a towel looped over his belt. A small band of curious club members, photographers, and reporters followed him.

Off to the side stood two boys about eleven, Joe Ullian and Fred Fischel. Both were too young to remember Ruth as a ballplayer yet old enough to know of his legend. They had ink pens in hand, but the sight of the imposing, 240-pound man kept them at a distance. Someone pointed them out to Ruth, and he headed their way. "Hi, fellows," he called out. "What's on your mind?"

Ruth signed their cards, posed for photos, and left them grinning before heading back to the sloping first hole.

During the practice round, course pro Russ Hale easily outdrove Ruth, who had been on a mission to become a more refined golfer. "I always could sock that white pill a mile but nowadays I am willing to sacrifice distance for accuracy," Ruth said. "I've been playing golf steadily this season, and my four previous rounds on courses in the metropolitan district were 78-75-74-73. But my tee shots are much straighter than when I was whaling the ball."

Though jovial on the course, Ruth, like Cobb, had wagered money on the outcome. He hoped to get Cobb to agree to a bet. "I always have wanted to be numbered among the very select few able to give Ty a drubbing at anything," he said. ". . . I've got a chunk of dough that says my game is good enough to top Ty's."

Ruth smoked cigars while he golfed, biting off the tips and chewing on them. He cussed when his shots went awry, but he remained a friendly presence. Around the fourteenth hole, his knees started aching—an old baseball injury acting up. Ruth sunk a fifteen-foot putt on the final green, giving him a 79 on the soggy, par-72 course. Not bad for a first try. From the trellised porch, club members applauded his final shot. He acknowledged them and then retired to the bar, sliding out of his shoes to give a bruised big toe some relief. He had clubbed his own foot in frustration.

"My swing was lazy today," he said between gulps. "The ball was fading on me."

As with Cobb, everyone always had questions for Ruth, and he obliged their curiosity as long as the scotch kept coming.

Ruth talked about Ted Williams, the young star of the Red Sox: "He's a natural, all right. I saw him last year, and he's got an easy swing and a hard swing. Anybody with a swing like that is going for homers. He can't help it." He reminisced about Fenway Park and some long-ago clout: "There was a Tanglefoot sign in right field behind the bleachers and I hit it, but only got a triple. In those days they wouldn't give you a home run if the winning run scored ahead of it. I must have lost fifty homers that way."

Fifty home runs? That was a stretch. As the afternoon grew long and the liquor continued to flow, Ruth became even looser with the facts. "I got even with Cobb," he said. "After we clinched the pennant one year, I told Huggins I was pitching. Well, I just laid the ball in there for the boys to hit, until I got to Cobb. I flattened him with a couple behind the knob and then struck him out the only two times I faced him. I'll have to remind him of that when I see him."

Of course, there was some truth to the story. He had pitched against Cobb in 1921 and struck him out. But he did it once, not twice. The game was in June, and the Yankees had not secured the title. And if Ruth had actually tossed a couple at Cobb's head, there would have been a brawl.

In recalling their encounters, Cobb and Ruth often exaggerated.

Cobb liked to tell of the time he tricked Ruth into striking out by faking an intentional walk. From center field, he supposedly ordered Hooks Dauss to pass Ruth. Dauss, as part of an elaborate trick, threw Ruth a strike. Cobb stormed the mound and chastised him and catcher Johnny Bassler. Again he ordered an intentional walk. And again Ruth watched a strike buzz past him, prompting Cobb to remove Dauss and Bassler for disobeying him. The new pitcher, Rufe Clarke, completed the ruse by ignoring Cobb's call for a walk and sneaking a third strike past him. It was a great pro-Cobb story that reinforced the notion that he had the brains to outwit a cocky Ruth. Except it never happened.

Ruth often related that one of his proudest moments occurred when he struck out Cobb, Crawford, and Veach in the ninth inning after loading the bases with nobody out in a 1-0 game. More fantasy. He might have been thinking of the September 21, 1916, game in which he fanned Cobb and Veach on six straight pitches and won 10-2.

Cobb and Ruth weren't the only players to embellish their careers. But as the two widely considered the game's best, did they really need to embroider their already-impressive accomplishments?

On Monday afternoon, while Ruth was in Boston, Cobb played a round at Fresh Meadow in New York. Battling strong winds, he shot an 85. Afterward, he went with Fred Corcoran to Toots Shor's place on West Fifty-first Street for dinner and drinks. DiMaggio and Sinatra were among the regulars at Shor's restaurant. Though crusty and boisterous, Shor, a former bouncer, knew how to treat the stars. He gave Cobb a secluded table and shielded him from the curious. Cobb and Corcoran talked the night away, Cobb worrying about his game. "Once you start to play poorly you get into a rut and stay there for some time," he said. "I haven't been hitting the ball well at all." It wasn't false modesty; Cobb was worried. Encouraged by the liquor, he began focusing on all the problems with his swing: how his hips moved too much, how he couldn't break his habit of lifting his right foot—baseball-style—before finishing his swing. Cobb and Corcoran drank and drank, and made it to Penn Station just before the midnight train departed for Boston. The next morning, Cobb awoke in a lower berth with a hangover. "You don't suppose that guy Shor has a bet on Ruth, do you?" he asked Corcoran.

It was Tuesday, and Cobb would have a day to recover. The big match would take place Wednesday, but Cobb was in a restless mood.

22

Notes, Goats, and Gamesmanship

Cobb shows off a novelty gift. NATIONAL BASEBALL HALL OF FAME LIBRARY, COOPERSTOWN, N.Y.

I N GOLF, AS IN BASEBALL, PSYCHOLOGY WAS PART OF TY COBB'S arsenal, and everyone expected him to deploy it against Ruth. Upon arriving in New York, Cobb had promised as much. He had, in fact, consulted by phone with Walter Hagen on the fine points of golf psychology. "I want to win this match and every little bit I can pick up to help me I will," he said. Hagen had advised Cobb on how to get Ruth's goat—as if Cobb really needed anyone's help in that arena.

Reporters tried to find out what specifically Cobb intended to do in Newton. Would he actually heckle Ruth? What would he say to upset him? Would he defy golf's genteel code of conduct? Cobb was vague on the details, but he pledged to open up with a taunt. "I won't need any prepared list of ribs for a guy like Ruth," he said. "I'll be able to think of plenty of things to burn him up by just looking at him. . . . I like Babe, and have great respect for him. We used to kid around a lot during ball games. Gosh, you had to do something. He was so blamed good."

But Ruth was taking no chances. He was guarding against Cobb's mental assault with one of his own. From the locker room at Commonwealth, he launched several preemptive volleys. Ruth knew the surest way to rile Cobb was to impugn his honor, and he did it in a teasing manner and with a hearty laugh. First, Ruth looked over his golf shoes and announced he would need to get another pair—with longer spikes to better defend himself. Then Ruth accused Cobb of having chickened out of their earlier date. Remember 1939? The train ride from Cooperstown to New York City? The men had agreed, but Cobb canceled, contending that he had a business engagement. Ruth said Cobb went to the World's Fair instead. ". . . I'll be waiting for him," Ruth told Boston reporters. "This time, he won't have any excuse—or is there a World's Fair going on in this town?"

Over several months, Cobb had been downplaying his own abilities and building up Ruth's. "It will be a rookie against an old-timer," he said. "I'm just a ham player."

Cobb was certainly up to something, and Ruth knew it. But it was unlike Cobb to reveal his strategy beforehand—to announce

his plans to taunt Ruth. Had he changed that much since his playing days? Was he willingly surrendering the element of surprise?

"I'll do everything possible to win," Cobb said.

~

Babe returned to Commonwealth on Tuesday morning, logging an
80 in his second practice round. He was changing in the locker
room and chatting with friends when Ty approached from behind
and tapped him on the shoulder. Ruth turned and greeted him. The
two hadn't seen each other in a year or two.

"Well, hello you old son of a bitch," Ruth said with affection.
"How are you?"

"Hi, Babe . . ."

And there the bantering and posturing began anew.

"I hear you're hitting them pretty well," Cobb said.

"Not bad. It looks tough for you. I'm going to knock your brains
out."

"Oh, you probably will, all right," said Cobb. "My shoulder's been
bothering me. I may not even be able to swing a club."

"Oh, yeah?"

"Say, they tell me you're hitting such a long tee shot I won't be
able to catch up with two of my little drives."

"Ehh, I'm just a control hitter."

"Do you ever shank?"

"Shank? Never heard of such a thing."

"But are you good on those short putts?" Cobb wondered. "I may
make you putt the little ones just to see if you can hole them."

"I don't expect you to give me nothing," Ruth replied.

"Well, all I'll expect is that you play as well as they say you do."

The long-ago rivals laughed at the give-and-take. It was like the
old days, only a lot more civil.

As Cobb changed, Ruth remarked to his friends, "Looks like he's
trying to talk me out of it. Maybe he doesn't think he can beat me
out on the course." Ruth might have been close on both counts.

Babe hung around until Cobb wandered outside. Trying to be

inconspicuous, he watched Ty tee off on the first hole. The ball whistled down the fairway. "That's not good enough," Ruth hollered. "You've got to hit them better than that if you expect to beat me tomorrow, Ty."

Ruth left for Fenway Park and spent the afternoon in the front row, watching the Red Sox pound first-place Cleveland 13–2. Fans cheered the sight of him, and Ruth in turn cheered when Jim Tabor clubbed a grand slam. Every Boston player got a hit except Ted Williams, who walked three times and made two outs. Williams was trying hard to impress Ruth. "It was the second time I've seen him," Ruth said. "I saw him whack a homer in the stadium last year. He's got power. . . . Wish they didn't walk him so much."

Back at Commonwealth, Cobb played his practice round by shooting multiple balls on each hole. He worked different angles and approaches, experimented with clubs, took notes like a frenzied stenographer, and welcomed the advice of his caddy. "I bow to your superior judgment," he said after the man recommended he use a four-iron rather than the three Cobb had requested. Cobb calculated his score as 78.

"He's conscientious," one of Ruth's moles told Babe later. "He may not hit a long shot but he's accurate."

During his ball-playing days, Cobb found there was rarely a challenge he couldn't meet by studying and analyzing it. He often spent hours in his hotel room reliving the day's game, figuring out what went right or wrong and plotting his action. He earned his reputation as a baseball thinker. But it was different with golf. The game perplexed him, and self-scrutiny didn't help. "I didn't have to think about what I was doing when I batted," he said. "But in golf I have to think about my back swing, my stance, my weight, and everything. The trouble is, I'm too conscious when I play golf. I think too much."

In his early golf years, Cobb relied only on himself, believing practice alone would improve him. It didn't. So he consulted professionals but found his habits difficult to break. "I'm all mixed up," he said. "I try to change, but it seems I'm better the old way. This is a funny game."

~

Both Cobb and Ruth were staying in downtown Boston at the plush Ritz Carlton, between Commonwealth and Newberry avenues. Across Arlington Street, in the public gardens, children played on the shaded landscape and dogs barked and tourists glided on the pond in swan boats.

Cobb hadn't been to Boston since 1928, when he played for Connie Mack. But lots of long-lost pals were showing up to reconnect with him. The fans he encountered along the way were receiving him warmly, too. What a change from the old days! In his hotel room, Cobb chatted with Joe Casey, a bit player who had spent parts of three seasons with Detroit. Casey, who lived in Massachusetts, had been at Fenway for the afternoon contest and was eager to talk baseball.

"I thought you might be out there at the ballpark," he said. "You don't see many games, do you, Tyrus?"

Cobb admitted as much, and gave Casey his usual spiel about how the game had changed before turning the subject to golf. "I did better today," he said. Cobb was relieved with his play at Commonwealth. He had executed his shots more proficiently in Newton than at Fresh Meadow. He felt confident, but he never liked to take these things for granted. Soon, Cobb excused himself. He said he needed to rest for a dinner party later that evening.

Ruth was already living it up on the roof of the hotel, which looked out over the Back Bay, speckled with boats. Over drinks, Ruth laughed with Fred Corcoran and a slew of friends and reporters. The sounds of a Cuban band reverberated across the floor.

The conversation ricocheted between baseball and golf, with Ruth always at the center. Johnny Corcoran, Fred's brother, razzed Ruth about how Cobb had salvaged a hole after hitting into a sand trap during his practice round. Ruth could sense a line of bullshit coming his way.

"What'd he get, a four?" he asked.

"No, he got a five," said Johnny Corcoran.

"I still think you're lying," Ruth replied.

Ruth bragged a bit about his own game. "I saw this big crowd gathered in front of the clubhouse today and I thought I'd give them a thrill by pitching in to the cup from about one hundred yards," he said. "I put everything I had into the shot but the damned ball stopped on the lip of the cup. It looked like it was going to roll right in, but that Cobb or somebody must have stuck some glue there and stopped it."

The stories and the drinks flowed for hours, and undoubtedly a few of the men got drunk. Maybe Ruth and Corcoran. Certainly a reporter or two. The ranks of sports reporters were filled with heavy drinkers. On occasion, when a peer would be passed out drunk, reporters would cover for one another by turning in ghost-written stories to their competitors' papers.

Cobb arrived at the party after it was well underway. Ruth spotted him, but Cobb sat at a different table. Pert Cuban dancers were shaking their shapely bodies on the stage. The sight brought a grin to Cobb's face.

"Woowww!" he roared.

"Same old Cobb," Ruth said to his tablemates.

The prospect of the old legends reliving their rivalry had been inspiring inky reams for several days. "These two have really been hot to have it out," offered Bill Cunningham of the *Boston Herald.* "This is no autograph carnival. It's a golf match for blood."

"In their heart of hearts, they are still fighting over the Civil War," noted Iffy the Dopester, the popular alter ego of *Detroit Free Press* editor Malcolm Bingay.

John Kieran of *The New York Times,* whose fame had multiplied as a panelist on *Information, Please!,* the nation's second-most-popular radio show, predicted an explosion. "Don't stand too close," he warned.

But it fell to Stanley Frank of the *New York Post,* writing a half year before America would be drawn into another world war, to characterize the match most distastefully. "Compared to Ruth and Cobb," he wrote, "Churchill and Hitler are old chums temporarily estranged by a slight misunderstanding."

The opening round was a day away. Though both men had predicted victory, Ruth had done it with more bluster, force, and confidence. At the hotel party, he dismissed talk of Cobb's performance during the practice rounds. "After all, it's what we do tomorrow that counts," he said.

Not entirely. Later that night in the privacy of his room, Ty Cobb reviewed his elaborate course notes and thought about his strategy.

23

Tee Time in Newton

Babe, Ty, and the trophy—with Spanky Joslyn, a resident of Golden Rule Farm. PRIVATE COLLECTION OF SPAULDING YOUTH CENTER

TWENTY-FIVE SCRUBBED AND SHINED BOYS FROM THE Golden Rule Farm crowded around Ty Cobb and Babe Ruth on Wednesday afternoon prior to their match. The scene made for one of those classic Ruth photos: the Babe, a gentle giant, surrounded by a troupe of admiring children. Ruth flung his right arm over Cobb's shoulder, and both of them mugged for the cameras while the children looked their way, some squinting into the sun. The boys, whose ages ranged from six to sixteen, had come down from Franklin, New Hampshire, to be part of the event, a benefit for their home.

Orphanages like Golden Rule Farm dotted the national landscape. There were hundreds of them, many much larger than the New Hampshire residence, which housed fifty or sixty troubled, neglected, homeless, or parentless boys. Three years earlier, Spencer Tracy and Mickey Rooney had starred in the Oscar-nominated *Boys Town,* a syrupy film that heightened affection for such institutions. Supporters described Golden Rule Farm as the Boys Town of New Hampshire.

Cobb and Ruth had agreed that all proceeds from the golf matches would go to charities. Golden Rule Farm qualified. A working dairy farm, it had recently fallen on hard times. Founded in 1914 by a minister, the home was being forced to abandon its current campus. The federal government was building a dam along the Pemigewasset River, which meant the farm property would be flooded seasonally. Though the operators had secured a new location and would be moving ten miles east to Northfield, New Hampshire, $50,000 was needed to renovate the facility. Actress Bette Davis, who had donated the silver cup that would be going home with either Cobb or Ruth, was a supporter of Golden Rule Farm.

BEST WISHES TO TY COBB AND BABE RUTH AND MAY THE BETTER MAN WIN, Davis wrote in a telegram from Hollywood. ALL HONOR TO BOTH FOR CONTRIBUTING THEIR FAME AND THEIR GAME TO SO SPLENDID A CAUSE.

By tee-off time, nearly a thousand spectators had paid the dollar admission fee and joined Cobb and Ruth on the picturesque grounds. Among them was former ambassador Joseph P. Kennedy, a Ruth fan of yore and father of a future president. Ex-Yankee Joe

Dugan was there, too, as well as Jesse Guilford, in the capacity of referee. Marshals wielding long bamboo poles marked the playing area, holding back spectators. Although Cobb had played baseball for much larger crowds, he had never golfed before such a gathering, and it set his nerves jangling. Maybe it was the closeness of the galley, the pregnant quiet, or his lack of confidence.

Cobb was anxious—and silent. Contrary to expectations, he wasn't saying a word to Ruth, let alone chucking insults at him.

Cobb's first drive drifted far right into the knee-high rough near the seventeenth hole. He tried to correct the errant shot but instead blooped the ball near the sixteenth hole. Four shots later, Cobb sunk his second putt. It had taken him six strokes.

"What's the matter, Ty? Too hot?" teased Ruth.

On a ball field, Cobb would have responded. But on the course, he ignored Ruth.

Not that Babe had done much better on the first hole. It had taken him five shots. But in match play it didn't matter whether you won the hole by one stroke or three. If it took you fewer strokes, you got the point.

Cobb rallied and won the second hole, which bordered a creek. He chipped to the green on his second shot, sinking his second putt for a par-4. The match was even. On the long third, Ruth jokingly admonished Cobb for placing his tee too far forward. Ruth was trying to ignite their diamond routine. But Cobb was having no part of it. Almost everyone had expected him to badger Ruth, but Cobb was employing a different tactic. He wasn't speaking. Without objection, Cobb moved his ball back. Soon, Ruth abandoned his teasing. "He wouldn't rise to the bait," he said later.

Babe took the third and fourth holes. The latter he chipped in from forty feet out—a pretty play and good for a birdie-4. "You can't beat that kind of luck," Cobb said. Ruth was on the verge of breaking the game open, and Cobb knew it. From the shaded porches of nearby homes, residents shouted encouragement to the former Red Sox star. "Over the fence, Babe," one yelled.

Worried about driving balls into the rough, Cobb began using a two iron from the tees, which raised Ruth's eyebrows. When Cobb grabbed his iron for one of the long holes, Ruth politely reminded him of the yardage. It was a sincere bit of advice, and it touched Cobb. But he knew what he was doing. He had his notes. He had rehearsed his shots yesterday. Cobb thanked Ruth and drove the ball with an iron.

The game turned in Cobb's favor on the fifth hole. Ruth stroked the ball to within eighteen inches of the pin—close enough for a friendly "give-me." Ruth paused, but Cobb didn't offer. He waited for Ruth to shoot. Ruth putted and missed. He slumped forward and rested his hands on his knees, staring into the turf and cussing his putter. He also flubbed a two-foot putt on the seventh, which provoked more muttering. Cobb putted smartly and took four straight holes.

The game moved slowly—annoyingly so for Ruth, whose legs had to ferry a good deal more weight. Normally, Ruth played a fast, impetuous game. He didn't linger over shots. Cobb, however, worked cautiously, taking multiple practice swings, darting far afield to check and double-check the flow of the fairway. He studied the lay of the land like a rookie surveyor, and he revisited his notes. Observers described him as grim and serious. His methods were deliberate and painstaking.

On the ninth hole, Cobb pelted a tree and ended up in a trap. Ruth capitalized, cutting Cobb's lead to one. A succession of strong putts kept Cobb in the game. He dropped them from ten, twenty, and eight feet on the next three holes, finally missing on the thirteenth.

Ruth got a chance to go ahead on the fourteenth when Cobb sliced his drive and landed his recovery shot to the right of the green. But Ruth stumbled, muffing an easy chip. He ended up on the edge of the same trap. After Cobb salvaged the hole, Ruth looked deflated. Cobb finished him off on the next one, sinking a ten-footer and taking an insurmountable three-hole lead with two holes to go. Cobb had won.

Incredulous, Ruth pivoted toward the spectators. "That man's a putting fool," he said. Ruth offered his hand to Cobb as polite applause rippled through the disappointed gallery. They completed the round, each adding another ten strokes. Their eighteen-hole scores were Cobb 81, Ruth 83.

Cobb couldn't mask his pleasure. He beamed near the clubhouse as he and Ruth posed with the winner's cup. In front of them stood nine-year-old Spanky Joslyn, a stripe-shirted lad who had been chosen to award the prize. Spanky lived at Golden Rule Farm. His mother had placed him there after losing her leg in an accident and being abandoned by the boy's father. Both Cobb and Ruth had genuinely soft hearts for such young fellows. The moment is frozen on the sports pages of the Boston papers. Cobb and Spanky are holding the cup and grinning at each other; Ruth is behind the boy, his meaty hand gently nuzzling the boy's arm.

"Well, I've got something to show my grandchildren," said Cobb, clutching the trophy. (And he wasn't kidding.) "I finally have beaten the Babe at something." As Cobb headed into the locker room to change, young fans called for the Babe to sign their admission tickets and manila-paged autograph books.

"This exhibition golf is more punishing than baseball," Cobb told reporters. "During my twenty-four years on the diamond, I never was under such terrific pressure as I was while coming from behind to beat the Babe. Maybe it was because both of us were so gentlemanly. He was awfully nice to me, and I tried to be equally so. Neither of us ever acted that way in a ball game."

The camaraderie between Ty and Babe didn't escape notice. Gap-toothed *Boston Herald* columnist Bill Cunningham served as the local tournament host. "These two traditional enemies are going to wind up liking each other if they don't watch out," he wrote. ". . . It wouldn't surprise me any to see them wind up with their arms over each other's shoulders singing 'Pals, Dear Old Pals' almost any time now."

Cobb was still gabbing when a sweaty Ruth lumbered into the changing room, his wrist tired. "I'd rather play thirty-six holes than sign those things for an hour," he cracked.

"Say," he remarked, looking at Cobb, "boy, you're a putting fool, aren't you? . . . You sure can use that putter. It's too hot for me. . . . I wish I could think of something really bad to do with that putter of mine."

Both gentlemen were endearingly gracious.

Cobb told reporters, "It was a great pleasure to play with him and a much greater pleasure to beat him."

"Don't get too excited about it, Ty," Ruth responded. "You know we play again at Fresh Meadow. . . ."

| Cobb | 6 | 4 | 6 | 5 | 4 | 4 | 5 | 3 | 6 | 5 | 3 | 4 | 5 | 4 | 4 | 3 | 5 | 5 | 81 |
| Ruth | 5 | 5 | 5 | 4 | 5 | 5 | 6 | 4 | 4 | 5 | 3 | 4 | 5 | 5 | 5 | 3 | 5 | 5 | 83 |

24

A Babe Among Friends

Ruth's golf swing—similar to his baseball swing. NATIONAL
BASEBALL HALL OF FAME LIBRARY, COOPERSTOWN, N.Y.

BABE AND CLAIRE RUTH CAUGHT A FLIGHT BACK TO NEW York shortly after the Newton contest. Ruth didn't let his disappointment over the defeat sour his attitude. He was embarrassed but remained friendly toward Cobb, even inviting him to join them on the airplane. "It's the only way to travel," said Ruth, managing to sound cheerful.

Cobb begged off. He and Corcoran would spend the evening in Boston, beginning a liquor-fueled celebration that would continue on the overnight train to Manhattan. They would stay up too late and drink too much, and Cobb would be hungover the next morning and have to cancel his practice. Fortunately for him, he had played the Fresh Meadow course earlier in the week and had already taken his notes.

On the flight home, Ruth must have pondered what had gone wrong at Commonwealth. Once on the green, he wasn't finding the cup. "I just couldn't sink even a two-foot putt," he lamented, "so what could you expect? When a guy has to give away so many strokes on the greens, he is lucky to stay close." Everyone had noted how well Cobb putted—and also that Ruth outdrove him on every hole. Their performance provided a convenient and much too simple analogy: In golf, as in baseball, Ruth was a long-ball slammer and Cobb a master of the short game.

But it wasn't just a matter of putts and drives. Cobb's behavior perplexed Ruth. He had expected Cobb to needle him throughout the match. Almost everyone had expected it, and Ruth had come prepared to return the favor. Instead, Cobb had given him the silent treatment. He hadn't been rude or curt, just silent. "He never said a word to me until after he had me licked," Ruth remarked. And then Cobb showered him with compliments. "The Babe is a darn nice fellow," he said. Ruth must have wondered whether it was all an act or whether Cobb's disposition had actually softened.

Cobb shrugged when asked about his nonconfrontational behavior. "Golf is different from baseball," he said innocently. "You don't do or say the same things you would on the diamond." He was right, of course. It's just that no one—Ruth included—thought Cobb would abide by golf's customs.

What frustrated Ruth so much was that he knew he was the better golfer, and he knew that he should have won. He hadn't played to his ability. Next, they would be performing in New York, his town, with his pals from St. Albans watching and rooting and expecting him to deliver. The pressure was real. Ruth did not want to lose again to Cobb, and he couldn't stomach the thought of being swept. But he wouldn't let that be known. Both men were too experienced and too publicity-conscious to stoop to public pettiness. They knew how to answer the questions. They could say the right things. Yes, I want to win. No, it isn't personal. I like Babe. I like Ty. He was one hell of a ballplayer; he used to cause me fits. On one level, most of it was true. They did like and respect each other, and it was just an inconsequential golf match after all, right?

But in another respect, it was so much more. For two decades, they had been compared relentlessly. It had started during their playing days and had continued into retirement. Who was the better player? Neither could escape the other when the topic surfaced, and the golf series reignited the debate. With a few exceptions, fans and experts saw Cobb and Ruth as the prime contenders for title of "greatest ever." Honus Wagner still had a handful of loyal supporters, including Ed Barrow of the Yankees. But by 1941, it had pretty much come down to Cobb and Ruth. Their names dominated the record books. "The greatest two baseball players who ever lived"—that's how Richards Vidmer of the *New York Tribune* described them after the Newton match.

In Cobb's mind, the issue had been settled forever in his favor—in 1936, when the Baseball Writers Association of America cast the most votes for him in balloting for the first class of Baseball Hall of Fame inductees. Cobb got 222 of a possible 226; Ruth and Wagner got 215. (The credentials of any writer who left either Cobb or Ruth off his ballot should have been burned.) According to his son Jimmy, Cobb was proudest of his Hall of Fame showing. First into the Hall of Fame! It got no better than that, Cobb believed. What more needed to be said?

Around that same time, perhaps influenced by the vote, even Ruth publicly acknowledged Cobb as the better player. Cobb, though he certainly agreed, often deferred to other authorities on the question. "Why not ask Connie Mack?" he once advised. "Let him be the judge. He has seen all the great ones." He said it as if he didn't know what Mack would say, as if Mack were a wild card, a sly Supreme Court nominee whose views had never been revealed. Of course, in recommending Mack as judge, Cobb knew fully how he felt. Mack was among his most ardent supporters.

Stan Baumgartner, who pitched against both, said you couldn't choose one over the other. "To say that Ruth was greater than Cobb or Cobb greater than Ruth is like comparing a California and a Florida orange," he said. "It all depends where you live, what you want, how you feel that particular day."

"We've found the old ball players and veteran managers almost evenly divided on the topic," reported Bob Considine of the *New York Daily Mirror.* "Some say they'd pick Cobb and their reasons generally are that he was the greatest batter, the greatest base runner, and the fiercest competitive force in baseball history. Some say Ruth, for he was the greatest slugger, one of the game's finest left-handed pitchers, and an incomparable producer of runs."

Among other eminent sportswriters, Harry Salsinger of *The Detroit News* and Fred Lieb of *The Sporting News* preferred Cobb (though Lieb would eventually switch sides). Dan Daniel of the *New York World-Telegram* and John Kieran of the *Times* favored Ruth. Said Kieran, "The name of 'Babe Ruth' was known in lands where the fame of no ball player ever had penetrated. . . . The Babe was 'the peepul's choice' by a heavy plurality."

For others, like Joe Williams, designating one was futile: "Even now, with all the records at your disposal, there is no way to tell for sure which was the better."

Clark Griffith, owner of the Washington club, offered perhaps the most diplomatic assessment. "Just let me say this: It would be like trying to choose between two twenty-dollar gold pieces."

Stanley Frank of the *New York Post* agreed. "If there never had been a Cobb, Ruth would be recognized, unanimously and unquestionably, as the greatest ball player of all time," he said. "Without Ruth in the picture, Cobb would be the unchallenged genius seen during the first century of baseball. . . . One man's superiority over the other with a ball bat never was established, and a golf club cannot settle the issue."

Certainly not. But that fact didn't lessen either man's desire to win. Both despised losing—in anything. The rivalry, though friendlier all these many years later, was as real and tangible as a wood club. It might be that the only thing at stake in the golf tournament was pride. But for Babe Ruth and Ty Cobb, that was no so small matter.

Said Grantland Rice, "They have been compared too long as ball players not to feel unusual pressure when they meet at golf."

~

The second match would be at Fresh Meadow Country Club in Flushing. The course, designed by A. W. Tillinghast, qualified as one of the area's finest. Several holes appeared in rankings by *American Golfer* as among the best in the nation. The layout measured 6,800 yards, and the fairways were wide, which would likely benefit Ruth. He had played Fresh Meadow many times, and had carded scores under 75. "Commonwealth is on the short side," Ruth said. "Naturally, Cobb had the advantage. Those cream puffs of his didn't handicap him a bit. But wait until we get on Fresh Meadow. You got to hit them a mile there. I'll have the advantage then."

Fred Corcoran described Fresh Meadow as one of Ruth's home courses and predicted his showing would be much better. "The Babe will find the long holes to his advantage. . . . I wouldn't be surprised to see him win."

What neither Ruth nor Corcoran knew was that Al Ciuci, the pro since 1931, was hard at work altering the course. The day before the contest, he and his crew attempted to make it easier on the baseball legends and more interesting for the fans. Ciuci had golfed dozens of times with Ruth, and earlier in the week had shot rounds with Cobb. He knew their games. He described Ruth as a free swinger and persistent slicer. "He wheels away from the line of flight on the back-swing, lifting his heels clear off the turf," he said. "At the top of his arc, Babe practically turns his back on the ball."

Hoping to create two-putt holes, Ciuci centered flags on all greens and designated the women's tees as the main ones, erasing about five hundred yards in distance. "This is a charity match," he said. Unknowingly, Ciuci may have shaved a couple of strokes off Cobb's game.

The history of Fresh Meadow was intricately tied to Ciuci's friend Gene Sarazen. The two had met at Beardsley Park, a public course in Connecticut where Ciuci, as course pro, allowed the sickly, diminutive sixteen-year-old—then known by his birth name, Eugenio Saracini—to hone his playing skills. Ciuci nurtured and encouraged the teen, promoting his abilities to noted Brooklawn pro George Sparling, who eventually and begrudgingly gave Sarazen a job, despite Eugenio's Italian ancestry. (Sparling preferred fellow Scotsmen.) Ciuci, said Sarazen, "first recognized that I was raw material from which a champion might be made."

Sarazen established himself by winning a U.S. Open and two PGA championships and defeating Walter Hagen in a challenge. But he played inconsistently in the mid-1920s. "I realized that my income had to be placed on a more stable basis than hit-or-miss slices of the tournament pot," said Sarazen. "I snapped up the chance to become the professional at the Fresh Meadow Club." He repaid Ciuci by bringing him on as an assistant. The two of them turned around the pro shop, quickly quadrupling sales.

"The times were good," said Sarazen, who palled around and occasionally golfed with celebrities like George Gershwin and Ed Wynn. But after losing the 1930 PGA Championship on his own course to Tommy Armour, Sarazen decided to leave Fresh Meadow, suspecting that a home-pro jinx had cost him the victory. His departure paid off two years later when Fresh Meadow hosted the U.S. Open and Sarazen turned in a brilliant performance that would ensure the course a spot in history. He shot the final twenty-eight holes in one hundred strokes, birdieing nine of them and bogeying only one.

"Gene," said Walter Hagen, "you've broken every record that I know of!"

Bobby Jones also applauded Sarazen: "When he is in the right mood, he is probably the greatest scorer in the game."

Fred Corcoran admired Sarazen and counted him among his dearest friends in golf, which may have explained the course's selection for the Cobb-Ruth match. That and the fact that the 1937 Montague-Ruth-Didrikson exhibition had been played there before a massive crowd.

~

On Thursday morning, Ruth headed to Fresh Meadow for a warm-up round. Finding it busy, he impatiently hustled over to St. Albans, "a honey" of a course, in his words. Although Ruth played throughout the metropolitan region, St. Albans rated as his favorite. Redesigned in 1923 by Tillinghast, it featured a 6,300-yard layout, plenty of sand bunkers, and two Hell's Half-Acre holes, each interrupted about three hundred yards out by forbidding hazards. Erased from the landscape north of today's JFK Airport after World War II, St. Albans offered Ruth a challenging, relatively private outing. It may also have reminded him of Tillinghast's St. Petersburg Country Club, better known as the Jungle Club. Before and during spring training in the mid-1920s, Ruth spent weeks there, several times—according to legend—driving a ball 360 yards on the 388-yard fourth hole.

Ruth struggled on the dewy greens of St. Albans Thursday. The thought of losing again to Cobb was affecting his game. He was growing frustrated, hindered by the same problem as in Newton: He couldn't putt worth a damn.

Dr. George Irwin, one of his golfing buddies, offered Ruth his Spalding & Bros. Cash-In putter. Ruth didn't recognize it, but he had earlier given it to Irwin as a gift. It worked. Ruth began sinking putts and gaining confidence. He liked the putter's feel. "I wish I'd seen it before," he said. His relief turned to exuberance as his successes mounted.

"Where's Cobb?" he joked, ready to start the match. "Boy . . . ," he called to his caddy, "wrap that club in gold cloth and carry it carefully over to Fresh Meadow. . . . What a putter!"

Ruth had found a secret weapon. "Watch me take him tomorrow," he said. "I can't be so terrible on the greens twice in a row, and that Fresh Meadow course is just tailored to my game. I'll more than make up for what he did to me yesterday."

Reporters tried to rev up the rivalry by inciting Cobb with tales of Ruth's day at St. Albans. But Cobb would have none of it. "The Babe's on the defensive now," he said in his slow, Georgia drawl. "Winning that first one was like taking the opener in the World Series. Babe's at a distinct disadvantage, as he well knows. The psychological edge is on my side. . . . In any case, let him go ahead and practice. I'll be there—don't worry about that."

~

It had been years since Cobb and Ruth had been in the news in such a big way. The Baseball Hall of Fame induction in 1939 had put them back on the sports pages, but the celebration came and went in a flash. The golf tournament, however, had been building for two months, and the press coverage had grown intense, especially in New York, Boston, and Detroit.

Cobb savored being in the spotlight again. While Ruth lived on the Upper West Side and never entirely escaped the public eye, Cobb resided in comparative seclusion, spending his days in his Atherton, California, home or his hunting lodge in Glenbrook, Nevada. His ball-playing chums—and, yes, despite claims to the contrary, he had friends—came to visit him there. His wife, Charlie, who had several times filed for divorce and in 1947 would follow through, lived separately. Occasionally, Cobb's adult daughters stayed with him. His sons, however, were elsewhere. Jimmy attended a military academy in New Mexico, and Herschel, married and with a child of his own, ran a Coca-Cola plant in Idaho. Ty Junior, studying to be a physician in Charleston, South Carolina, had little to do with him.

The golf matches with Ruth gave Cobb many things: a competitive mission, an exciting diversion, a chance to shape his image, and a dose of warm fan affection. In Boston, Cobb had encountered men who remembered seeing him play.

"I wish you were back on those base paths and I were back in the stands calling you names," one Sox fan told Cobb. "Ah, those were the days!"

"Yeah, I used to love them, too," Cobb said.

The golf tournament was generating news stories across the country, and dozens of cities were expressing interest in hosting Cobb-and-Ruth events of their own. Corcoran hinted that a summer tour could be launched successfully. Cobb might have gone for it. But Ruth quickly snuffed that talk. "Traveling gets me down," he said. "I like to play, but I don't want to hop all over the country to do it." Ruth was even having doubts about playing the Detroit leg.

Every New York paper promoted the Fresh Meadow match, and all the top-name columnists feverishly sold it. Expectations ran high for a turnout that would dwarf that in Newton. "A much larger crowd is expected," reported one paper. "At least twice as large," forecasted another. Admission prices had been reduced from $1.50 to $1 after the wrong figure got printed on tickets. Free buses would be running regularly from the Queens subway line to the country club. All proceeds would be going to the U.S.O. The last time an exhibition featuring Ruth had received as much play, more than ten thousand fans swarmed onto the course at Fresh Meadow. This had all the ingredients of another huge gate.

"Everywhere I've gone, there has been talk of watching these two swingers in action," said Corcoran.

Given the potential turnout, Ruth got Corcoran to issue a notice that no autographs would be signed during the competition. "I got a kink in my left arm from signing 'Babe Ruth' on everything from match covers to handkerchiefs," Ruth complained.

The Giants would be in town at the Polo Grounds, but the first-place Brooklyn Dodgers—now outdrawing the Yankees—had the day off, and the Yanks, also in first, were playing in Philadelphia. There would be little competition. A big payday for the U.S.O. looked certain.

Play-off at Fresh Meadow

Ruth and Cobb decide who will tee off first. NATIONAL
BASEBALL HALL OF FAME LIBRARY, COOPERSTOWN, N.Y.

⌒

T HE PASTORAL LANDSCAPE OF QUEENS AND LONG ISLAND
gave birth to a dazzling array of golf courses and country
clubs in the late 1910s and early 1920s. It was a picturesque playground, mostly for privileged sportsmen. Within miles of today's
Long Island Expressway, between the current Van Wick Expressway and Belt Parkway, one could find layouts designed by Tillinghast, Alister MacKenzie, Seth Raynor, and the lesser-known

Devereux Emmet and Tom Wells. Among them were Fresh Meadow, St. Albans, Pomonok, Oakland, Queens Valley, and Hillcrest. Most would vanish after World War II, their valuable land purchased, scraped, and graded for new homes, schools, stores, and hospitals. (Fresh Meadow would suffer that fate, too, though the club itself would relocate and continue into the twenty-first century.) In 1941, most of the courses remained vibrant and alive.

Hours before Friday's scheduled three o'clock start, Cobb decided to take his practice strokes away from the gaze of reporters and fans. He chose Pomonok Country Club, just west of Fresh Meadow. Pomonok had been renovated three years earlier—in time to host the 1939 PGA championship, at which Henry Picard defeated Byron Nelson in a play-off on the thirty-seventh hole. Pomonok offered an interesting, intimate layout that included a peculiar 108-yard seventeenth hole rimmed by sand traps. Aside from privacy, Cobb had another reason for warming up there rather than heading directly to Fresh Meadow: psychology. "I never believe in reaching a battle site too early," he said. "You're apt to get jittery if you hang around in that tense atmosphere. I follow the policy employed by football teams and arrive on the scene of action at the last possible moment."

Cobb got to Fresh Meadow in time to trade a few humorous jabs with Ruth in the humid locker room. He laughed about the clip that Ruth used to keep his curvy, crisply parted, slicked-back hair off his forehead. "I never thought I'd live to see the day when Babe would be pinning up his locks with one of those gimcracks they sell in beauty parlors. . . ."

"Pipe down, Ty. You're jealous. . . ."

"Oh, boy, I've got the Babe's goat. . . . Just look at him sweat."

"You're all dried up, Cobb, like one of those California prunes. . . ."

"When you're my age, Babe, you won't be able to walk eighteen holes. . . ."

Ruth may have been heavier than Cobb, but he didn't look it on this day. He had dressed stylishly, wearing two-toned shoes, cuffed slacks, and a collarless, button-up shirt that was pressed and tucked.

Cobb was rumpled by comparison, his shirt hanging over his waist, a tattered, fingerless glove on his right hand.

Ruth headed to the first tee before Cobb, who was slow making his appearance. Ruth bided his time with a double scotch in one hand and his new putter in the other. He was showing it off. "I'm counting on this babe to help me," he said, hoisting the blade.

When Cobb finally emerged, he and Ruth took several moments to satisfy the newsreel photographers, whose whirring machines would soon pose a distraction to Cobb. Ty and Babe hammed it up for those who would see their exploits on movie-house screens. Ruth, brown as a football, chuckled as he patted Cobb's bald goose head. With a U.S.O. banner featuring Franklin Roosevelt as a backdrop, Ruth took a swing at a ball as Cobb, behind him, craned his neck as if following its flight. They even evoked their baseball roots, deciding who would go first, as if picking sides in a sandlot game, scaling the shaft of a club with their fisted hands, one atop the other.

Fresh Meadow boasted a meandering, three-story clubhouse that sat atop a hill near the center of the course. Its black-and-white, Shakespearean-style exterior was visible from much of the terrain. One fact could not have escaped Ty and Babe as they stood before the building at the first tee: There was no crowd. Dozens of men and teenage boys stood scattered along the porch watching from behind a wall of shrubs. Others specked the grass near the tee. But they weren't jostling for position. They weren't nudging to get a better view. There was no need.

If the turnout disheartened them, Ty and Babe didn't show it. They kept the mood light initially. Ruth needled Cobb by revealing one of his secret weapons, a cane chair that he intended to cart along the course and threatened to use should Cobb dilly-dally. As its name implied, it was a single-legged wooden cane topped with a metal perch that in theory would cradle Ruth's sizeable caboose should he choose to rest it. The chair testified to Cobb's painfully deliberate style of play.

A speedy, quick-acting whiz on the ball field, Cobb moved like mud on the links. Much to Ruth's frustration, Cobb squandered time, spending several minutes on each shot, manicuring the turf with his hands, selecting and reselecting clubs, strolling a hundred feet or more from his ball to survey the grounds, and delaying putts until the sound of movie cameras subsided. He played with all the abandon of a blindfolded man feeling for the edge of a cliff.

"I don't think he does it to annoy me," Ruth said. "They tell me Cobb has always been a sleepwalker on a golf course. . . . It takes that guy four hours to snail his way around. . . . I can feel myself getting older."

Cobb knew his pace bothered Ruth, but he defended it, saying he had become a more measured golfer at the recommendation of a pro in San Francisco. "Ruth grumbles about my slowness," he said. "Well, I play deliberately."

His calculated style was designed to mute what observers—and Cobb himself—viewed as his most glaring liability: a volatile disposition. Commentators had been wondering about it for weeks. Would Cobb explode? Would he lose his temper? Observers who had watched both men over the decades believed that Cobb's temperament would be his undoing. Though he appeared to have mellowed since his baseball days, Cobb was by nature more tightly wound than Ruth. He exuded a tense energy that many thought would be detrimental to his game.

"While a fellow who is steamed up can go on playing ball," said Frank Graham of *The New York Sun*, "he can't go on playing golf—or, at least, he can't go on playing it very well."

Another columnist described Ruth as better equipped emotionally for golf. "Those taut nerves which made Ty outstanding on the diamond may not be conducive to good golf," he said.

Of all the authorities weighing in on the issue, none had played more golf with both Ruth and Cobb than Grantland Rice. While "Babe is no phlegmatic philosopher when he misses a shot . . . he hasn't the tension Cobb carries," Rice wrote. "Cobb is one of the greatest competitors that ever lived, but winning golf demands a firm control of the nerves and brakes on any mental upheaval. In this respect, the Babe has the edge."

Cobb knew it was a problem. "Flashes of temper helped on the diamond," he said. "When I got mad, I could make monkeys out of rival infielders. They'd throw the ball around recklessly, and I'd cash in on their wild throws. But the same intensity . . . is a handicap in golf. . . . I start snatching the club up and hitting from the top of my swing when I let myself get excited." Thus, the tortoise tempo.

Cobb had kept his emotions in check at Newton. He hadn't exploded there, but this was a new day in Flushing, full of intriguing possibilities and promises.

The first hole at Fresh Meadow stretched a relatively straight 437 yards, bordered by a series of bunkers on both sides of the fairway. Ruth hadn't a chance to use his cane chair before Cobb got in the opening dig as Babe launched a long wild drive. Ignoring Al Ciuci's plans, both men insisted on shooting from the original tees. Ruth's ball fell left of the fairway among the woods.

"Where'd you go, Babe?" Ty asked, facetiously scouring the horizon. It was a payback for Ruth's remark at Commonwealth.

Cobb clubbed his first down the middle but frittered away his clean drive with wild shots, allowing Ruth to salvage the hole for a par-4.

The second, at 395 yards, gave Cobb headaches. About three-fourths of the way to the green, the fairway narrowed and turned sharply to the left. Cobb skidded his drive among the maples. On his follow-up shot, he strained to finesse the ball past a large tree but struck bark. It might have been an appropriate place for a blowup, but Cobb restrained himself. After Ruth sunk his ball on a fourth shot, Cobb conceded with a pickup, getting a six. Ruth was up by two holes.

Cobb and Ruth split the third, which also had an abrupt dogleg, and the fourth, a cozy 188-yard par-3. Like many Fresh Meadow holes, the fourth featured cavernous bunkers and bottleneck greens. Cobb remained down by two, but he could feel his game improving. "Now I'll get him," he announced. And he did.

Although having difficulty finding the fairway from the tee, Cobb executed nice recoveries, chipped smartly, and putted beautifully on the next four holes, dropping them from as far as eighteen feet out. On the 578-yard, two-wood fifth, he scored a par-5, cutting Ruth's lead to one hole.

The sixth was, in the view of Gene Sarazen, "the most dangerous hole" at Fresh Meadow. "It was 428 yards long and menaced from tee to green along the left by a stout line of trees," he said. "This tight left side placed a heavy premium on straightness off the tee, but that was only half the battle. To carry the pond that nosed well into the fairway on the right, you had to bang a tee-shot that carried 220 yards." Ruth double-bogeyed, allowing Cobb to tie the match.

Cobb carried the seventh and eighth holes as well. In winning four straight, he had single-putted every hole, expending a miserly four strokes to Ruth's wasteful eleven. It was a splendid streak, and it allowed Cobb to storm ahead by two. Well, mosey ahead would be more accurate.

Ruth looked stunned. He felt the match slipping away. If he couldn't break Cobb's hold by the turn, he might not get another chance. He grew more solemn and serious, and bore down. As if struck by superstition, Ruth began averting his eyes from Cobb, staring instead into the feathery turf. Cobb smelled blood. It was a critical moment, and both sensed it as they played the 143-yard ninth.

Ruth's first shot, an iron, drifted off the fairway to the right. Cobb replied with a beauty to the far edge of the green, which sloped toward the hole. Ruth, in a trap beneath a clubhouse walkway, faced a difficult recovery. As Ruth prepared to chip, Cobb committed a breach of golf etiquette that may have changed the direction of the match. Looking like a guard in the tower of a fortress, Cobb stationed himself directly above Ruth and just yards away, his eyes burning Ruth. One witness generously suggested Cobb was unaware that his sentrylike watch from atop the green violated golf decorum. Others felt Cobb was trying to freeze Ruth. Despite the stare-down, Ruth chipped to within fifteen feet. Cobb flubbed his first putt and then another as Ruth dropped his. The crowd near the clubhouse cheered Ruth loudly.

The frivolity that had existed two hours earlier evaporated in the hot sun, replaced by a serious air unbecoming at a celebrity charity match. Both men reverted to the competitiveness that had brought them acclaim on the diamond. They stopped speaking to one another. Cobb no longer applauded Ruth's good plays, and Ruth clapped for Cobb only as an afterthought. After Ruth threw back a drink, he and Cobb began the final nine like two men who suddenly remembered why they had disliked each other two decades earlier.

Cobb claimed the tenth hole with a par-4. But Ruth dropped a twenty-five-foot putt on the hospitable eleventh green, which funneled gently toward the cup, and he evened the match with a par-3 on the forest-hugging twelfth. They tied on the next three holes, both men squandering opportunities. Ruth missed eighteen inches from the thirteenth flag, and Cobb, after coming within four feet of a hole in one on the 219-yard fourteenth, failed to sink an easy putt.

On the sixteenth, Ruth challenged the strength of his cane seat. It held him fine, though uncomfortably. Cobb, in the words of one witness, "looked like an old woman who had swallowed her store teeth." The tension of which Grantland Rice had warned had taken residence on his face. On the 587-yard, par-5 hole—Fresh Meadow's longest—Ruth plunged ahead on sharp work with his irons. But Cobb rallied yet again on the seventeenth, which bordered a stone wall. Cobb exploited a Ruth bomb that careened off a tree. They were tied.

Ruth saved his farthest tee shot of the day—280 yards—for the eighteenth, which was interrupted by bunkers 350 yards out. Cobb swatted his ball into the rough behind bushes. Ruth put his second shot near the green's far edge. Cobb continued off the fairway in the rough, not far from a barn. Ruth found the green on his third shot. When it looked hopeless for Cobb, he came up with a sterling play, popping his ball over the trees and back on the fairway. Ruth's putt missed the hole by two inches. Several spectators flinched. Ruth looked skyward in disbelief and then turned away in frustration.

Realizing that the match hung on his next shots, Cobb deliberated for ten minutes with his caddy. Cobb wanted to use a six iron, but his caddy insisted on an eight. Ruth took refuge in the shade while Cobb's discussion exploded into an argument. Eventually, the caddy talked Cobb into using the six, and he chipped to within fifteen feet. "I didn't know I was so strong, but the kid convinced me," Cobb said. "Maybe it was just a case of my misjudging the range." Ruth sank his putt, and Cobb did the same. They were tied, forcing a play-off.

On the nineteenth hole, Ruth sliced his drive and took two more strokes to get on the green. Cobb, meanwhile, had hooked right, recovered on the next shot, and gotten to within twenty feet on the third. Both men moved closer to the hole on their first putts. Ruth sunk his second. When Cobb blew his next one—a six-footer—the hometown crowd cheered. One exuberant young man hopped around, thrusting his fist in the air. Cobb snatched the ball and shook Ruth's hand without making eye contact.

Ruth had won. Amid the cheers and congratulations, a fan reminded Ruth that he would have to play Cobb in a deciding match in Detroit. Babe bristled. "That's out," he said. "That Cobb drives me nuts with his stalling. Geez, you could play thirty-six holes while you go around once with him. I can't go through four hours of this again. I'm satisfied to let it lay."

The contest had lasted three hours and thirty minutes. The Yankees could have played two games in that time.

The match frustrated Cobb, whose drives stayed on the fairways only three times. "I could have used a putter off the tee" and it wouldn't have mattered, he said. For his part, Ruth had three-putted most of the holes. "I would have knocked his brains out if I was putting," he said. Each had shot an 85 on the par-70 course, with not a birdie in sight.

Afterward, amid the soothing spirit of the locker room, some of the stress from the afternoon faded. The conversation turned to baseball, and the mood lightened between Cobb and Ruth as someone conjured Ruth's days as a pitcher.

"Why, old baldy here was lucky to get a foul off me," Ruth said.

"How did you pitch to Cobb, Babe?"

"High and on the inside. I just blew Ty down—had him sprawling in the dust half the time. Them was tough days. If a batter so

much as dug his heels into the dirt as though he meant to take a
toehold, we pitchers felt it was a personal insult. We loosened up
his spikes by dusting him off. If he didn't duck, it was his hard
luck."

"Dig up the averages, Babe," Cobb retorted, "and you'll find I hit
plenty of your beanballs. . . ."

For some of the reporters who had long been covering Cobb and
Ruth, it didn't matter how poorly either had golfed, and it mattered
less who had won. "The old timers in the gallery could close their
eyes," wrote Joe Williams. "They could see the Babe in the stadium.
They could see Ty out in Detroit. . . . After all these years, it was the
Babe and Ty trying to do it again. Who cares whether they can play
golf? Even at their worst they were still the best."

It was a sentiment that Grantland Rice embraced. The sight of
them together inspired this poem:

> *I can see them again as they took the field*
> *In the years that used to be—*
> *When the dust flew high and the fences reeled*
> *From a swing that was full and free.*
>
> *There was the crash of the blasting ash,*
> *And the flame on a shining spike,*
> *A sudden whirl and a sudden dash—*
> *With Cobb on the scoring pike.*
>
> *There was the lull with the bases full*
> *As the big Babe gripped his mace—*
> *And the thunder roared as the runners scored*
> *In the wake of a winning pace.*
>
> *I can see them still in the phantom host*
> *That starred in the summer plot,*
> *When the Georgia Ghost was a nation's toast*
> *And Babe was the king of swat.*

It was still light out when Ruth, friend Paul Carey, and writer Bob Considine departed Fresh Meadow after 7:30. They had celebrated the victory over a few drinks in the clubhouse, where Ruth was reminded—and conceded—there would be a third and final match in the Detroit area. "We'll get together again," he promised.

Ruth sat in the front seat beside the chauffeur so that he could extend his weary legs and control the radio. The car was hot, and the windows were open. His face damp with sweat and his wet hair combed back, Ruth dialed the tuner to WOR and his favorite show, *The Lone Ranger.*

"Pipe down," he said, when Considine tried to ask a question.

The show mesmerized Ruth. In this episode, a couple of desert scoundrels were determined to prevent two settlers from drawing water from the only hole in the region. In coming to their rescue, the Ranger and Tonto found themselves in trouble. "That poor bastard is sure in a spot," said Ruth. Or maybe he said "that poor son of a bitch" or "that poor prick." We can't be sure. In retelling the incident, Considine replaced the offending words with hyphens.

By eight o'clock, the Lone Ranger had prevailed, much to Ruth's relief. Ruth turned to Carey and Considine and reflected on his long history with Cobb. "We never had a real fight, but started for each other several times," he said. "Hell, there can't be any real fights in baseball. Somebody's always jumping in to hold you back. Half the guys can't fight anyhow. All they do is scratch or they fight crazy. When Cobb fought Billy Evans, he got a hold of Billy by the necktie and kept swinging him around in a circle, belting him while he swung. What kind of fighting is that?"

The chauffeur pulled up to the tollbooth of the steel-towered Triborough Bridge. The worker recognized Ruth.

"Hi, Babe. I heard you win, one-up."

"Yeah, pal, one-up," Ruth answered. "Can't lose them all."

After crossing the Harlem River into Manhattan, Ruth told his driver to head down to 106th Street. They slowed as they drove through an Italian neighborhood, where several people recognized Ruth.

Ruth waved to an Italian grandmother. "I forget her name but she's a nice old lady," he said. "One day, I stopped to talk to her, coming in from the club, and she told me her old guy was real sick. Dying. She started to cry, and all that. So I said, 'That old guinea ain't going to die, Mother. What are you carrying on for? He's going to be okay.' And damn if he didn't get well, like I said."

At the stoplight, someone yelled, "How's it go, Babe?"

"Can't complain. How's it with you?" Ruth answered. "DiMaggio must go good up in this section," he said to Considine, who would soon leave the sports beat to become a war correspondent. He would later collaborate on Ruth's end-of-life autobiography.

Indeed, DiMaggio was doing well in most sections of New York. That afternoon in Philadelphia, he had singled and homered, extending his hitting streak to thirty-nine games. He was pulling fans into ballparks. In the twelve-game home stand that had ended on Thursday, the Yankees had drawn 220,000 spectators to the Bronx—a per-game average of about 18,333.

But in the next day's papers, DiMaggio found himself sharing the headlines with Cobb and Ruth:

RUTH IS WINNER ON 19TH HOLE

BABE AND TY SHOW OLD FIGHTING SPIRIT

BABE TURNS THE TABLES ON BASEBALL RIVAL

REVENGE!

RUTH BEATS COBB IN OVERTIME

THE BABE EVENS GOLF SERIES

Ty and Babe could still captivate the sporting world.

Ruth	4	4	5	4	6	6	5	6	3	5	4	3	6	3	5	5	6	5	5	90
Cobb	5	6	5	4	5	5	4	5	4	4	5	4	6	3	5	6	4	5	6	91

26

Pulling for Joltin' Joe

JOE DI MAGGIO, Yankees

O N THE WAY HOME TO THE WEST COAST, TY COBB DE-
toured toward Detroit, arriving Sunday, June 29, two days
after the Fresh Meadow match. DIMAGGIO EQUALS COBB'S STREAK,
blared the headline atop *The Detroit News* sports page. With a hit
against Philadelphia's Johnny Babich, a Pacific Coast League rival
determined to deny DiMaggio, the Yankee Clipper had tied Cobb's
1911 forty-game mark.

"I was stopped by Ed Walsh," Cobb recalled. "He walked me a
couple of times that day. I'm not sure, but I think he walked me the
last time I went to bat. That record stood for a long time"—eleven
years, until George Sisler topped it.

Cobb spent Sunday afternoon at Briggs Stadium, where a parade of friends and acquaintances came, sat, talked, and had pictures taken with him, as if documenting history for their grandchildren. Team owner Walter Briggs shared his box with Cobb. Harry Heilmann, who described Cobb as the best friend he ever made in baseball, dropped by for a quick hello. He was now a beloved broadcaster. Detroit manager Del Baker and St. Louis coach Fred "Bootnose" Hofmann, a former Ruth teammate, chatted with him about the golf tournament. Cobb and umpire Harry Giesel laughed about Giesel's first major-league call, when he thumbed out Cobb on an attempted steal in 1925. Even $45,000 Tiger prospect Dick Wakefield, who had debuted days earlier, made sure to get in a photo. The idea was to record the former star with the future one, though the latter part of the equation would fail to materialize.

The Tigers won, and in Washington so did the Yankees, with DiMaggio getting hits in both games of a doubleheader, tying and surpassing Sisler's American League record of forty-one straight.

"So Joe broke the record?" Cobb asked while entertaining that evening at the Statler Hotel near Grand Circus Park. "Well, that's a great thing for baseball. . . . That's quite a feat, batting in forty-two consecutive games, and he may run it far beyond that. . . . The kids come up and do bigger and better things each year."

DiMaggio unmistakably claimed the record on July 2 when he surpassed Wee Willie Keeler, the sprite subscriber to hitting them where they ain't. Some baseball observers would have given DiMaggio the nod even if he hadn't. They discounted Keeler's forty-four-game streak because it occurred in 1897, when foul balls didn't count as strikes. But DiMaggio made the point moot by hitting a home run off Boston's Dick Newsome. After the game, someone marked a baseball with "45." DiMaggio showed it to his wife, former showgirl Dorothy Arnold. He grinned so big that you could see his gold-capped molar.

Already among the most famous athletes in America, DiMaggio rose to new heights during the streak, becoming a celebrity outside of baseball. Within weeks, "Joltin' Joe DiMaggio," the raucous, horn-infused romp by Les Brown and His Band of Renown, would top the charts. DiMaggio's run had grown to forty-eight games when the leagues took a few days off for the July 8 All-Star Game.

The midsummer contest, hosted at Briggs Stadium in Detroit, had the feel of a DiMaggio celebration: bands played, patriotic bunting fluttered along the stands, and the loudest cheers—excepting those for hometown favorite Rudy York—went to the Yankee center-fielder. Twenty-year-old phenomenon Teddy Williams, armed with a movie camera, made sure to film DiMaggio during batting practice. A legion of former stars—Dizzy Dean, Mickey Cochrane, Eddie Collins, Tris Speaker—watched DiMaggio from the stands. Speaker undoubtedly with a quietly critical eye, for fans were mentioning DiMaggio in the same breath as Speaker, some suggesting that Joe—not Tris—belonged beside Ruth and Cobb in the greatest-ever out-field. But Speaker had his defenders in the press, even in New York. "Younger fans, unwilling to believe that the game has known a bet-ter ball player than DiMaggio, want to know where he comes in," wrote Frank Graham in the *Sun*. "As a matter of fact, he doesn't come in at all. Not yet."

Cobb and Ruth weren't at the game. Ty was back on the West Coast, refining his golf stroke, and Ruth was still in Bretton Woods, New Hampshire, vacationing after a July 4–6 holiday tournament. He was staying at the opulent Mount Washington Hotel, situated near thousands of acres of woodlands. He loved the resort. "You know what kind of country that is," he said. "You hate to leave it."

At the All-Star Game, baseball clown Al Schacht had hoped to do a skit about Cobb and Ruth. He had ordered special masks for the occasion, but they failed to arrive on time.

The game was expected to be an American League romp, led by Joe D. and Bobby Feller, who had brought his own trainer. Feller shut out the National Leaguers through the first three innings, fac-ing nine hitters and striking out four of them, and DiMaggio dou-bled in the eighth, starting a rally that closed a deficit. But the glory went elsewhere. In the ninth, with DiMaggio on first and Joe Gor-don on third, Ted Williams faced Claude Passeau, who had struck him out earlier. The count went to two balls, one strike. Passeau had snuck a knee-high fastball past Williams in his previous at bat, and Williams expected him to try it again. "So I just put all I had in that next swing," he said.

Williams drilled the ball, and it took flight. The ball stung the green-wood facing of the third deck, right below the press-overflow section. It bounced back onto the field. The home run ended the game and gave the American League a dramatic victory. In the locker room, manager Del Baker kissed Williams on the cheek. "Boy," said Williams, "I bet my mother in San Diego turned a somersault on that one."

Williams's season was being overshadowed by DiMaggio's, but he was batting above .400 and would continue to do so, becoming the first major leaguer to exceed the figure since Bill Terry in 1930. More significantly, from Cobb's perspective, might have been his age. Ted Williams wouldn't turn twenty-three until August. Cobb was twenty-four before reaching .400 the first time.

In the years prior to the golf tournament, both Cobb and Ruth were seeing signs that their baseball records weren't invincible. Rogers Hornsby had retired with a .358 batting average, nine points shy of Cobb, and Jimmie Foxx had crossed the five-hundred-home-run threshold. Mel Ott, at thirty-two, was nearing four hundred. Three years earlier, Hank Greenberg, with fifty-eight home runs, had come close to tying Ruth's season mark.

Williams's average and DiMaggio's streak prompted Cobb to innocently suggest that the strike zone be widened by two inches, which got plenty of folks chortling. "I'd just love to know," said Del Baker, "what Ty Cobb would have said if somebody had advanced that proposal when he was an active player."

Cobb considered himself a perceptive judge of talent. Although he liked what he saw of Williams, he recognized that Williams had been playing in the majors for fewer than three years. But DiMaggio had been around since 1936 and had been an All-Star every season. Cobb had invested years in him. He knew DiMaggio back when he played with the San Francisco Seals of the Pacific Coast League, and Cobb had helped him with his batting and with negotiating his first contract with Yankees general manager Ed Barrow.

"He wrote out a letter to Barrow, saying the $4,000 was too low a salary," DiMaggio would recall. "I copied the letter in my hand-writing and signed my name." They went back and forth a couple of times, with Cobb fashioning the responses and the offers steadily increasing. Contrary to baseball legend, Barrow never sus-pected Cobb was involved, DiMaggio said. "He knew that my brother Tom was acting as my agent and thought that all the nego-tiating was done by Tom and me." Barrow even rewarded Tom DiMaggio with two new suits.

In the late 1930s, Cobb became a regular at Joe DiMaggio's Grotto on Fisherman's Wharf. DiMaggio saw him frequently in the off-season.

"He comes in my joint, and I just sit there and listen to him," he said. "What a man he is! I just keep my trap shut and listen. . . . Ty's made it possible for me to take a lot of shortcuts. Every time I see him, I pick up something—something I might never have thought about. For instance, this past winter he told me the way he used to break his batting slumps, and I'm going to try it this year, if I get in one."

Cobb liked to proffer advice, especially to the talented ones, and he heaped it on DiMaggio. Don't rush from the ballpark after the game, he said. Hang out in the locker room, talk with your teammates, review the contest, let your body cool down before you take a shower and head outside. Don't practice too much be-fore you play, save your strength for the long days of summer, Cobb counseled.

"Golly, when I first came up, I used to run myself ragged shag-ging flies before the game," DiMaggio said. "I asked [manager] Joe McCarthy if it would be all right with him if I did like Ty used to, and he said okay."

Cobb had even bet money that DiMaggio would hit .400 in 1939; DiMaggio reached .381, a league-best (and a career-best, it would turn out). "I let him down at the end of the season," DiMag-gio said. "He gave me a talking-to about it."

The only problem was that Cobb's advice just kept coming, whether or not its presumed beneficiary wanted it. Once he got something in his mind, Cobb wouldn't let up. And so it happened that, with the golf tournament attracting press attention and DiMaggio adding to his hitting streak and Cobb frequently finding himself before packs of reporters, he got the chance to share more thoughts about DiMaggio. Cobb tried to be delicate, in his own way.

"It ill becomes me to say anything about this, but. . . ."

"DiMaggio is a hell of a ball player, but . . ."

"I don't want to be criticizing or knocking the fellow, understand? . . . But . . ."

"Don't get me wrong. Joe is great, but . . ."

Cobb made it clear that DiMaggio was not living up to his potential. Despite DiMaggio's streak, it was the other guy, Williams, who was flirting with .400.

"Joe's friends would like to see him condition himself better through the winter," Cobb said. "He should hunt, walk a lot. His off-season letdown is too pronounced. . . . He hasn't begun to approach his peak. If he only conditioned himself in the winter by walking or hunting to keep his legs in shape, he'd be so far ahead of the others that it wouldn't even be close. . . . Would he hit the dead ball? He'd hit anything. . . . He is one of the greatest hitters, quickest fielders, surest throwers, and fastest runners I've seen. . . . You know, I don't know quite how to say this. . . . It's just an idea of mine. But I think DiMaggio could be even greater than he is."

Babe Ruth didn't criticize DiMaggio in the same way. But he appreciated other players more. Maybe it had something to do with DiMaggio being anointed as the next Ruth. Babe preferred Charlie Keller's style of play. "Boy, can that guy sock a ball," he said. "DiMaggio bats straightaway and doesn't get them up like that Keller."

Twelve days before the final Cobb-Ruth golf match, Joe DiMaggio went hitless against the Cleveland Indians, concluding his streak at fifty-six games. Cobb, meanwhile, was in training, promising friends he'd defeat Babe Ruth in their final match.

"I'll beat him for sure," he said.

27

Ty, Tris, and Babe in Cleveland

Baseball's greatest outfield as of 1941: Cobb, Ruth, and
Tris Speaker. ERNIE HARWELL COLLECTION, DETROIT PUBLIC
LIBRARY

~

Ty COBB AND BABE RUTH AGREED TO MEET TRIS SPEAKER IN
Cleveland three days before their July 29 golf match in
Michigan. Speaker had asked them to come to town for the baseball federation's annual amateur day. It promised to be a grand
weekend for the three players most often proclaimed as the all-
time trinity of the outfield. While the exiled Joe Jackson—and now

DiMaggio—received consideration on such rolls, Cobb, Ruth, and Speaker got tagged more often as the greatest trio.

The Texas-born Speaker played in the shadow of Cobb and Ruth. From 1907 through 1919, Cobb won the American League batting title every year except 1916, when Speaker slipped past him. Speaker's lifetime average of .345 placed him a few spots behind the Georgia Peach and a couple in front of the Bambino. He frequently led the league in doubles, accumulating nearly eight hundred of them over his career—a mark that remained untouched into the twenty-first century. But Speaker was best known for his sparkling defense. Contemporaries described him as a master artist. He roamed center field, they said, with the fluidity and grace of a stallion on the plains. Almost no one questioned Speaker's station as the best defensive outfielder.

He and Cobb had clicked almost immediately. Not so with Ruth. As late as the early 1920s, Speaker had suggested Ruth would do better to give up slugging and concentrate on pitching. Their mutual dislike spanned much of their careers but eased in Speaker's final seasons as both men grew and as Ruth's personality won over Speaker. By the 1930s, they found themselves golfing together, genuinely appreciating each other's company.

In the late afternoon of Wednesday, July 23, Ty Cobb departed alone by train from Reno, Nevada. The two-day journey took him over rock and river, reversing a path traveled by prospectors and pioneers. Cobb enjoyed train travel; he rarely flew. Perhaps the rail reminded him of his playing days. Or maybe he appreciated the panoramic views of mountains and prairies or found the rhythm of the ride relaxing. Or possibly he just hated airplanes. He had taken his first flight in 1915. "I can't say I would like the sport as a steady diet, but one flight was interesting," he said. On the train, Cobb probably passed the time by reading, writing, and socializing. Like his father, he appreciated history, collecting books about Napoleon, whom he viewed as a remarkable man. "I never tire of digging up something about his life," he once said.

Cobb also read newspapers, and not just the stock pages, though they were of particular interest, his wealth having topped a million long ago. Occasionally—as Bugs Baer, John Kieran, Grant-land Rice, and others could testify—he wrote columnists hand-written letters in his trademark green ink, mostly to correct their errors and to shape the way he would be remembered. Kieran got a letter clarifying details of Cobb's fight with Billy Evans. Rice received numerous letters over the years, and Baer heard from him after falsely claiming that a barber sharpened Cobb's spikes. Cobb spent much time denying variations of that myth.

Cobb encountered his spiking reputation wherever he went. He couldn't escape it, and it irritated him. It seemed to him that some-times all anyone remembered about his playing days could be summed up in the panels of a comic book: A demon-eyed runner barrels toward an innocent infielder and leaps into a midair slide, razor spikes flashing in the sun, as the hesitant, heroic fielder tries to place a gentle tag while evading an assault.

He dealt with that image in press and radio interviews, in talks with fans, and at social gatherings. No matter how friendly the questioner, the underlying implication—that he had been a dirty player—pierced Cobb.

While playing a round of golf with Cobb, Grantland Rice, and John "Mysterious" Montague in 1938, Hal Sims, a famous bridge player in an era when bridge players could become famous, felt im-pelled to broach the subject with Cobb. "Ty, I've always admired you," he said. "As a ball player, you were in a world apart. But tell me this if you will: Why did you have to spike so many men?"

Rice cringed. For a while, Cobb didn't say anything. But Rice knew it was only a matter of time. He recognized the anger rising in Cobb's face. Midway through their golf match, Cobb exploded. He grabbed Sims's arm, and the two pudgy fellows almost threw punches. Later, over dinner, Cobb told Rice, "I only remember intentionally spiking one man in twenty-four years." (In other inter-views, Cobb admitted to four or five victims.) There were eviden-tiary photos that seemingly contradicted Cobb, one showing him plunging his spikes into the belly of catcher Paul Krichell, trying to dislodge the ball in a 1912 game.

Much depends on how one defines "intentionally spiking." In

Cobb's view—backed by the rule book—the base path belonged to the runner. A fielder blocking his path risked being spiked because Cobb wouldn't hesitate to clear his rightful lane. Those incidents, from Cobb's perspective, weren't any more intentional than when a fielder landed his blades on Cobb's legs after leaping for a throw. The shiny white scars that striped his limbs attested to the frequency of those occurrences.

It was a rough game, particularly in Cobb's early years. The first time Cobb slid headfirst into a base, veteran shortstop Kid Elberfield ground his face into the dirt. Over time, Cobb perfected the feet-first fade-away slide, which when employed properly required he have both feet near the ground—not in someone's flesh. And what of those colorful stories about his filing his spikes or having someone do it for him? Pure fantasy, Cobb contended. An invention of writers; never happened, he said. Period.

Throughout the Newton and Flushing golf matches, journalists alluded to Cobb's spikes and his fights with Billy Evans, Charles Schmidt, Buck Herzog, and others.

In Boston, a cheery fan had reminisced with Cobb about the first time he saw him play. "You were on second and you started to steal third," he said. "You came into the bag with your spikes so high it looked as if you were sliding on the back of your neck. There was an argument over the decision. The third baseman swung at you with his fist. You swung back and a regular free-for-all started."

Cobb must have been in a forgiving mood. "Yeah," he said, "that Larry Gardner and I always had a lot of trouble."

With Ruth, the press usually focused on the saintlier side of his image: his affection for children, his hospital visits, and the healing power of his home runs. It was there in the column Considine had written about Babe driving through the Italian neighborhood. It was everywhere.

The golf tournament prompted one Detroiter to write the Hearst *Times* with a rich tale of being rescued by Ruth in 1923 as a ten-year-old. The boy had slipped into the park early, seeking autographs from a group of Yankee players who were in a disagreeable mood. They grabbed him. "Two of them held me while the others sharpened up a knife obtained from the grinning refreshment stand clerk," he recalled. They stripped off his pants and waved the knife over his body. The boy wrenched himself free, ran off in tears, and conveniently slammed into Ruth, crumbling at his feet.

"The Babe picked me up in his arms," he said.

"Hey, kid! What's wrong?" Ruth asked.

The boy explained what had happened. Ruth grew indignant, took the boy by the hand, and marched over to the players.

"He seemed thirty feet tall," the man remembered.

Ruth hurtled toward his teammates.

"He hit them with express-train speed," the man said. "Two of the men went down like tenpins. . . . His mammoth fist lashed out like a streak of light and crashed against the chin of another player, who sailed over the counter of the stand and disappeared with a crash of coffee cups. . . . Babe Ruth made those guys shine my shoes, put back on my pants, and made each one of them apologize to me."

If Cobb had seen the story, he would have shaken his head and wondered how the hell anyone could believe such horseshit. Ruth had always benefited from that kind of coverage. As a player, he had always been the favorite of photographers for his willingness to pose doing just about anything. Survey the papers of the 1920s and you'll find an agreeable Ruth captured in myriad situations. There's Babe Ruth with a tuba and Babe Ruth dressed as Santa Claus and surrounded by Odd Fellows. There's Ruth standing with kids on crutches and beside those in hospital beds. There's the Babe engaging a uniformed chimp, hurling snowballs, boxing, bowling, golfing, playing football on a beach, fishing on a boat, diving in a one-piece tank-topped bathing suit, hoisting a day's catch after a turkey hunt, and maneuvering through a sea of children at an orphanage. He always visited the orphanages.

For decades, Cobb had been losing the public-relations battle to Ruth. What would happen when he was no longer around to charm

the reporters and counter the growing and exaggerated stories?
He needed all the irrefutable evidence he could gather. He needed
something new, something permanent, to remind everyone that
he had been better than Ruth. He needed to gather one more victory against his old rival, one more undeniable triumph that would
stand eternally.

~

Cobb's two nights aboard the train proved uncomfortable because
of a faltering air-conditioning system. On Friday afternoon, the
train pulled into Chicago's Union Station about the same time that
Babe and Claire Ruth were arriving in Cleveland. The Ruths had
flown in from New York. Speaker met them at the airport and
drove them to the Hotel Carter, at Ninth and Prospect streets, less
than a mile from Lakefront Stadium.

Claire Ruth frequently traveled with Babe. She tried to keep him
on a tight rein, which was easier and less necessary in 1941 than in
1929 when they married. For a while, she golfed with him. But
that didn't work well for either one. "I didn't like the game and
gave it up when I realized that my duffer play ruined his own ex-
cellent game," she said. Claire resigned herself to the life of a golf
widow.

They rarely went to ball games anymore. Partly, that related to
Babe's frustration at being excluded from the sport. But Claire also
attributed it to autograph hounds. "I find myself passing over a
steady stream of cards and papers for Babe's signature," she said.
"We wind up reading about the game in the papers."

"And," Babe added, "if I don't sign them all, I'm a heel."

Ruth wasted little time in his Cleveland hotel room. He wanted
to get in a round of golf. "I need to beat that guy Cobb," Ruth remarked with false urgency.

Speaker, who may have been a better golfer than either Ty or
Babe, counted Cobb among his best chums in baseball and certainly wouldn't have embraced Ruth's mission. But he was always

up for a game, and so they headed over to the Country Club of Cleveland, where Billy Burke served as course pro. Burke, minus a ring finger he lost in a foundry mishap, won the 1931 Open at Inverness in Toledo, succeeding Bobby Jones. Burke edged George Von Elm by one stroke in the 144-hole marathon. And he did it with steel-shafted clubs, which helped popularize them. Since 1934, he had been pro at the private course in Pepper Pike, about fifteen miles east of downtown Cleveland. It had been designed by Howard Toomey and William Flynn, the latter a childhood friend of Francis Ouimet and creator of Cherry Hills in Denver. (Burke would remain pro there into the early 1960s.)

It was hot, and Ruth and Speaker got their fill in nine holes. In the locker room afterward, Ruth stripped out of his clothes and started shooting the bull about his playing days.

"You know, when I was pitching against Cobb," he said, "I used to yell at that Peach, 'Get ready to go down, you so-and-so. This one's coming right at your dome.' And he'd drop or get back. We didn't fool around in those days. We'd tell those hitters we were throwing it at them, and they'd duck. Take Joe Jackson. Once I saw him at the Boston ballpark get hit right on the head. A ball sailed off Joe's dome and bounced all the way over those stands in Boston. What did Joe do? Hell, he just walked to first base without even taking off his cap."

Ruth felt modern ballplayers weren't as tough as those of his generation. Of course, no ballplayer in the history of the world ever viewed the guys who came after him as more robust than his own peers. Ruth was no different.

"I remember one time we were playing an exhibition game when I was with the Yanks. I'm on second base and Gehrig is at the plate. Well, one of those corn-leaguers hit Gehrig right on the head. Down goes Lou, like he was shot. They rushed a piece of ice from the dugout and I trotted in from second to see what was going on. Well, the trainer is rubbing the ice around the back of Gehrig's neck and then around across his mouth. And what do you suppose that Gehrig was doing? Every time the ice passed his

mouth, he'd stick out his tongue and lick it! That was enough for
me. I went back to second base."

Wherever Ruth went, people wanted to hear the stories. He
could spin them, and others drew closer as he did. He was the
Babe, after all.

Speaker nodded at Ruth. "Most people think of this big guy as a
home run hitter," he said. "I don't! I remember him as a pitcher.
What a pitcher, too!"

Soon, they were talking about Ruth's twenty-nine scoreless innings in the World Series. "Yes, sir," Ruth confirmed. "Twenty-nine
scoreless innings."

That night at the hotel while awaiting Cobb's arrival, Ruth and
Speaker entertained a few acquaintances with still more stories of
their ball-playing days. Eventually, though, the topic turned to the
Georgia Peach and golf.

"That Cobb is a nut about the game," Ruth said. "He's too serious
for me. Yeah, and he's too slow. Why, in our last match I pulled out
a chair on him."

Speaker recalled the first time he had played with Cobb, in the
1910s. "Ty burned up because he could not beat the game after a
couple of rounds and told me it was a lousy game and bad for ball
players," said Speaker. "Look at him now. You can't chase him off
the course."

Shortly before midnight, Cobb—his face a shade or two darker
from weeks in the sun—stepped off the train in Cleveland and
asked a *Cleveland Plain Dealer* reporter where Ruth was and
what he had said about him. Ruth had commented about Cobb's
increasing weight. Cobb laughed: "Well, the Babe is eating pretty
good, too."

Cobb joined the hotel celebration. For the next forty-eight
hours, the three men were nearly inseparable. Within days of their
reunion, pictures of them would be splashed on sports pages
across America, with taglines heralding them as OUTFIELD ACES, THE
ALL-TIME DREAM OUTFIELD, and BASEBALL'S IMMORTALS. Bodies loose,
eyes sparkling, arms tossed over shoulders—they looked truly

delighted. On Cobb's face, there was not a hint of the elaborate plan that he had hatched and likely refined on his long journey.

~

A sweltering heat wave struck the Cleveland area Saturday. It was so hot that the pavement was buckling in spots. By afternoon, temperatures were approaching one hundred degrees. Thousands were seeking relief at bathing beaches. But Cobb, Ruth, and Speaker decided to golf. They headed over to the Country Club and invited Billy Burke to round out their foursome.

Ruth and Cobb looked to be melting in the sun. Ruth mopped sweat from his face with a hand towel, and Cobb worried over his vulnerable, unprotected skull, rubbing his hand across his head as if trying to disrupt a burn. The unflustered Burke kept his tie tightly knotted.

Cobb missed an inordinate amount of shots. Putts that he would have made at Fresh Meadow drifted away from the cup. "Don't know what's wrong with me," he said. "I'm sure off." Cobb's misplays registered with Ruth, just as he had hoped they would. Burke won the round with a 71, Speaker shot a 77, Ruth a 79. Cobb topped 80.

At the hotel that evening, a confident Ruth picked at one of Cobb's sore spots. "I can remember when we had our spikes sharpened before each game," he said, casting an accusatory glance at Cobb. "I can also remember when I got spiked three times in one game."

One imagines they were all boozy by then.

"Twenty-nine scoreless innings . . . ," Speaker repeated. "I don't know who ever matched it."

~

Early Sunday afternoon, Ty and Babe shared a ride to cavernous Lakefront Stadium, where the Indians played Sunday and evening games.

"You know, Babe, there's one thing in baseball I wish you hadn't done," said Cobb. "I wish you hadn't gone over to the National League after you left the Yankees. You should have stayed in the American League always. You ought to be in there right now in some kind of a job."

At the ballpark, where temperatures threatened to again top one hundred, Cobb and Ruth reluctantly nudged into their baseball flannels. "This is the last time I'll ever put this thing on," Ruth said. (It wasn't, though.)

Fifteen thousand fans came out for the Federation League fundraiser. It was a decent crowd for such an event, but Lakefront Stadium still felt empty. With a capacity exceeding seventy-eight thousand, it often did. Fans clustered in the stands between first and third bases, coming to life when the three baseball legends, accompanied by a brass band and drum corps, marched from the outfield to home plate.

Cobb got in a few words before the public-address system failed. "I am honored and happy to be here," he said as the microphone scratched and sizzled. Ruth and Speaker silently saluted the crowd, and then Ruth put on a hitting demonstration, launching a few balls over the fence.

Their appearance concluded near the stands, where a mass of raucous boys swarmed around them, thrusting programs and pens at the middle-aged men. Several lads reached out to touch them as if doing so might fill them with baseball magic. One boy about nine stood atop the fence and steadied himself by resting his right hand like a crown on Ruth's head.

The temperature dropped to eighty in Cleveland Sunday evening, July 27. It was a few degrees cooler beside Lake Erie at the D&C Boat Docks, where Cobb and Ruth boarded the steamer *City of Cleveland,* which would ferry them and hundreds of other passengers to Detroit by seven o'clock the next morning.

The five-hundred-foot boat—a floating hotel, really—had the ambience of a traveling party. Rows of lights marked each of its decks and shimmered on the rippling water. Fueled by coal-burning boilers, the side-wheeled vessel powered through the great lake, its tall stacks spewing dark, shadowy clouds into a moonless night sky. Although the heyday of the steamer was drawing to a close, the *City of Cleveland* and its sister ship, the *City of Detroit,* promised pleasant journeys and numerous amenities: beautifully appointed public areas, sumptuous meals, musical entertainment, and nicely furnished parlor rooms, some with private verandas. It was a festive, relaxed way to travel.

Cobb and Ruth stayed up late drinking. "Babe again was all smiling confidence," Cobb said later, "and he killed a good part of a quart of Scotch. And the next day . . . he looked slightly ill." Ruth disembarked first from the steamer on Monday morning, puffing a breakfast cigar. In deference to the temperature, he had already shed his sport coat.

Detroit, like much of the nation, had been suffering through a heat wave for two weeks. The city had seen nothing like it in twenty years. Day after day, the mercury rose into the nineties, often exceeding one hundred. Doctors advised residents to stay in the shade, avoid exertion, drink fluids, consume light meals, and eat salt three times a day. During the morning and afternoon, thousands took refuge at beaches and in the Detroit River. At night, families slept atop blankets beneath the stars on Belle Isle, the almost-one-thousand-acre park designed by Frederick Law Olmsted.

On Sunday, twenty thousand people had escaped to the "air-conditioned" big tent of the Ringling Brothers and Barnum and Bailey Circus. Two hundred thousand pounds of ice were used to cool the pavilion for the afternoon and evening shows. Thousands of people were turned away because spectators were unwilling to squeeze closer on the bench seats. The most comfortable place to be—climatewise—was inside the enclosed, twenty-six-foot cage wagon of the show's supreme attraction, Gargantua, THE WORLD'S MOST TERRIFYING LIVING CREATURE! The five-hundred-pound gorilla, touring with the first Mrs. Gargantua, circled the hippodrome in the relative comfort of seventy-six degrees.

"Unless this heat spell ends . . . ," wrote Iffy the Dopester of the *Detroit Free Press,* "Old Iffy is picking on Cobb to win. . . . The Big Bambino is not what you would call a hot-weather go-getter."

Iffy's friend Harry Salsinger, sports editor of the competing *Detroit News,* was also ecstatic that Ty and Babe were back in town. Although he had been reporting baseball since 1907, when he came to the *News* as a twenty-year-old cub reporter, he was only in his midfifties. But he was beginning to sound like a curmudgeon. A tall, dignified man, Salsinger was respected by his journalistic peers, who eventually elected him president of the Baseball Writers Association of America. He had seen a lot of players over the years, and Cobb was his favorite.

In the locker room, he delighted in telling the young athletes about Cobb's feats and deeds. He told them how hard Cobb played, how he worked furiously to achieve his goals, about the four times that he stole three bases in an inning, about his sizzling competitive nature. Usually, they listened politely and feigned interest. Sometimes, after he departed, they rolled their eyes. On a rare occasion, a player might challenge him.

"I'll be perfectly frank with you," one star told Salsinger. "I don't believe Cobb did any of those things you tell about. You just imagine them. There are several dozen better ball players in the game today than Cobb ever was."

The response flustered Salsinger. When he looked out at the ball field these days, he saw what it lacked: players with color, zest, and fire. There was not a Cobb or a Ruth among them. While he recognized Joe DiMaggio as the best of the current batch, he dismissed him in a second breath as "purely mechanical."

"DiMaggio plays baseball superbly well, but he plays it without dash, glitter, shimmer, glow, or apparent enthusiasm," he wrote. "There is nothing spontaneous about his play, nothing inspiring. He does everything exceedingly well but with no more emotion than a diesel engine."

Cobb and Ruth were part of a golden era. "They were giants," he said. And now they were in Detroit together for one last game.

28

Cobb's Secret Weapon

Cobb takes a practice swing. NATIONAL BASEBALL HALL OF
FAME LIBRARY, COOPERSTOWN, N.Y.

I N THE FIRST HALF OF THE TWENTIETH CENTURY, GROSSE ILE offered a summer haven for some of Detroit's wealthiest automotive entrepreneurs. Located in the Detroit River, ten miles south of the big city and a mile west of Canada, the island—actually a collection of islands—played host to the Fishers, the Oldses, and the Knudsens. Henry Ford bought canal property there, and in 1939 his top assistant, security chief Harry Bennett, built the mysterious Pagoda House on a portion of it. For a while, Mickey Cochrane was his neighbor. Bennett's home had a tunnel that connected to a boat-house. Two tunnel entrances were concealed, one behind a sliding cabinet, the other behind a sliding wall in a bedroom closet. Given Bennett's violent clashes with union organizers, most believed the tunnel provided an escape route should Bennett be attacked.

Magnificent homes, some erected in the 1840s, dotted the land-scape. The hilly east side of the island offered splendid views of the freighters and steamers that cruised by just hundreds of yards off-shore. It was a gentle playground for the well-to-do, a scenic refuge from the stifling city, a place where daughters of affluent industri-alists could comfortably ride their horses.

The Grosse Ile Golf and Country Club, near the southern tip of the island, played a central role in the social life of residents. Since 1921—thanks to a $350,000 loan floated by tire company founder (and Tigers part-owner) John Kelsey—it had included an eighteen-hole course designed by Donald Ross. The course was, residents boasted, one of the first in the country to feature an in-ground wa-tering system.

For three years, Grosse Ile had been home to a small naval sta-tion, located less than a mile from the country club, which officers frequented in their free hours. In August, contingents of Royal Air Force cadets would begin arriving at the base as part of a program to train British pilots. They would receive ground-school instruction there before heading to Pensacola, Florida, for flying exercises. As if anticipating the mix of Brit pilots and U.S. sailors, the Trenton The-atre across the river offered an enticing double feature the week of the Cobb-Ruth match: *Naval Academy,* a "stirring drama of three boys," and *Scotland Yard,* a romantic adventure set in London.

The world was becoming an increasingly frightening place in the summer of 1941. Germany had invaded Russia, providing yet more evidence of Adolf Hitler's grand ambitions. War was raging in several countries, and reports about the battles dominated news on radio and in print. American men were being drafted into service in preparation for a fight, and sports heroes were not immune. In fact, polls showed the public wanted it that way, seven in ten re-spondents saying athletes should receive no special consideration.

Hank Greenberg, first baseman for the defending American League champion Tigers, had become the first major-league star selected to serve. A U.S. senator, noting that Greenberg had taken a sizeable pay cut, applauded him. "To my mind," he said, "he's a bigger hero than when he was knocking home runs." On May 6, in his final game before induction, Greenberg had slugged two home runs at Briggs Stadium. It was an emotional day at the park, with fans giving the six-foot-four hero a warm send-off. Greenberg's teammates presented him with a gold watch that featured their signatures in miniature on the back, and Mrs. Briggs, the owner's wife, hugged him farewell.

"So long, boys," Greenberg said as he left the locker room. "I'll be back again next year."

He wouldn't, of course. "I was just hoping to go in and get my service done and then come back and resume my career," Greenberg would recall. "It was a one-year draft, and war hadn't been declared yet and I thought I'd return for the 1942 season. Little did I know . . ." It would be four and a half years before he returned to the majors. Feller, DiMaggio, Williams, and other ballplayers would serve as well, beside golfers like Jones, Snead, and Hogan.

Although Americans sensed that they would be drawn into the war, few imagined the devastating manner in which it would happen. The week of June 14, newsstands were lined with copies of *Collier's* magazine. The cover story? IMPREGNABLE PEARL HARBOR.

~

No one wanted a Fresh Meadow turnout. Not Ruth. Not Fred Corcoran. Most of all, not Cobb. Not in Detroit. Not in his town. In an attempt to bolster attendance, Corcoran enlisted two more figures in the U.S.O. fund-raiser: the legendary Hagen and John "Mysterious" Montague.

Hagen loved baseball as much as Cobb and Ruth loved golf. He had played semipro ball in Rochester, New York, considered a career in the sport, and even arranged to try out with Philadelphia in 1914. (He wisely skipped the date in favor of a golf tournament.)

After winning his second U.S. Open, Hagen became head pro at Oakland Hills in the Detroit area and more closely followed the exploits of Cobb and the Tigers. While he didn't stay long at the club, Hagen remained a booster of the team. He worked out with Mickey Cochrane's squad at spring training in 1934, even donning a uniform. A year later, as the Tigers prepared for their World Series against Chicago, Hagen joined them on the field for a warmup exercise, a game of pepper.

He enjoyed the ball field and ballplayers. At a Red Sox camp one spring, Hagen took to the mound in an attempt to strike out Sam Snead, another ball-playing golfer. But Hagen's arm wasn't sharp, and Snead nailed his pitches. Over the years, Hagen had golfed with numerous major leaguers, including Jimmie Foxx, Rube Marquard, and, of course, Babe Ruth.

Hagen knew Ruth well from their covert outings during spring training. In 1927, he had introduced the British Ryder Cup team to Ruth and baseball, shepherding them to Yankee Stadium to see a game and to meet his comrade. Although Hagen was more charming, he shared with Ruth a passion for living large. They spent freely and drank proficiently and caroused together, partying until morning with spirited showgirls. Babe and Haig helped make the 1920s roar.

Writers who leaned toward baseball described Hagen as "the Babe Ruth of golf." Undoubtedly, some golf writers found the converse description worked as well. By extension, Bobby Jones must have been "the Ty Cobb of golf." Weeks after the Grosse Ile contest, in one of the Ryder Cup challenge matches that replaced the international competition during the war years, Jones would assemble a squad to face Hagen's team at the Detroit Golf Club and pull off an upset before twelve thousand fans.

Hagen spent much of his time in Michigan. He stayed at the Detroit Athletic Club or the Book-Cadillac Hotel, attending ball games just down Michigan Avenue. "He can't eat dinner any night until he gets all the big league scores and who pitched for each team," said Corcoran.

Before the Cobb-Ruth series began, Hagen had shared with

Cobb his insights into Ruth the golfer. "One thing I noticed peculiar to Babe's game, and to that of most ball players, was that for
the length of time an average ball game consumes Babe was a fine
golfer," Hagen said. "He could concentrate. After the hour and fifty
minutes' duration of a ball game, or about the eleventh hole as golf
is played, the Babe began to slop his shots away."

Indeed, during the marathon matches in New York and Massachusetts, Ruth won only two holes after the twelfth flag—and one
was the play-off hole. Cobb would have found Hagen's observation
invaluable and illuminating, and it would have given him even
more reasons to play a protracted, cautious, calculated game.

Cobb left nothing to chance. On Monday, the day before the piv-
otal match, he arrived at Grosse Ile Golf and Country Club and did
a bit of investigating. He inquired around the clubhouse, solicited
advice, and then took action, securing what he hoped would provide him a decisive advantage: a crackly-voiced, dark-haired fifteen-
year-old caddy.

Young Pete Devany lived on Grosse Ile, golfed a fine game, and
knew the layout exceptionally well. But he had never caddied for
anyone other than his father, who just happened to be Joe Devany,
the club pro and one of Walter Hagen's numerous pals. His dad
wasn't young Pete's only connection to golf. His maternal grandfather, Wilfrid Reid, played on the English teams that won the French
and Swiss opens in the early part of the 1900s. He then came to
America and designed San Francisco's Lakeside Golf and Country
Club, which evolved into the Olympic Club. Reid, who played
against Ouimet, Harry Vardon, and Ted Ray in golf's "greatest game
ever," was pro at Seminole Country Club in Palm Beach, where the
Devanys spent their winters. Additionally, Pete's younger sister,
Pat, was a budding prodigy; she would tour the country at sixteen
and for a while live with Babe Didrikson and her husband. Pete Devany knew his golf. More importantly, he knew the course.

Cobb got onto the fairways before Ruth on Monday—a necessity
really, given the pace of his game. He shot several balls in his warm-
up round, approaching the holes from prismatic angles, picking his
caddy's mind, and recording his discoveries in a notebook. Three

pals from his Detroit days—Joe Lessel, Bill Monahan, and Fred Wirth—joined Cobb on the outing, but it was the teenager who received much of his attention.

Pete's gig not only made him a celebrity among friends, it landed him on the front page of the *Trenton Times,* a local paper that trumpeted this cumbersome slogan beneath its nameplate. JUST LIKE A LETTER FROM HOME—ALL THE GOOD NEWS YOU WANT TO READ ABOUT, AN OPINION OR TWO, PRINTED IN LARGE READABLE TYPE.

"Anyone can give advice," said Pete, who downplayed his role. "Anyone familiar with a golf course can give pretty good advice, too. It isn't the advice so much; it is the actual shot that counts. It is pretty tough to do what you should even after you know what should be done."

Cobb charmed the boy, treating him as a confidant, escorting him down the fairway with his arm across his shoulders. In return, Pete shared every bit of his expertise. "He's a swell guy," Pete said of Cobb.

Ty and his entourage finished eighteen holes and retired to the grillroom before the cooling rains arrived. Cobb was relaxing at a table when the downpour began. He watched as Ruth and his party—two newspaper executives and a club officer—charged off the ninth green and took cover.

They settled at the table beside them.

"What did you shoot?" Cobb asked.

"Oh, 41 or 42."

"Oh, yeah?"

"What did you do the first nine in?"

"Forty," said Cobb, though really there was no way to tell with his having used several balls.

"Over your head, heh?"

Cobb chortled something about Babe's weight.

"Hell," said Ruth, "I was up to 265. Don't eat much either. Don't know how the old suet piles up but it does. I'm still swinging out there. But I don't get the snap in the wrist like I did in baseball. It's that snap in the wrist that counts both in golf and baseball. That's how Ted Williams hits—the snap in the wrist. Boy, he can hit it, too. But you don't have to be big to hit a ball hard—golf ball or baseball—it's that wrist action that does the business."

Despite three-putting most of the greens, Ruth said he felt satisfied with the nine holes he golfed. "I'm ready for Ty," he said.

And Cobb was ready for him.

29

For Eternal Bragging Rights

The Cobb-Ruth matches attract reams of newspaper coverage.

∿

I NSIDE THE GROSSE ILE CLUBHOUSE ON TUESDAY AFTERNOON, July 29, 1941, Ty Cobb was growing anxious. More than two thousand fans, many in white shirts and straw hats, were swarming about the course. Hundreds were still pouring over the bridges that connected Grosse Ile to the mainland. Others were arriving by boat, docking outside friends' homes. Spectators milled around the country club awaiting the four o'clock start, lingering beneath shade trees to escape the throbbing sun. The turnout, estimated at three thousand, looked to be three times larger than the numbers in Newton and Fresh Meadow combined.

"This is completely a Cobb gallery," remarked Fred Corcoran. "Every man and woman is here to see Cobb win."

The gathering crowd made Cobb tense and fidgety. The fans had never bothered him so in baseball. But this was different. There was no wooden fence or brick wall to keep them back. They stood right beside you; they seemed more than spectators. Cobb thumbed through the notes he had taken the day before and plotted. Earlier, he had been on the course driving balls, his caddy Pete shagging for him. What disquieted Cobb most on this occasion was that this was his crowd. They had come to see him. One needed only to look at their faces to realize that many of these folks—the bulk in their forties, fifties, and sixties—had seen him play on the ball field. They had come, he felt, expecting to watch the Georgia Peach of yesteryear once again turn back the Babe. They expected him to win, and Cobb didn't want to disappoint.

The celebrity-speckled gallery included a legion of his baseball teammates: Cochrane, Bobby Veach, Clyde Manion, Davy Jones. The old catcher Roger Bresnahan was there, up from Toledo; former hockey stars Normie Smith and Hec Kilrea, too. Mayor Ed Jeffries had come out, as had a couple of judges, a former Tiger team physician, and scads of local notables. Among them was John Roesink, onetime owner of the Negro league Detroit Stars and a longtime friend of both Ruth and Cobb. And, of course, the pencil-mustached Harry Salsinger and his former boss, the droopy-jowled Malcolm Bingay ("Iffy the Dopester")—"Sal" and "Bing" to Cobb—were watching as well.

"I went out to see the game for just one reason," Bingay would explain. "I wanted to see if the years had dimmed the fierce competitive spirit of Cobb."

In the clubhouse, Ruth acted as if he hadn't a worry. He breezed about the room exhibiting the gregarious personality that made him so popular among fellow players. He chatted with friends and tried to ease Cobb's nerves. It's not like they were playing for World Series money, right?

"The trouble with you is that you're too tight," Ruth said to Cobb. "You're jittery. You can't win any matches that way. You ought to be loose and relaxed."

"I'll be loose and relaxed when it counts," Cobb replied. But deep down, Cobb probably did wish he could be more loose and relaxed. He liked that about Ruth. He envied how Ruth could be the life of the party and how others perked up in his company.

That morning, neither Ruth nor Cobb would hazard a bold prediction on the outcome, though Ruth tried unsuccessfully to get Cobb to wager money.

The sun had been broiling the Grosse Ile landscape without a break all afternoon. The air was steamy, and the fairways radiated heat. Joined by Hagen and Montague, Cobb and Ruth teed off about four o'clock. Cobb looked unnerved, dropping the first hole on six shots, two over par, as Ruth bogeyed. Cobb bore down and sunk a twenty-foot putt on the second green, halving the hole with Ruth, whose shirt was already streaked with sweat.

On the 498-yard third hole, Ruth launched his drive out of bounds and struggled to recover. Cobb plodded up the fairway with grave care, getting to within eighteen feet of the flag on his fifth shot. He huddled on the green with his caddy, Pete, and asked his advice for the first time that afternoon. Pete whispered his recommendation, and they crouched to consider the flow of the land. Cobb sunk the difficult putt, took the point, and got showered with cheers.

"Same old Ty!" someone hollered.

Pete was ecstatic.

Ruth was drenched. After tying him on the fourth hole, Ruth dropped the next four.

"Take me out!" he yelled to the gallery.

"You want a pinch hitter?" someone asked.

"Yeah!"

Cobb was playing as if his everlasting salvation depended on the outcome. He studied his notes, and he conferred continually with his caddy. Always, he took a practice swing. Sometimes two.

By the halfway point, with Cobb ahead by four holes, Ruth appeared to resign himself to defeat. His goal seemed to change from winning the match to entertaining the crowd. Ruth's levity and humor balanced Cobb's seriousness. Ruth laughed it up with Montague, Hagen, his caddy, and the spectators. He chatted and teased. He played the fool, pretending to try to push over a tree that blocked the path of his ball. Twice, he lay on the greens, crossed his arms over his chest, and closed his eyes, gently protesting Cobb's protracted style of play. Spectators embraced Ruth's carefree attitude. Through his antics, he was reinforcing all their warm and treasured memories of him.

On the twelfth hole, Ruth lampooned Cobb, kneeling on the turf and theatrically lining up his shot. "Guess I'll look over a putt, too," he declared.

Cobb ignored him.

"That guy's so slow he'd stop a funeral," Ruth said. "I should have taken along a studio couch."

Ruth took the twelfth and thirteenth holes, but Cobb still held a substantial advantage. He was up by three, with five holes left. On the fourteenth, facing a forty-foot putt, Cobb flashed Ruth a quizzical look, inquiring whether the long shot might qualify for a "give-me."

No way, said Ruth.

Cobb proceeded to sink the putt, squelching Ruth's rally and thrilling the gallery.

Ruth muttered about Cobb's short game.

By the fifteenth hole, as the contest dragged toward its fourth hour, daylight had begun to dim. Hagen jokingly struck a match to help Ruth see his ball. The Babe missed the cup and admonished himself. "Beautiful shot, Ruth," he said. He was almost out of holes.

On the sixteenth green, Cobb tapped in an eighteen-inch putt and captured the victory. He was up three, with two holes remaining. The play ended there. Cobb had won, and Ruth congratulated him. Cobb was delighted and gracious.

"I am more gratified by the turnout than by my victory," he said. "You know, Detroit is my adopted hometown. It was here that I climbed to baseball heights and it sure was one of the greatest thrills of my life to see so many of my old friends. And it is satisfying to know that they turned out in such numbers."

Cobb and Ruth had not played memorable golf. They missed par by fifteen and eighteen holes, respectively. Cobb shot a 78 for sixteen holes, Ruth an 81. Six times they pelted spectators with errant drives. With nothing on the line, Hagen shot a forgettable round—a 75—while Montague turned in the best score, a 70. Of course, the details didn't matter. Cobb had won.

Afterward, in the dressing room, he cheerfully expounded on whatever subjects the reporters suggested: the health benefits of golfing, DiMaggio's pursuit of an $80,000 salary, the changing nature of baseball.

Cobb took time to sign a scorecard for his caddy, Pete Devany, bestowing a sizeable tip on him—though Pete would politely decline to reveal precisely how much. Cobb told Pete he would like to play a round with him sometime when in town.

Ruth, meanwhile, sat outside on the clubhouse steps, surrounded by boys seeking his signature. Cobb may have taken—as he described it—THE LEFT-HANDED HAS-BEENS GOLF CHAMPIONSHIP OF NOWHERE IN PARTICULAR, but Ruth, with his antics and lighthearted approach, had won the crowd.

The congratulatory telegrams poured in all evening. For a while, Cobb and Ruth celebrated together with 120 other folks at Mickey Cochrane's island home. Eventually, Cobb left for the Statler Hotel, where he threw a private, intimate dinner for some longtime Detroit friends: pilot Jimmy Doolittle, photographer Bill Kuenzel, Harry Salsinger, and Malcolm Bingay.

Doolittle, who in time would be flying missions over Japan, told Bingay he had been a Cobb fan as a boy in St. Louis.

"What interested you in Ty Cobb?"

"Speed!" said Doolittle. "Just speed! I wanted to see him go around those bases."

Doolittle didn't need to do a sales job on Bingay, who once wrote this of Cobb:"What Shakespeare was to literature, Beethoven was to music, Caruso was to tenors, Napoleon was to warfare, Lincoln was to statesmanship, Newton was to physics, Ty Cobb was to baseball—peculiar, alone, unique; the apotheosis of the apple slappers. . . . Like they speak of the Elizabethan era, or the Renaissance, or the glory that was Greece and the grandeur that was Rome, it is well for historians to speak of the Cobbian age."

Ty Cobb and Babe Ruth had staged their final promotional picture on Monday at Grosse Ile. It ran the day of the event in some Detroit papers. It was unlike any other they had taken to that point. It wasn't just the pose of them face-to-face, gently knocking fists. Or the apparent spontaneity of it, with Cobb fleshy and barechested, a white shower towel draped around his neck. It was the way they looked at each other. Cobb was beaming at Ruth with his robin-egg-blue eyes, and Ruth was beaming back at him. They looked comfortable and at ease. They looked like two long-lost pals who had finally found each other after a remarkable journey.

And in some ways, they were.

Ruth	5	4	7	4	5	4	6	6	5	7	5	5	3	5	5	5	81
Cobb	6	4	6	4	4	3	5	5	5	6	5	6	4	5	5	5	78

The Later Years

A final meeting: Ty and The Babe in 1947. ERNIE HARWELL
COLLECTION, DETROIT PUBLIC LIBRARY

~

TY COBB AND BABE RUTH LIVED ON OPPOSITE COASTS, SEPA-
rated by twenty-seven hundred miles, a distance made
greater by Cobb's reluctance to fly and Ruth's desire to stay near

his home. In the years after their golf tournament, they came together on at least two occasions.

In 1945, Cobb was called upon to coach a team in *Esquire* magazine's East-West Classic. Cobb was reluctant to take the assignment at first. "You don't want an old has-been," he said. "I've been out too long and the kids wouldn't be interested in me." But when told that the teenage players had been clamoring for him, Cobb relented. "If you mean that," he said, "I'll do anything you say." He agreed to manage the West team, which made Ruth a natural choice for the East. For ten days in New York, assisted by Mel Ott, Carl Hubbell, and others, Cobb and Ruth supervised late-August workouts with squads of young prospects, among them future Philadelphia pitcher Curt Simmons. Cobb delighted in working with the young players and showered attention on his favorites. Ruth was at his most rotund, somewhat less involved than Cobb, and more of a figurehead. But he took part, and his team prevailed in the showcase exhibition at the Polo Grounds.

Cobb and Ruth saw each other for the final time two years later on Sunday, September 28, 1947. Yankee owner Del Webb flew Cobb in from Nevada on his private plane. Ruth was a withered figure. He had been battling throat cancer, and the Yankees, who soon would be facing rookie Jackie Robinson and the Dodgers in the World Series, wanted to honor Ruth by raising money for his foundation. The call went out to old-timers willing to participate in a two-inning exhibition. From all across the country, they came to see the Babe one more time. Former Yankee teammates Waite Hoyt, Earle Combs, Wally Pipp, Bob Meusel, and Joe Dugan were there. Boston's Golden Outfield of Harry Hooper, Duffy Lewis, and Tris Speaker came, too, along with a cast of former stars that included eighty-year-old Cy Young, Chief Bender, Jimmie Foxx, and Charlie Gehringer.

Unable to play, Ruth watched in a fully buttoned overcoat as Cobb, sixty-one, led off in the first inning. Cobb told catcher Wally Schang that he hadn't swung a bat in years, and persuaded Schang to back away from the plate in case the bat slipped from his hands.

Schang obliged, and then Cobb dropped a beauty of a bunt to joyful cheers. If he had been four steps quicker, he might have beaten the throw.

After the brief game, Ruth stepped to the microphone as twenty-five thousand fans cheered. In a raspy, weak voice, his words merely a whisper, he thanked the crowd and acknowledged its kindness with a wave. Either before the exhibition or afterward, someone thought to snap one last picture of Cobb and Ruth together. Whether from pain or medication or emotion, Ruth's eyes were wet when Cobb laid his hand on Ruth's right shoulder. The moisture caught the flash of the camera.

The next summer, on the evening of August 16, 1948, Ruth died at Memorial Hospital in New York. In the days that followed, eighty thousand people—from anonymous tykes in their parents' arms to the city's most famous figures—paid their respects at Yankee Stadium, walking past his casket for a final view of the Babe. Days later, the city stopped for his funeral at St. Patrick's Cathedral. President Harry Truman said a whole generation of former boys mourned his death. "Babe Ruth had all the qualities of a hero," he said.

Cobb knew he would never match Babe Ruth's popularity. "People tell me I was the greatest player who ever lived," he said. "And maybe I am—as far as the way I played baseball. . . . [But] I wish I could have been more like the Babe. When he died, an entire nation mourned."

Through the first half of the century, Cobb continually captured the top spot in player rankings, outpolling Ruth, for example, in a 1942 survey of former professional players. After Babe died, however, he began accumulating the honors. In 1950, United Press International named him the top ballplayer of the 1900s—an honor Cobb had captured four years earlier, when Ruth was still alive.

The statistics hadn't changed, but Cobb's image was deteriorating as Ruth's rose. Two of Cobb's sons, Herschel and Ty Junior, died in the early 1950s. In occasional fits, Cobb grew more publicly critical of the current crop of stars, contending that Joe DiMaggio and Ted Williams played a brand of ball that would have kept them from succeeding during his era. But he tempered those views at other times.

In the autumn of his life, while on the East Coast for the Baseball Hall of Fame festivities that he so cherished, Cobb would sometimes head to New York, drive past Babe Ruth's apartment along Riverside Drive, and get weepy reminiscing about his former rival. "He was the most natural and unaffected man I ever knew," Cobb said. "God, how I miss him."

Cobb didn't like how Ruth had changed the game, but he honored his abilities as a ballplayer and trumpeted his talents. And Ruth returned the tribute. "At times," Ruth said, "we wanted to cut each other to ribbons. But I have a sincere and honest respect for Ty Cobb."

Cobb's persona cracked further after his July 17, 1961, death, undermined by an unflattering piece written for *True* magazine by biographer Al Stump. TY COBB'S WILD TEN-MONTH FIGHT TO LIVE captured Cobb in the most bitter, miserable months of his life, after the deaths of two sons and while in the throes of cancer and alcoholism. Stump's story provoked a backlash in *The Sporting News* and elsewhere, with Cobb's contemporaries coming to his defense. "Why should an author wait until the idol of millions was locked in that mausoleum at Royston, Georgia, to type such caustic and scathing prose?" asked Sid Keener, director of the Baseball Hall of Fame. Another scribe described Cobb as "a wonderful and warm-hearted man, tops in character and everything else." Wrote George Sisler, "I always liked Cobb. He played to win."

But Cobb's reputation continued to plummet. By 1969, Major League Baseball had voted Ruth as its greatest player. When Pete Rose toppled Cobb's career-hits record in 1985, a fresh flourish of negative publicity conjured a brutal caricature of Cobb. It got to the point where any reference to Cobb—even the most casual— reinforced the notion that he was the meanest, nastiest, dirtiest player to ever wear a uniform. In Ken Burns's acclaimed documentary, *Baseball,* one authority described Cobb as the single black mark in the game's history. In the movie *Field of Dreams,* a ghostly player noted that Cobb wasn't invited to play in the cornfield because everyone hated him. The perception of Cobb as a person was altered further—perhaps permanently—by Stump's merciless 1994 biography and *Cobb,* the scathing movie it spawned. A fan from the era of the Georgia Peach would be stunned by how he is portrayed today.

Cobb's standing as a baseball player has changed, and not just because of the emergence of newer stars. Current baseball analysts and historians, viewing on-field achievements through different prisms, have concluded that Babe Ruth was the best ever—and that Cobb wasn't even runner-up. *Total Baseball,* as the official encyclopedia of baseball, placed Nap Lajoie and Willie Mays higher, and statistical guru Bill James calculated that Honus Wagner, Lefty Grove, Stan Musial, and Hank Aaron all had greater career value. But in his time and for those who saw him play, Cobb stood with Ruth in a class above all others. "I know enough of fame on the diamond to realize that it lasts just as long as the ability is there to win it," Cobb had said in 1916. "I shall have my day like all the rest, and whatever I have done will be forgotten. . . ."

In his final decades, Ty Cobb lived in several houses. He returned to Georgia for the last years of his life and built a home on Chenocetah Mountain, which, he said, was the "highest place between here and Key West." Fittingly.

Wherever he lived after 1941, whether in California or Nevada or Georgia, Cobb kept two mementos on his mantle. One was a reminder of his first-of-class induction into the Baseball Hall of Fame. The other was the Bette Davis trophy from Newton, the first leg in THE HAS-BEENS GOLF CHAMPIONSHIP OF NOWHERE IN PARTICULAR.

Acknowledgments

FOR MORE THAN NINE DECADES, ANY KID WHO HAS LOVED BASE-ball has come to know Ty Cobb and Babe Ruth. Their names tower over the sport even today—though to a lesser degree than when I was growing up in the early 1970s. It has been my privilege and pleasure to research and write *Ty and The Babe,* and it would not have been possible without the support of the talented Pete Wolverton, associate publisher of Thomas Dunne Books. Pete gave me my break with *The Final Season,* for which I will always be thankful, and he has edited and guided three of my four baseball books. I've enjoyed working with him again, as well as with Katie Gilligan, Joe Rinaldi, and Matt Baldacci of St. Martin's Press.

Throughout my adventure in book writing, I've been fortunate to have the support and encouragement of Philip Spitzer, the only agent with whom I've been associated. I treasure his advice, wisdom, and friendship. His assistant, Lukas Ortiz, has also been invaluable.

Many people helped this book become a reality by offering their expertise, providing assistance, or sharing memories. I am indebted to the families of Babe Ruth and Ty Cobb, particularly Julia Ruth Stevens, Linda Ruth Tosetti, Peggy Cobb Schug, and Brent Stevens. The recollections of Ernie Harwell, Elden Auker, Jimmy Lanier, Lew Matlin, Rip Collins, Sara Cochrane Bollman, Bill Glane,

Sheila Ryan, Marcia Woodley, Bud Donaldson, and the family of Spanky Joslyn also shaped this work. Likewise, fellow writers and researchers Richard Bak, Phil Bergen, Charlie Bevis, Dave Black, Stan Byrdy, William Cobb, Wesley Fricks, Bob Hector, George Maskin, Wayne McElreavy, David Michelson, Leigh Montville, and Doug Vogel illuminated aspects of the story. Daniel Black of the *Newton Tab*, George Sweda of *The Cleveland Plain Dealer*, and Zack Stanton, my oldest son, assisted with areas of research. Further, *Ty and The Babe* benefited from the knowledge and kindness of Dale Petroskey, Jim Gates, Tim Wiles, Claudette Burke, Dan Holmes, Freddie Berkowski, and Pat Kelly of the National Baseball Hall of Fame Museum and Library, Greg Schwalenberg of the Babe Ruth Museum, Candy Ross of the Ty Cobb Museum, Pat Zacharias and Vivian Baulch of the *Detroit News* library, Josie Walters-Johnson and Jan McKee of the Library of Congress, Teresa Gray of the Grantland Rice Collection at Vanderbilt University, Mark Patrick of the Ernie Harwell Collection at the Detroit Public Library, Doug Stark and Jaime Mikle of the U.S. Golf Association, Ward Clayton of the PGA Tour, Glenn Greenspan and Jill Maxwell of Augusta National, Dave Verduci, Paul Calligaro of the Grosse Ile Country Club, Claire Koester and Nancy Karmazin of the Grosse Ile Historical Society, Susan Abele of the Newton Historical Museum, Terry Jacoby of the *Grosse Ile Camera*, Susan Calegari of the Spaulding Youth Center, Leigh Webb and Colin Cabot of the Franklin Historical Society, Jeffrey Suchanek and Bill Marshall of the A. B. "Happy" Chandler Collection at the University of Kentucky, the staff at the MacDonald Public Library in New Baltimore, Michigan, the Suburban Library Cooperative of Southeast Michigan, and members of the Society for American Baseball Research.

Finally, for their inspiration and encouragement throughout the years, I thank my wife, Beth Bagley-Stanton; my sons, Zack, William, and Taylor; my father, Joe Stanton, who is my guiding light; and Mike Varney, whose rich friendship I cherish and to whom this book is dedicated.

Appendix
Ty Cobb Versus Babe Ruth: Game by Game

Ty Cobb and Babe Ruth played against each other in more than two hundred games. This appendix spotlights their hitting performances in each of those games. It includes only the games in which both men appeared. Ruth arrived in the major leagues in the summer of 1914, as Cobb was midway through his tenth season. Although Ruth pitched against Detroit on July 16 of that year, he did not face Cobb in that contest—or any other until May 1915.

1915
May 11: Detroit 5, Boston 1 at Navin Field
Ty: 3 for 3
Babe: 1 for 2
Babe surrenders a single to Ty in their first encounter. Cobb collects two singles and a walk off of Ruth, scores one run, and drives in another. Ruth doubles and knocks in Boston's only run.

July 9: Detroit 15, Boston 4 at Navin Field
Ty: 1 for 2
Babe: 0 for 0
The Tigers hammer Ruth and two other pitchers. Cobb scores three runs.

August 25: Boston 2, Detroit 1 at Navin Field
Ty: 1 for 5
Babe: 0 for 2
Ruth holds Cobb hitless over eight and two-thirds innings. The Red Sox win in the thirteenth inning.

August 26: Detroit 7, Boston 6 at Navin Field
Ty: 2 for 4
Babe: 0 for 1
Honored before the game on the tenth anniversary of his Detroit debut, Cobb gets two hits, scores twice, steals a base, and disputes a close play by grabbing umpire Silk O'Loughlin's arm after being called out on an attempted theft. Ruth fails in a pinch-hit attempt.

September 20: Boston 3, Detroit 2 at Fenway Park
Ty: 1 for 3
Babe: 1 for 3
In the final game of a wild four-game series that sees Cobb mobbed by hundreds of angry Red Sox fans, Babe Ruth extinguishes the Tigers' pennant hopes 3–2, holding Cobb to one single and a run-producing sacrifice over seven and two-thirds innings. Boston goes on to win the pennant and the world championship.

1916
May 24: Boston 4, Detroit 0 at Fenway Park
Ty: 1 for 3
Babe: 2 for 3
Ruth shuts out the Tigers, allowing Cobb one hit while getting two for himself and scoring a run.

June 9: Detroit 6, Boston 5 at Navin Field
Ty: 2 for 4
Babe: 3 for 3
Ruth scores a pair and gets his fifth career home run, his first-ever against Detroit. The Tigers rally in the final two innings.

July 20: Detroit 3, Boston 2 at Fenway Park
Ty: 3 for 6
Babe: 0 for 2
Cobb scores the winning run after Ruth throws wildly to first in the thirteenth inning, allowing Ty to advance to second on an infield hit and to come home on a single to right.

July 29, game one: Detroit 10, Boston 8 at Navin Field
Ty: 1 for 3
Babe: 0 for 0
Cobb scores twice. Ruth starts on the mound and lasts just a third of an inning.

July 29, game two: Detroit 7, Boston 3 at Navin Field
Ty: 1 for 2
Babe: 1 for 1
Ruth belts a pinch-hit triple in the eighth and scores moments later.

July 31: Boston 6, Detroit 0 at Navin Field
Ty: 1 for 4
Babe: 2 for 4
Ruth holds the Tigers scoreless, records two hits, holds Cobb to one, and gets Ty to end the game on a grounder.

August 1: Boston 6, Detroit 2 at Navin Field
Ty: 0 for 4
Babe: 0 for 1
Ruth appears as a pinch hitter.

August 24: Boston 3, Detroit 0 at Fenway Park
Ty: 0 for 1
Babe: 1 for 2
Ruth shuts out Detroit and allows three hits, none for Cobb. Babe gets a hit and scores a run.

August 25: Detroit 2, Boston 1 at Fenway Park
Ty: 1 for 4
Babe: 0 for 1
Cobb doubles.

August 26: Detroit 2, Boston 1 at Fenway Park
Ty: 2 for 4
Babe: 1 for 1
Ruth scores the only Red Sox run after a pinch-hit double in the ninth.

September 21: Boston 10, Detroit 2 at Navin Field
Ty: 0 for 4
Babe: 2 for 4
Ruth strikes out Cobb and Bobby Veach on six straight pitches, holding Ty hitless while pounding two hits, including a long triple. With both teams battling for first, the series breaks midweek attendance records in Detroit.

1917

May 11: Boston 2, Detroit 1 at Navin Field
Ty: 1 for 3
Babe: 2 for 4
Ruth wins his seventh straight game and gathers two hits to Cobb's one. He even fans Ty with a runner on third. "Ruth made Tyrus look cheap . . . ," reports *The Boston Globe*. "The Red Sox bench warmers gave Tyrus a great riding, getting just what they were after—his goat." In the ninth, Cobb daringly tries to take third on an infield out. But Ruth darts to the abandoned third base and swats Cobb with the ball, executing a rally-killing double-play.

June 6: Detroit 3, Boston 0 at Fenway Park
Ty: 2 for 5
Babe: 1 for 2
Ruth loses a pitching battle.

June 9: Detroit 1, Boston 0 at Fenway Park
Ty: 2 for 4
Babe: 0 for 0
The Tigers complete a sweep of the Red Sox. Ruth, appearing as a pinch hitter in the ninth, walks and is replaced by a runner.

July 11: Boston 1, Detroit 0 at Navin Field
Ty: 0 for 2
Babe: 2 for 3
Babe permits only one hit while collecting two of his own, including a triple, and pelting Cobb with a pitch.

August 10, game one: Boston 5, Detroit 4 at Fenway Park
Ty: 1 for 4
Babe: 1 for 3
Ruth pitches, hits a home run, and scores twice in the first game of a doubleheader.

August 11, game two: Detroit 5, Boston 0 at Fenway Park
Ty: 3 for 4
Babe: 0 for 0
Cobb leads with a double and two runs scored. Ruth pinch-hits.

August 27: Detroit 5, Boston 1 at Navin Field
Ty: 3 for 4
Babe: 1 for 4
Cobb drives in two. Ruth pitches and gets a double. "It seems to be impossible to classify this Ruth," comments *The Detroit News*. "He's hired to pitch, he prefers to hit, and he's developed into a great fielder."

September 19, game one: Detroit 5, Boston 2 at Fenway Park
Ty: 2 for 4
Babe: 0 for 0
Ruth pinch-hits; Cobb scores twice.

September 20: Detroit 1, Boston 0 at Fenway Park
Ty: 1 for 4
Ruth: 0 for 3
Babe loses a pitcher's duel.

1918
May 15: Boston 5, Detroit 4 at Fenway Park
Ty: 0 for 4
Babe: 1 for 3
Cobb has an off day, coming to the plate three times with runners in scoring position and failing to drive in any of them. Ruth pitches and gets a double. The Sox win in the ninth.

Appendix

May 16: Boston 7, Detroit 2 at Fenway Park
Ty: 2 for 4
Babe: 1 for 3
Each contributes a run.

May 17: Boston 11, Detroit 8 at Fenway Park
Ty: 2 for 3
Babe: 0 for 5
Ruth struggles, striking out with the bases loaded. Cobb robs him of a hit on a fine defensive play.

May 18: Boston 3, Detroit 1 at Fenway Park
Ty: 0 for 3
Babe: 1 for 4
Ruth doubles off the wall in center as Boston sweeps the series.

June 1: Detroit 4, Boston 3 at Navin Field
Ty: 0 for 0
Babe 0 for 1
The Tigers prevail in thirteen innings. Both men get into the game as pinch hitters. Cobb walks and, thus, the box score shows no official at bat.

June 3: Boston 5, Detroit 0 at Navin Field
Ty: 0 for 1
Babe: 1 for 5
Ruth homers in his second straight game as Dutch Leonard no-hits the Tigers. Cobb, who has been injured, pinch-hits.

June 4: Boston 7, Detroit 6 at Navin Field
Ty: 1 for 1
Babe: 1 for 3
Ruth homers yet again. It marks his first three-home-run series. Five of his fifteen career home runs have come against the Tigers. Cobb gets a pinch-hit single and scores.

July 20: Boston 5, Detroit 1 at Fenway Park
Ty: 1 for 4
Babe: 0 for 3
Ruth slams into the wall in left field, stealing a hit from Cobb.

July 22, game one: Boston 1, Detroit 0 at Fenway Park
Ty: 1 for 4
Babe: 0 for 3
Joe Bush three-hits the Tigers.

July 22, game two: Boston 3, Detroit 0 at Fenway Park
Ty: 2 for 4
Babe: 0 for 4
Carl Mays four-hits the Tigers.

August 6: Boston 7, Detroit 5 at Navin Field
Ty: 2 for 5
Babe: 2 for 4
Both men score.

August 7: Detroit 11, Boston 8 at Navin Field
Ty: 3 for 4
Babe: 2 for 4
Cobb scores four times.

August 8: Boston 4, Detroit 1 at Navin Field
Ty: 2 for 3
Babe: 1 for 4
Ruth pitches for the win.

1919
May 21: Detroit 6, Boston 5 at Navin Field
Ty: 2 for 5
Babe: 0 for 3
Cobb triples and Ruth scores a run.

May 24: Detroit 5, Boston 3 at Navin Field
Ty: 2 for 4
Babe: 0 for 1
Cobb scores twice as the Tigers sweep Boston.

June 5: Boston 2, Detroit 1 at Fenway Park
Ty: 1 for 4
Babe: 1 for 1
Ruth, the starting pitcher, hurts his knee stumbling back to third while on the bases. Cobb produces a run-scoring triple.

June 7: Detroit 10, Boston 5 at Fenway Park
Ty: 2 for 4
Babe: 1 for 3
Ruth homers. Cobb triples, steals a base, executes a sacrifice, and scores twice.

July 20: Boston 8, Detroit 0 at Navin Field
Ty: 2 for 3
Babe: 0 for 5

July 21: Detroit 6, Boston 2 at Navin Field
Ty: 3 for 4
Babe: 2 for 4
Ruth, pitching and batting fourth, homers in the ninth—to that point, the longest ball hit out of the Detroit park.

July 22: Detroit 2, Boston 1 at Navin Field
Ty: 2 for 3
Babe: 0 for 4
Cobb leads the Tigers, driving in the first run and scoring the second.

July 23: Boston 8, Detroit 1 at Navin Field
Ty: 1 for 4
Babe: 1 for 5

July 29: Detroit 10, Boston 8 at Fenway Park
Ty: 1 for 5
Babe: 3 for 5
Despite Ruth's brilliant offense—two doubles, a two-run homer, and three runs scored—the Tigers defeat the Red Sox.

July 30, game one: Detroit 3, Boston 1 at Fenway Park
Ty: 0 for 3
Babe: 0 for 2

July 30, game two: Boston 3, Detroit 2 at Fenway Park
Ty: 4 for 4
Babe: 0 for 4
Ruth starts at first but takes the mound in the eighth, fanning three but not Cobb, who gets a double.

July 31: Boston 2, Detroit 1 at Fenway Park
Ty: 1 for 5
Babe: 4 for 6
The game ends in controversy when Detroit catcher Ed Ainsmith gets called for interfering with a Boston runner in the twelfth inning. Ruth leads with four hits, including two doubles and a game-winning single.

August 23: Detroit 8, Boston 4 at Navin Field
Ty: 0 for 4
Babe: 1 for 4
Ruth hits a grand slam in the third but Cobb rallies the Tigers in their half by starting a triple steal and scoring the first in a six-run barrage.

August 24: Boston 8, Detroit 7 at Navin Field
Ty: 1 for 5
Babe: 3 for 5
Ruth homers twice in an eleven-inning victory.

August 25: Boston 5, Detroit 4 at Navin Field
Ty: 3 for 5
Babe: 2 for 4
Ruth homers again. It marks his first four-home-run series. He also singles in the winning run. The Tigers' ninth-inning rally falls short by one run as Cobb gets tagged at home plate trying to stretch a triple into an inside-the-park home run.

September 17, game one: Detroit 7, Boston 6 at Fenway Park
Ty: 2 for 3
Babe: 1 for 3
The Tigers rally for four in the ninth.

September 17, game two: Boston 2, Detroit 1 at Fenway Park
Ty: 0 for 3
Babe: 0 for 2
Umpire George Moriarty tosses Cobb and manager Hughie Jennings for arguing a called ball that loads the bases in Boston's two-run sixth.

September 18: Detroit 8, Boston 2 at Fenway Park
Ty: 2 for 5
Babe: 1 for 3
Cobb belts a triple and scores twice.

1920

May 24: Detroit 3, New York 1 at Polo Grounds
Ty: 1 for 4
Babe: 2 for 3
Ty and Babe—"the supermen of baseball," according to *The New York Times*—face each other for the first time in New York. Ruth outshines Cobb with a single and a triple, but Cobb's team wins, with Ty contributing a single, a run, and sparkling defensive play.

May 25: New York 4, Detroit 3 at Polo Grounds
Ty: 0 for 4
Babe: 1 for 3
Ruth knocks a two-run homer in the first inning.

May 26: New York 4, Detroit 1 at Polo Grounds
Ty: 0 for 4
Babe: 2 for 3
Ruth homers again.

July 8: Detroit 4, New York 3 at Polo Grounds
Ty: 1 for 1
Babe: 1 for 4
Hampered by a knee injury, Cobb makes his first appearance in a month, driving in the go-ahead run on a pinch-hit single in the ninth inning. Cobb fakes a double steal, allowing Harry Heilmann to score the Tigers' fourth run. The Yankees get one in the ninth but it's not enough. Ruth's triple extends his hitting streak to twenty-two games.

July 10: New York 7, Detroit 6 at Polo Grounds
Ty: 2 for 4
Babe: 2 for 4

Cobb singles in the tying run in the ninth. Ruth contributes a home run and a double and steals third base. The day prior, with Cobb sidelined, Ruth hits a home run and scores three times.

July 11: New York 6, Detroit 5 at Polo Grounds
Ty: 2 for 4
Babe: 1 for 1

Ruth homers—his third of the series—and walks three times. Cobb homers, too.

August 5: Detroit 7, New York 1 at Navin Field
Ty: 3 for 5
Babe: 1 for 2

Ruth homers. Cobb doubles, singles twice, scores once, and knocks in two runners.

August 6: New York 11, Detroit 7 at Navin Field
Ty: 1 for 5
Babe: 2 for 4

Ruth blasts two homers, bats in four runs, and scores three.

August 7: New York 7, Detroit 3 at Navin Field
Ty: 3 for 5
Babe: 1 for 4

Ruth doubles and scores two runs. Cobb singles twice and scores once. Even the Detroit papers are saying that Ruth has dethroned Cobb as baseball's biggest name.

August 8: Detroit 1, New York 0 at Navin Field
Ty: 2 for 3
Babe: 0 for 3

The largest crowd of the season turns out to see Ruth, who grounds out three times and gets caught stealing after a walk. The spotlight belongs to Cobb, who singles and doubles and scores the game's lone run on a wild pitch.

August 21: Detroit 10, New York 3 at Polo Grounds
Ty: 1 for 4
Babe: 0 for 3
A rowdy crowd of thirty thousand hassles Cobb for comments attributed to him in newspapers—comments he denies making—saying that pitcher Carl Mays should be banned from baseball after killing Ray Chapman with a pitch. After his rocky reception, Cobb bows to the stands and gestures grandly toward the press box, blaming reporters for the reception. During the game, Ruth circles all the bases thinking he has hit a home run, only to be called back on a foul ball.

August 22: Detroit 11, New York 9 at Polo Grounds
Ty: 5 for 6
Babe: 0 for 3
Cobb leads the Tigers. When he takes third on a close play and is called safe by umpire Dick Nallin, New York fans hurl bottles onto the field in protest.

August 23: New York 10, Detroit 0 at Polo Grounds
Ty: 2 for 3
Babe: 1 for 2
Ruth doubles and scores three times as Carl Mays gets the victory in his first game back since hitting and killing Ray Chapman. Ruth plays strong defense, throwing out Cobb and others trying to stretch hits.

August 24: Detroit 5, New York 3 at Polo Grounds
Ty: 0 for 3
Babe: 1 for 4
Ruth singles and drives in a run; Cobb scores on a walk.

September 12: New York 13, Detroit 6 at Navin Field
Ty: 3 for 5
Babe: 0 for 2

September 13: New York 4, Detroit 2 at Navin Field
Ty: 1 for 3
Babe: 1 for 3
Ruth's two-run clout gives the Yankees the lead.

September 14: New York 13, Detroit 3 at Navin Field
Ty: 1 for 5
Babe: 0 for 2
Ruth scores twice after walks, tying Cobb's American League record of 147 runs in a season.

1921

May 10: New York 2, Detroit 1 at Navin Field
Ty: 0 for 4
Babe: 1 for 4
Ruth's opening-inning home run, with Roger Peckinpaugh on base, provides the Yankees all the runs they need to defeat the Cobb-managed Tigers.

May 11: Detroit 2, New York 1 at Navin Field
Ty: 1 for 4
Babe: 2 for 4
Cobb robs Bob Meusel of a home run on a leaping catch, throws out Ruth trying to stretch a single, and then engineers a fake steal that allows Donie Bush to score the winning run. Ruth gets nailed attempting to steal home. "HEAD WORK OF COBB DOES IN YANKEES," says the headline in *The Washington Post*.

May 12: New York 11, Detroit 10 at Navin Field
Ty: 1 for 3
Babe: 3 for 5
Cobb doubles and scores two runs, but Ruth triumphs with a home run and a triple, driving in the tying run and scoring the winning one in the ninth. Ruth predicts he will hit sixty home runs.

May 13: New York 6, Detroit 4 at Navin Field
Ty: 2 for 4
Babe: 1 for 2
Cobb doubles and triples and scores twice, but the Yankees prevail.

June 11: New York 7, Detroit 6 at Polo Grounds
Ty: 3 for 3
Babe: 1 for 2
Ruth erases Cobb's fine performance (two doubles, a single, two runs) with a game-tying three-run homer in the seventh.

June 12: New York 12, Detroit 8 at Polo Grounds
Ty: 2 for 5
Babe: 3 for 4
Before the game, Ruth snubs Cobb by refusing a photographer's request that the
two stars have a picture taken together. Throughout the game, they trade taunts until
they nearly come to blows after Ty needles Ruth following a strikeout. Ruth tallies
two doubles and a home run, his nineteenth. Reports the *Detroit Free Press*, "This
was one of the wildest games ever staged here and kept a crowd of nearly thirty-two
thousand all stirred up." *The New York Herald* agreed: "Fight was in the air all day."

June 13: New York 13, Detroit 8 at Polo Grounds
Ty: 1 for 5
Babe: 2 for 3
Ruth asks Miller Huggins to let him pitch and gets revenge against Cobb. After
walking Cobb and getting him to fly to center, Ruth strikes out Ty to the delight of
the crowd. He also launches two home runs, one estimated at more than 450 feet.

June 14: New York 9, Detroit 6 at Polo Grounds
Ty: 1 for 5
Babe: 2 for 3
Ruth crushes two more home runs, giving him six in the series against Detroit. Cobb
hits one, too.

July 16: New York 5, Detroit 4 at Navin Field
Ty: 1 for 1
Babe: 0 for 5
Cobb pinch-hits and scores a run.

July 17: New York 8, Detroit 5 at Navin Field
Ty: 0 for 1
Babe: 0 for 3

July 18: New York 10, Detroit 1 at Navin Field
Ty: 0 for 1
Babe: 1 for 2
Ruth, after being walked four times, pounds a ball an estimated 560 feet in the
eighth.

July 19: New York 6, Detroit 5 at Navin Field
Ty: 0 for 1
Babe: 1 for 5
Ruth doubles in the seventh and scores the winning run after catcher Ed Ainsmith throws wildly while trying to pick him off a base.

August 4: Detroit 8, New York 3 at Polo Grounds
Ty: 2 for 3
Babe: 2 for 3
Cobb records a triple and a home run while scoring three times. Ruth doubles twice and scores twice.

August 5: New York 7, Detroit 3 at Polo Grounds
Ty: 0 for 4
Babe: 1 for 3
Ruth scores after a three-base error.

August 6: Detroit 9, New York 8 at Polo Grounds
Ty: 1 for 4
Babe: 1 for 3
Ruth collects his thirty-ninth home run but costs the Yankees the game by dropping a shallow fly in left field, allowing the winning run. Cobb contributes a triple and a run.

August 26: New York 10, Detroit 2 at Navin Field
Ty: 1 for 4
Babe: 0 for 4
Cobb homers and scores both Tiger runs.

August 27: New York 7, Detroit 5 at Navin Field
Ty: 2 for 3
Babe: 1 for 3
Ruth and Cobb each score a run.

August 28: Detroit 7, New York 3 at Navin Field
Ty: 2 for 4
Babe: 3 for 5
The Detroit win allows Cleveland to lengthen its lead over the Yankees. Ruth knocks three doubles; Cobb singles twice, takes a pitch to the head, and scores two times.

September 18: New York 4, Detroit 2 at Polo Grounds
Ty: 1 for 4
Babe: 2 for 4
Nearly thirty-six thousand watch New York reclaim first place.

September 19: Detroit 10, New York 6 at Polo Grounds
Ty: 3 for 6
Babe: 0 for 5
Cobb and the Tigers knock the Yankees out of first again. Cobb plays a big role with a bases-loaded single in an eight-run eighth inning.

September 20: New York 4, Detroit 2 at Polo Grounds
Ty: 1 for 3
Babe: 1 for 4
Ruth contributes a key single to a three-run fourth inning, putting the Yankees back in first.

September 22: New York 12, Detroit 5 at Polo Grounds
Ty: 0 for 5
Babe: 0 for 5
Ruth and Cobb conclude their bitter 1921 face-offs by going hitless.

1922
June 14: Detroit 6, New York 2 at Navin Field
Ty: 2 for 4
Babe: 1 for 3
Visiting Detroit for the first time since returning from suspension, Babe Ruth gets booed by Tiger fans. He singles and scores once. Cobb scores and contributes a run-producing double.

June 15: Detroit 2, New York 1 at Navin Field
Ty: 1 for 3
Babe: 0 for 2

The Tigers knock the Yankees out of first. Ruth scores New York's only run after walking. Cobb begins the key eighth-inning Detroit rally, leading off with a hit and scoring the tying run.

June 16: Detroit 9, New York 4 at Navin Field
Ty: 1 for 5
Babe: 1 for 3

Ruth and Cobb try to antagonize each other throughout the contest by waving theatrically at one another. Cobb scores after a bunt single.

June 17: Detroit 9, New York 8 at Navin Field
Ty: 2 for 5
Babe: 0 for 4

A crowd of twenty-five thousand—the largest ever on a Saturday at Navin Field—watches Detroit sweep the Yankees. Fans jam into foul territory and into the outfield, separated from the action by ropes. Ground rules are established mandating that a ball hit into the crowd in the air will be a triple. Nine triples are recorded, two by Cobb. The home rule sparks a major dispute in the seventh when Aaron Ward drives a long ball into center. Cobb drifts back to the rope barrier. With the ball still in the air, fans open a path for Cobb who steps into the mob and catches the fly. Ward is called out. Led by Babe Ruth—who was hit by a pitch earlier in the game—the Yankees argue the call. The Tigers convince the umpire that fans have been encroaching further and further into the playing area. Manager Miller Huggins protests the game. Ruth continues to struggle against Detroit, getting four infield outs in the game and only two singles in the series.

July 19: Detroit 5, New York 1 at Polo Grounds
Ty: 2 for 4
Babe: 1 for 5

Cobb scores the first run. Ruth strikes out twice and begins—uncommon for him—choking up on the bat when the count reaches two strikes.

July 20: New York 5, Detroit 1 at Polo Grounds
Ty: 1 for 2
Babe: 1 for 3
Ruth scores twice.

July 21: New York 7, Detroit 5 at Polo Grounds
Ty: 2 for 4
Babe: 1 for 4
Cobb belts a three-run homer and a double. Ruth continues to press. In four at-bats, he sees just nine pitches.

July 22: Detroit 2, New York 0 at Polo Grounds
Ty: 2 for 5
Babe: 0 for 3
In the ninth inning, with their team down and Ruth hitless—in twenty-seven at-bats against the Tigers this season he has but five singles—New York fans urge Miller Huggins to send a pinch hitter up for Ruth. "Who's going to bat for Ruth?" fans yell.

August 6: New York 11, Detroit 6 at Navin Field
Ty: 1 for 4
Babe: 3 for 6
Thirty thousand people—the largest crowd ever at Navin Field—turn out to see Ruth and the Yankees. Police officers lock the gates, repelling thousands of fans who will mill around the stadium, leaving them to watch from trees and telegraph lines. Ruth hits a home run and a double and scores three times. Cobb, in a race with George Sisler for the batting title, gets a double and is robbed of two hits on fine defensive plays.

August 7: New York 4, Detroit 3 at Navin Field
Ty: 0 for 3
Babe: 4 for 5
Cobb tries to turn back a streaking Ruth by starting rookie star Herman Pillette in a second straight game. Ruth gets two doubles.

August 8: Detroit 2, New York 1 at Navin Field
Ty: 2 for 4
Babe: 1 for 3
A big gust blows one of Ruth's long high drives out of the stands and into Cobb's glove for an out.

August 9: New York 8, Detroit 3 at Navin Field
Ty: 2 for 4
Babe: 1 for 5
Ruth cracks a home run after being deprived earlier when Cobb makes what long-time baseball writer Harry Salsinger describes as one of the greatest catches ever at Navin Field. Cobb climbs over collapsed bleachers and leaps at the fence to deny Ruth a four-bagger in the first inning.

August 16: Detroit 7, New York 3 at Polo Grounds
Ty: 0 for 4
Babe: 2 for 4
Ruth gets a double and a home run, but Detroit rallies for four in the ninth. Cobb's main contribution is a lengthy argument with Carl Mays, whom he accuses of trying to hit him.

August 17: New York 7, Detroit 1 at Polo Grounds
Ty: 0 for 4
Babe: 2 for 3
Ruth shows his versatility by dropping a bunt single in the seventh when Cobb and the rest of the Tigers play him deep.

September 19: New York 4, Detroit 3 at Navin Field
Ty: 0 for 3
Babe: 2 for 3
Ruth records a home run and a triple, getting thrown out at the plate on the latter while foolishly trying to stretch it into a round tripper.

September 20: New York 6, Detroit 5 at Navin Field
Ty: 1 for 3
Babe: 1 for 4
Cobb's strategy backfires when he has Ruth walked to load the bases and Wally Pipp follows with a three-run triple.

September 21: New York 9, Detroit 8 at Navin Field
Ty: 3 for 4
Babe: 2 for 4
Cobb scores three times; Ruth gets a double and his thirty-fifth home run.

1923

May 12: New York 3, Detroit 2 at Navin Field

Ty: 2 for 4

Babe: 1 for 4

Despite being greeted by a chorus of boos, Ruth leads New York with a home run at the newly expanded Navin Field.

May 13: Detroit 4, New York 1 at Navin Field

Ty: 1 for 4

Babe: 0 for 4

The attendance record falls in Detroit with 40,884 paying customers flowing through the turnstiles at Navin Field. It takes police fifteen minutes to herd the crowd into the overflow area of the outfield.

May 14: New York 16, Detroit 11 at Navin Field

Ty: 2 for 6

Babe: 1 for 6

Ruth doubles off the wall, just missing a home run, and robs Cobb of a triple in the game's best defensive play.

May 15: New York 9, Detroit 5 at Navin Field

Ty: 1 for 4

Babe: 3 for 4

Ruth homers and triples and alertly throws out Cobb at third base.

June 17: New York 9, Detroit 0 at Yankee Stadium

Ty: 0 for 4

Babe: 3 for 5

Ruth homers and scores twice before fifty-two thousand fans in the inaugural season of Yankee Stadium. Cobb fails to get the ball out of the infield.

June 18: Detroit 11, New York 3 at Yankee Stadium

Ty: 2 for 5

Babe: 1 for 4

Cobb gets a double and a fluke home run on a ball that takes a single bounce over the outfield fence untouched. One of Ty's scorching foul balls results in a fan being removed from the stands after being struck "in a vital spot," according to a newspaper report.

June 19: New York 6, Detroit 5 at Yankee Stadium
Ty: 2 for 5
Babe: 1 for 3
The Tigers rally in the ninth but fall short. Cobb scores the final run by plowing into catcher Fred Hoffmann and jarring the ball loose.

June 20: Detroit 9, New York 7 at Yankee Stadium
Ty: 3 for 5
Babe: 0 for 2
Cobb scores twice. "Ty is still the greatest of them all," says *The New York Times.*

July 21: New York 3, Detroit 2 at Navin Field
Ty: 0 for 0
Babe: 1 for 4
Suffering from a sore shoulder, Cobb appears in only one game in the New York series—as a pinch runner. And he scores.

August 9: Detroit 11, New York 3 at Yankee Stadium
Ty: 3 for 5
Babe: 1 for 2
Cobb leads with three singles, two runs, and three RBIs. Ruth walks three times and scores once.

August 11, game one: New York 10, Detroit 4 at Yankee Stadium
Ty: 0 for 5
Babe: 2 for 3
An estimated fifty-seven thousand fans turn out for the doubleheader.

August 11, game two: New York 9, Detroit 8 at Yankee Stadium
Ty: 2 for 4
Babe: 1 for 3
Ruth slaps his twenty-eighth home run and scores twice. Yankee fans boo Cobb for having Ruth walked in the seventh.

August 12: Detroit 5, New York 2 at Yankee Stadium
Ty: 1 for 3
Babe: 3 for 4
Ruth turns in a strong game, getting a double and a home run, stealing bases, moving past Harry Heilmann in the batting race, and tying Cy Williams in the home run contest. But the Tigers win with Cobb scoring twice.

August 22: Detroit 6, New York 3 at Navin Field
Ty: 0 for 3
Babe: 2 for 3
Ruth doubles and gets caught stealing.

August 23: Detroit 2, New York 1 at Navin Field
Ty: 1 for 4
Babe: 0 for 2

August 24: New York 7, Detroit 1 at Navin Field
Ty: 3 for 5
Babe: 1 for 4

September 24: New York 12, Detroit 4 at Yankee Stadium
Ty: 0 for 3
Babe: 2 for 3
Ruth has a grand game, scoring three times, stealing a base, and getting two doubles.

September 25: Detroit 5, New York 4 at Yankee Stadium
Ty: 1 for 1
Babe: 0 for 3
Going into the eighth, with the Tigers down 3–2, Cobb pinch-hits, singles, and scores the tying run.

September 26: Detroit 8, New York 3 at Yankee Stadium
Ty: 1 for 4
Babe: 1 for 3
Tigers break a 3–3 tie with five runs in the tenth, an attack that includes a Cobb single.

1924

May 23: New York 7, Detroit 6 at Yankee Stadium
Ty: 4 for 5
Babe: 2 for 3
Cobb and Ruth score a pair of runs each. Ruth homers.

May 24: Detroit 7, New York 3 at Yankee Stadium
Ty: 1 for 4
Babe: 1 for 3
Ruth and Cobb double; Cobb scores once.

May 25: Detroit 6, New York 5 at Yankee Stadium
Ty: 1 for 5
Babe: 2 for 4
With forty-five thousand New York fans watching, Cobb pops a two-run blast to start
the Detroit scoring in the sixth. Ruth and Cobb score a pair each.

May 26: New York 8, Detroit 2 at Yankee Stadium
Ty: 0 for 3
Babe: 2 for 3
Ruth clouts a home run.

June 11: Detroit 7, New York 2 at Navin Field
Ty: 3 for 3
Babe: 1 for 2
Cobb leads the attack with two triples, a single, and three runs. "Ty had another of
those brilliant days of his that are becoming like gems in a cluster ring—close
together and very sparkling," praises Bert Walker in *The Detroit Times*. Cobb also
engages umpire Billy Evans in an argument after Ruth is called safe stealing third.

June 12: New York 10, Detroit 4 at Navin Field
Ty: 2 for 4
Babe: 2 for 2
Ruth belts his fifteenth home run with Earle Combs aboard. The next inning, Tiger
pitcher Sylvester Johnson strikes Ruth with a pitch—on orders of Cobb, Babe
suspects. Cobb drives in two on singles and gets tossed out trying to steal third.

June 13: New York 9, Detroit 0; victory by forfeit at Navin Field
Ty: 0 for 4
Babe: 0 for 2
Tension between Cobb and Ruth contributes to a Friday the 13th riot on the ball field. Bob Meusel charges the mound after being struck by a pitch. The field explodes in fights, with a clenched-fisted Ruth confronting Cobb and accusing him of directing beanballs. Fans floods onto the field and police struggle to maintain control. The league suspends Meusel and pitcher Bert Cole and fines Ruth.

June 14: New York 6, Detroit 2 at Navin Field
Ty: 1 for 4
Babe: 2 for 5
Almost forty thousand fans jam Navin Field, hoping for a replay of the previous day's violence. But mounted officers assure a peaceful afternoon. The fans fill temporary circus seats that have been erected in the outfield. Ruth collects two ground-rule doubles; Cobb gets one. The win gives the Yankees sole possession of first.

July 21: Detroit 9, New York 7 at Yankee Stadium
Ty: 0 for 5
Babe: 1 for 5
Ruth triples and makes a superb run-saving catch, but Cobb, though hitless and booed by Yankee fans, plays with zeal and sparks Detroit's seventh straight victory.

July 22: Detroit 3, New York 1 at Yankee Stadium
Ty: 1 for 4
Babe: 0 for 4
The Tigers knock the Yankees from first place.

July 23: New York 4, Detroit 3 at Yankee Stadium
Ty: 2 for 4
Babe: 2 for 5
Ruth returns the Yankees to first with a solo shot in the eleventh inning. Cobb gets the blame for the loss, getting thrown out at the plate in the sixth and picked off second in the eighth. "In the Kitty League, they would call this bush baseball," reports *The New York Times*.

July 24: Detroit 5, New York 4 at Yankee Stadium
Ty: 2 for 5
Babe: 1 for 3

Cobb scores twice, and the Tigers reclaim first when the game is called after the eighth inning to allow the Yankees to catch a 5:15 train to Indianapolis for an exhibition game.

August 3: Detroit 5, New York 2 at Navin Field
Ty: 1 for 4
Babe: 1 for 4

A record crowd of 42,712 watches Detroit move back into first. The superstitious Tigers keep a good-luck gamecock on their bench.

August 4: New York 9, Detroit 8 at Navin Field
Ty: 2 for 5
Babe: 2 for 4

Ruth belts a three-run blast and the Yankees win in the eleventh inning, regaining the top spot in the league.

August 5: New York 9, Detroit 2 at Navin Field
Ty: 1 for 4
Babe: 3 for 5

Ruth clouts his thirty-fifth home run with two runners on base.

August 6: Detroit 5, New York 2 at Navin Field
Ty: 1 for 2
Babe: 1 for 2

Ruth homers in a third straight game, but Cobb and the Tigers prevail in the rain-shortened contest.

August 22: Detroit 8, New York 6 at Yankee Stadium
Ty: 2 for 6
Babe: 1 for 5

Ruth robs Cobb of extra bases on a leaping catch but Ty contributes a two-run single to the twelfth-inning victory.

August 23: New York 8, Detroit 1 at Yankee Stadium
Ty: 2 for 4
Babe: 1 for 5
Ruth begins a six-run sixth inning with a single.

August 24: Detroit 7, New York 2 at Yankee Stadium
Ty: 1 for 4
Babe: 1 for 4
Cobb and Ruth both circle the bases, but Ty's long ball gives the Tigers the advantage. The Yankees remain in first, just ahead of Washington and Detroit.

September 19: Detroit 6, New York 5 at Navin Field
Ty: 1 for 5
Babe: 1 for 4
Cobb scores the winning run in the ninth inning, knocking the Yankees out of first place and behind Washington.

September 20: Detroit 6, New York 5 at Navin Field
Ty: 2 for 4
Babe: 0 for 3
Playing like a man possessed—stealing bases, crashing into the scoreboard—Cobb leads Detroit while getting his two hundredth hit of the season and setting a record by reaching the plateau nine times.

September 21: Detroit 4, New York 3 at Navin Field
Ty: 3 for 4
Babe: 1 for 3
More than forty thousand fans watch the Tigers sweep the Yankees and take the season series, thirteen games to nine. Cobb scores on a squeeze play and draws Lou Gehrig into an argument that gets Gehrig ejected. Ruth performs poorly in the September series, collecting only two singles. The Yankees will finish the season in second, behind Washington.

1925

June 14: New York 8, Detroit 3 at Yankee Stadium
Ty: 0 for 3
Babe: 2 for 4
Ruth homers, scores twice, and robs Cobb of a round trip with a leaping catch. *The New York Times* derides spectators for treating Cobb harshly: "Twenty years from

now the same fans will be boasting to their offspring that they saw the great Tyrus Raymond Cobb play ball."

June 16: Detroit 5, New York 3 at Yankee Stadium
Ty: 0 for 5
Babe: 2 for 3
Ruth homers again and contributes a double. Cobb commits a two-run error but his Tigers win.

June 17: Detroit 19, New York 1 at Yankee Stadium
Ty: 3 for 6
Babe: 0 for 4
Aided by wild pitching, Detroit scores thirteen times in a forty-nine-minute hitting barrage. Cobb provides the highlight: a grand slam.

June 18: Detroit 6, New York 3 at Yankee Stadium
Ty: 4 for 4
Babe: 0 for 4
Cobb puts Detroit ahead with another home run.

August 6: New York 10, Detroit 4 at Yankee Stadium
Ty: 0 for 1
Babe: 0 for 4
Ruth scores a run and Cobb, limited by a bruised hip, fails while pinch-hitting.

August 8, game one: Detroit 9, New York 3 at Yankee Stadium
Ty: 1 for 5
Babe: 1 for 3
Ruth and Cobb each score a run. In the second game, in which Ruth did not play, Cobb gets three hits and scores the winning run. The Yankees try—and fail—to catch Cobb off base. Lou Gehrig engages Cobb in conversation as pitcher Bob Shawkey, ball in hand, unsuccessfully sneaks up behind Tyrus. A day earlier, while coaching first, Cobb tries to upset Gehrig by claiming he is intentionally stepping on the feet of Tiger runners. Failing to incite Gehrig, Cobb turns to the grandstand and good naturedly tries to convince Yankee fans of Gehrig's infractions.

August 18: New York 5, Detroit 2 at Navin Field
Ty: 0 for 0
Babe: 2 for 5
After Ruth crushes an eighth-inning homer, Cobb pinch-hits and walks to load the bases.

September 26: New York 3, Detroit 1 at Yankee Stadium
Ty: 0 for 1
Babe: 1 for 4
Ruth scores; Cobb fails to convert while pinch-hitting. Cobb does not appear in the following four games against New York. But Ruth blasts three more home runs in the series—all after the Knights of Columbus present him with a chest containing fifty pieces of silver.

1926

May 7: New York 7, Detroit 6 at Yankee Stadium
Ty: 1 for 5
Babe: 1 for 3
Ruth contributes a two-run blast.

May 8: Detroit 7, New York 5 at Yankee Stadium
Ty: 1 for 3
Babe: 2 for 5
Ruth leads the Yankees with a three-run homer; Cobb provides a key two-run single and scores once.

May 9: Detroit 14, New York 10 at Yankee Stadium
Ty: 4 for 4
Babe: 0 for 3
With fifty-five thousand New York fans as witness—the biggest crowd at Yankee Stadium since 1924—Cobb puts on a memorable show, slugging two home runs and scoring three times. Teases *The New York Times*: "As soon as the young fellow gets the hand of things, they will let him play every day."

May 10: New York 13, Detroit 9 at Yankee Stadium
Ty: 1 for 4
Babe: 1 for 3
Gehrig and Ruth hit back-to-back home runs.

June 8: New York 11, Detroit 9 at Navin Field
Ty: 1 for 6
Babe: 3 for 5
Babe homers twice, with Gehrig on base both times.

June 9: New York 4, Detroit 3 at Navin Field
Ty: 0 for 0
Babe: 1 for 4
Suffering through a slump, Cobb benches himself but enters the game as a pinch runner in the ninth.

June 11: New York 9, Detroit 3 at Navin Field
Ty: 0 for 1
Babe: 1 for 3
Cobb fails in a pinch-hitting role.

August 10: Detroit 5, New York 3 at Navin Field
Ty: 1 for 1
Babe: 1 for 3
After sitting out the previous three games against New York, Cobb pinch-hits and drives in the winning runs.

September 11: New York 10, Detroit 8 at Navin Field
Ty: 0 for 1
Babe: 3 for 4
Ruth leads a ninth-inning rally with a three run home run. Cobb pinch hits in the ninth.

1927

April 12: New York 8, Philadelphia 3 at Yankee Stadium
Ty: 1 for 4
Babe: 0 for 3
The largest crowd ever to see a game—seventy-two thousand—cheers Cobb in his first game as an Athletic, providing vindication after gambling charges are dropped. Ty and Babe pose for photos together before the game.

April 13: New York 10, Philadelphia 4 at Yankee Stadium
Ty: 2 for 4
Babe: 2 for 4
A slowing Cobb stretches a single into a double but gets nailed at home on a throw by Bob Meusel. Ruth scores twice.

April 14: New York 9, Philadelphia 9 at Yankee Stadium
Ty: 1 for 4
Babe: 1 for 3
Both Cobb and Ruth score two runs apiece before the three-hour game is called for darkness after ten innings.

April 15: New York 6, Philadelphia 3 at Yankee Stadium
Ty: 1 for 4
Babe: 2 for 4
Babe slugs a solo homer, scores two runs, and gets a standing ovation after throwing out Al Simmons at the plate.

April 20: Philadelphia 8, New York 5 at Shibe Park
Ty: 0 for 3
Babe: 0 for 4

April 21: New York 13, Philadelphia 6 at Shibe Park
Ty: 2 for 5
Babe: 1 for 2
Ruth walks four times, gets a bunt single, and scores twice. He has only one RBI in the young season. Teammate Lou Gehrig has nineteen.

April 23: Philadelphia 4, New York 3 at Shibe Park
Ty: 2 for 4
Babe: 1 for 5
Ruth homers; Cobb triples and scores two times.

May 1: New York 7, Philadelphia 3 at Yankee Stadium
Ty: 2 for 4
Babe: 2 for 4
Babe homers twice.

May 30, game one: Philadelphia 9, New York 8 at Shibe Park
Ty: 0 for 2
Babe: 2 for 5
Cobb tallies three runs.

May 30, game two: New York 6, Philadelphia 5 at Shibe Park
Ty: 1 for 4
Babe: 2 for 4
Ruth scores three times and wins the game with an eleventh-inning home run.

May 31, game one: New York 10, Philadelphia 3 at Shibe Park
Ty: 0 for 3
Babe: 1 for 4
Ruth homers.

May 31, game two: New York 18, Philadelphia 5 at Shibe Park
Ty: 3 for 4
Babe: 3 for 6
Babe homers again. Cobb and Ruth each score a pair of runs.

September 2: New York 12, Philadelphia 2 at Shibe Park
Ty: 1 for 3
Babe: 1 for 3
Ruth gets his forty-fourth home run; Gehrig gets numbers forty-two and forty-three.

September 3: Philadelphia 1, New York 0 at Shibe Park
Ty: 0 for 4
Babe: 2 for 4
Lefty Grove holds the Yankees to four hits, two by Ruth.

1928
April 11: New York 8, Philadelphia 3 at Shibe Park
Ty: 1 for 2
Babe: 1 for 3
Cobb and Tris Speaker are honored before the game with free radios. Ruth scores three runs.

April 13: New York 8, Philadelphia 7 at Shibe Park
Ty: 2 for 5
Babe: 1 for 4
Cobb drives in two runs.

April 20: Philadelphia 2, New York 1 at Yankee Stadium
Ty: 2 for 4
Babe: 0 for 4
Cobb scores the winning run in the ninth after leading off with a triple, spoiling the Yankees' home opener.

April 21: Philadelphia 10, New York 0 at Yankee Stadium
Ty: 3 for 6
Babe: 0 for 4

May 24, game one: New York 9, Philadelphia 7 at Shibe Park
Ty: 3 for 6
Babe: 1 for 4
Despite an otherwise fine performance before forty-five thousand spectators, Cobb ends the game on a blazing drive back to pitcher Waite Hoyt, stranding two runners in the ninth.

May 24, game two: Philadelphia 5, New York 2 at Shibe Park
Ty: 0 for 4
Babe: 2 for 3
Ruth contributes a double and a home run.

May 25, game one: New York 4, Philadelphia 2 at Shibe Park
Ty: 1 for 4
Babe: 0 for 2

May 25, game two: New York 9, Philadelphia 2 at Shibe Park
Ty: 1 for 3
Babe: 3 for 5
Ruth leads the attack with two home runs, a double, two runs scored, and four RBIs.

May 26: New York 7, Philadelphia 4 at Shibe Park
Ty: 0 for 3
Babe: 1 for 3
Cobb scores after getting a walk; Ruth drives in two.

May 28: New York 11, Philadelphia 4 at Shibe Park
Ty: 1 for 5
Babe: 2 for 2
Ruth brings in three.

June 20, game one: Philadelphia 10, New York 5 at Yankee Stadium
Ty: 3 for 4
Babe: 1 for 3

June 20, game two: New York 9, Philadelphia 3 at Yankee Stadium
Ty: 1 for 2
Babe: 2 for 5
Though Cobb continues to contribute at the plate, he is showing signs of his age in the field. In this game, he falls facefirst in the outfield chasing a drive. In May, he dropped a fly ball. In July, he will launch a wild throw to home plate.

June 21: New York 4, Philadelphia 0 at Yankee Stadium
Ty: 1 for 3
Babe: 1 for 4
A second game follows but gets canceled—voiding Cobb's two doubles and Ruth's home run.

June 27: New York 7, Philadelphia 4 at Shibe Park
Ty: 0 for 2
Babe: 1 for 3
Ruth helps fuel a four-run rally in the eighth, driving in a run.

June 28: New York 10, Philadelphia 4 at Shibe Park
Ty: 1 for 5
Babe: 3 for 5
Babe homers twice, drives in three, and scores three.

June 29: Philadelphia 6, New York 4 at Shibe Park
Ty: 3 for 5
Babe: 1 for 3
Cobb contributes three singles to successful Philadelphia rallies.

July 1, game one: New York 12, Philadelphia 6 at Yankee Stadium
Ty: 1 for 4
Babe: 1 for 3
With sixty thousand fans watching, New York pummels the Athletics. Cobb gets a double and scores a run; Ruth drives in two. But Lou Gehrig, with five RBIs and two home runs, propels the Yankee offense.

July 1, game two: New York 8, Philadelphia 4 at Yankee Stadium
Ty: 1 for 5
Babe: 0 for 3

September 11: New York 5, Philadelphia 3 at Yankee Stadium
Ty: 0 for 1
Babe: 1 for 3
In his last major-league at bat, coming before sixty thousand fans just moments after Ruth belts a tie-breaking home run, Cobb pinch-hits in the ninth and unceremoniously pops out to the shortstop.

Bibliography

NEWSPAPERS

Atlanta: *Journal.*
Augusta: *Chronicle.*
Boston: *Evening Transcript, Globe, Herald, Post.*
Chicago: *Daily News, Herald-American, Tribune.*
Cleveland: *Plain Dealer, Press.*
Detroit: *Free Press, Journal, News, Saturday Night, Times.*
Los Angeles: *Times.*
New York: *Brooklyn Eagle, Daily News, Evening Journal, Herald, Herald-Tribune, Journal American, Mirror, Morning Telegraph, Post, Sun, Times, Tribune, World, World-Telegram.*
Philadelphia: *Inquirer.*
St. Louis: *Globe-Democrat, Post-Dispatch.*
Washington: *Post.*

OTHER PERIODICALS

Numerous articles in *The Sporting News* proved beneficial, as did pieces in *Baseball Magazine, Collier's, Life, Literary Digest, Sporting Life,* and other periodicals. The most helpful are noted here:

"Babe Ruth Is Supernormal," *Literary Digest,* October 1, 1921.

Beasley, Norman. "Ty Cobb's Opinion of Babe Ruth," *Physical Culture,* October 1920.

Bisher, Furman. "A Visit with Ty Cobb," *Saturday Evening Post,* June 14, 1958.

Cobb, Ty. "The Baseball Riddle," *American Legion Monthly,* April 1931.

———. "They Don't Play Baseball Any More," *Life,* March 17, 1952.

———. "Tricks That Won Me Ball Games," *Life,* March 24, 1952.

Cravath, Cactus. "What the Batting Records Have Cost Me," *Baseball Magazine,* July 1918.

Lane, F. C. "A Day with Cobb," *Baseball Magazine,* April 1916.

———. "The Season's Sensation," *Baseball Magazine,* October 1918.

———. "Secret of My Heavy Hitting," *Baseball Magazine,* August 1921.

Lieb, Frederick. "Ruth Originator of the Big Inning," *The Sporting News,* July 12, 1950.

———. "Meet the American Idol," *Independent and Weekly Review,* August 14, 1920.

Reynolds, Quentin. "Ty Cobb's Dream Team," *Collier's,* June 17, 1939.

Rice, Grantland. "The Durable Cobb," *Collier's,* April 3, 1926.

———. "The Winner's Way," *Collier's,* July 10, 1926.

Robinson, Arthur. "My Friend Babe Ruth," *Collier's,* September 20, 1924.

"Ruth Supernatural," *Literary Digest,* July 25, 1925.

Salsinger, H. G. "Cobb or Ruth—Which Was Tops?" *The Sporting News,* May 24, 1950.

"Spanking Baseball's Baby and Petting Its Paragon," *Literary Digest,* September 19, 1925.

Stoddart, Dayton. "What Baseball Has Taught Ty Cobb," *Collier's,* July 19, 1924.

"Ty Cobb Remains King of All Batsmen," *Literary Digest,* January 17, 1920.

WEB SITES

I referred to these Web sites more than a handful of times: www.baseballlibrary.com, www.retrosheet.org, www.baseball-reference.com, www.sabr.org, and www.baseball-guru.com (Bill Burgess's Ty Cobb postings).

BOOKS

Alexander, Charles. *Ty Cobb* (Oxford: Oxford University, 1984).

Bak, Richard. *Cobb Would Have Caught It* (Detroit: Wayne State University, 1991).

———. *Peach: Ty Cobb in His Times and Ours* (Ann Arbor: Sports Media Group, 2005).

The Barry Halper Collection of Baseball Memorabilia (New York: Sotheby's, 1999).

Beim, George, with Julia Ruth Stevens. *Babe Ruth: A Daughter's Portrait* (Dallas: Taylor, 1998).

Bevis, Charlie. *Mickey Cochrane* (Jefferson: McFarland, 1998).

Bingay, Malcolm. *Detroit Is My Own Home Town* (New York: Bobbs-Merrill, 1946).

Byrdy, Stan. *Augusta and Aiken in Golf's Golden Age* (Charleston: Arcadia, 2002).

Cobb, Ty. *Busting 'Em* (New York: Edward J. Clode, 1914).

———, edited by William R. Cobb. *Memories of Twenty Years in Baseball* (Marietta: William R. Cobb, 2002).

———, with Al Stump. *My Life in Baseball* (New York: Doubleday, 1961).

Connor, Anthony. *Voices from Cooperstown* (New York: Collier, 1982).

Corcoran, Fred, with Bud Harvey. *Unplayable Lies* (New York: Duell, Sloan and Pearce, 1965).

Cramer, Richard Ben. *DiMaggio: The Hero's Life* (New York: Simon & Schuster, 2000).

Creamer, Robert. *Babe: The Legend Comes to Life* (New York: Simon & Schuster, 1974).

———. *Baseball in '41* (New York: Viking, 1991).

DiMaggio, Joe. *Lucky to Be a Yankee* (New York: Rudolph Field, 1946).

Eig, Jonathan. *Luckiest Man: The Life and Death of Lou Gehrig* (New York: Simon & Schuster, 2005).

Fleitz, David. *Shoeless: The Life and Times of Joe Jackson* (Jefferson: McFarland, 2001).

Fleming, G. H. *Murderer's Row: The 1927 New York Yankees* (New York: Morrow, 1985).

Fountain, Charles. *Sportswriter: The Life and Times of Grantland Rice* (Oxford: Oxford, 1993).

Frost, Mark. *The Greatest Game Ever Played* (New York: Hyperion, 2002).

Gallico, Paul. *The Golden People* (New York: Doubleday, 1965).

Gay, Timothy. *Tris Speaker* (Lincoln: University of Nebraska, 2005).

Gershman, Michael. *Diamonds: The Evolution of the Ballpark* (Boston: Houghton Mifflin, 1993).

Graham, Frank. *A Farewell to Heroes* (New York: Viking, 1983).

Greenberg, Hank, with Ira Berkow. *Hank Greenberg:The Story of My Life* (Chicago:Triumph, 1989).

Hagen Walter, as told to Margaret Seaton Hick. *The Walter Hagen Story* (New York: Simon & Schuster, 1956).

Harwell, Ernie. *The Babe Signed My Shoe* (South Bend: Diamond, 1994).

Holmes, Dan. *Ty Cobb: A Biography* (Westport: Greenwood, 2004).

Holtzman, Jerome. *No Cheering in the Press Box* (New York: Holt, Rinehard & Winston, 1974).

Holway, John. *The Last 400 Hitter* (Dubuque:William C. Brown, 1992).

Hoyt, Waite. *Babe Ruth As I Knew Him* (New York: Dell, 1948).

Kaufman, Louis, Barbara Fitzgerald, and Tom Sewell. *Moe Berg* (Boston: Little Brown, 1974).

Kelley, Brent. *In the Shadow of the Babe* (Jefferson: McFarland, 1995).

Lane, F. C. *Batting* (Cleveland: Society for American Baseball Research, 2001).

Lieb, Fred. *Baseball As I Have Known It* (New York: Grosset & Dunlap, 1977).

Lowe, Stephen. *Sir Walter and Mr. Jones* (Chelsea: Sleeping Bear, 2000).

McCallum, John. *Ty Cobb* (New York: Praeger, 1975).

Meany, Tom. *Babe Ruth* (New York: A. S. Barnes, 1947).

Montville, Leigh. *The Big Bam* (New York: Doubleday, 2006).

Mosedale, John. *The Greatest of All:The 1927 Yankees* (New York:Warner, 1975).

Pirrone, Dorothy Ruth, with Chris Martens. *My Dad, the Babe* (Boston: Quinlan Press, 1988).

Reisler, Jim. *Babe Ruth: Launching the Legend* (New York: McGraw-Hill, 2004).

Rice, Grantland. *The Tumult and the Shouting* (New York: Barnes, 1954).

Ritter, Lawrence. *East Side, West Side* (New York: Total Sports, 1994).

———. *The Glory of Their Times* (New York: Quill, 1984).

Robinson, Ray. *Iron Horse: Lou Gehrig in His Times* (New York: Perennial, 1991).

Ross, Donald. *Golf Has Never Failed Me* (Chelsea: Sleeping Bear Press, 1996).

Ruth, Babe, as told to Bob Considine. *The Babe Ruth Story* (New York: Dutton, 1948).

Ruth, Claire, with Bill Slocum. *The Babe and I* (New York: Avon, 1959).

Sarazen, Gene. *Thirty Years of Championship Golf* (New York: Prentice-Hall, 1950).

Seidel, Michael. *Streak: Joe DiMaggio and the Summer of '41* (New York: McGraw-Hill, 1988).

Shore, Josselyn. *The Story of the Fresh Meadow Country Club* (New York: Country Club, 1985).

Smesler, Marshall. *The Life That Ruth Built* (Lincoln: University of Nebraska, 1975).

Smith, Ken. *Baseball's Hall of Fame* (New York: Grosset and Dunlap, 1952).

Smith, Robert. *Babe Ruth's America* (New York: Crowell, 1974).

Snead, Sam, with George Mendoza. *Slammin' Sam* (New York: Donald Fine, 1986).

Sobol, Ken. *Babe Ruth and the American Dream* (New York: Ballantine, 1974).

Society for American Baseball Research, editor Tom Simon. *Deadball Stars of the National League* (Washington: Brassey's, 2004).

Stanton, Tom. *The Final Season* (New York: Thomas Dunne, 2001).

———editor. *The Detroit Tigers Reader* (Ann Arbor: University of Michigan, 2005).

Stevens, Julia, with Bill Gilbert. *Major League Dad* (Chicago: Triumph, 2001).

Strege, John. *When War Played Through* (New York: Gotham, 2005.)

Stump, Al. *Cobb: A Biography* (Chapel Hill: Algonquin, 1996).

Taylor, Dawson. *The Masters* (New York: A. S. Barnes, 1973).

Thorn, John, et al. *Total Baseball,* sixth edition (New York: Total Sports, 1999).

Wagenheim, Kal. *Babe Ruth: His Life and Legend* (New York: Henry Holt, 1974).

Walsh, Christy. *Adios to Ghosts* (New York: self-published, 1937).

Wexler, Daniel. *The Book of Golfers* (Ann Arbor: Sports Media Group, 2005).

——— *Missing Links* (Chelsea: Sleeping Bear, 2000).

Williams, Peter, editor. *The Joe Williams Baseball Reader* (Chapel Hill: Algonquin, 1989).

Williams, Ted, with John Underwood. *My Turn at Bat* (New York: Fireside, 1988).

Wood, Allan. *1918: Babe Ruth and the World Champion Boston Red Sox* (Lincoln: Writers Club, 2000).

Index

Note: Pages with photos are indicated by italics.

288   *Index*

Pomonok Country Club (New York,
New York), 193
portable bleachers, Navin Field (Detroit,
Michigan), 100-101
Pratt, Del, 67, 105
Prohibition, 103, 142
psychology, golf challenge, 171-172

"rabbit ball" (baseball design), home
runs, 89
racism, Cobb, Ty, 55-56
Radcliffe, Ted, 56
rain-delay authority, 62
Ray, Ted, 225
Raynor, Seth, 192
Reach Baseball Guide, 65
Reid, Wilfrid, 225
Rice, Grantland, x, 59, 65, 90, 97, 107,
113, 124, 143, 144, 146-147,
151, 155, 156, 187, 195, 200, 211
Rice, Kit, 151-152
Rickenbacker, Eddie, 115
Rickey, Branch, 49, 147
Rivers, Alex, 7-8, 104-105
Rivers, Ty Cobb, 8
Roberts, Cliff, 143
Robinson, Frank, 112
Robinson, Jackie, 55, 56, 235
Robinson, Wilbert, 67, 113
Rockefeller, John D., 129
Rockne, Knute, x
Roesink, John, 107, 124, 229
Rogers, Will, 43-44
Rooney, Mickey, 178
Roosevelt, Franklin D., 9, 17, 142, 194
Rosburg, Bob, 145
Rose, Pete, 112-113, 237
Ross, Donald, 222
Rousch, Edd, 46
Rowland, Pants, 78, 99
Roy L. Doan Baseball School (Jackson,
Mississippi), 10-11
rule changes, baseball, 62-63, 89, 130
Runyan, Paul, 155
Runyon, Damon, 27
Ruppert, Jacob, 60-61, 122, 134
Ruth, Babe, *15, 40, 51, 64, 71, 83, 91,
98, 109, 133,* 146, *153, 177,
183, 192, 209, 234*

1915 season, 33-38, 41
1916 season, 40-43
1917 season, 44
1918 season, 46-49
1919 season, 51-53, 57-59, 63
1920 season, 66-70, 72-76
1921 season, 79-80, 83-90
1922 season, 92-94
1923 season, 94-95
1924 season, 99-102, 105-115
1925 season, 121-124, 130
1926 season, 127-131
1927 season, 133-135
"Babe" nickname, 27
baseball career, 28, 30
Baseball Hall of Fame (Cooperstown,
New York), 12-14, 16-17, 19-20,
185
baseball strategy, 81, 116-117
base running, 81
base stealing, 81
bats, 94-95
Boston Red Sox contract, 60-62
Brooklyn Dodgers, 9-10
childhood of, 29, 41, 56-57
death of, 236
endorsements, 104
Esquire's East-West Classic, ix-x
finances of, 123, 130, 132
golf, 61, 96-97, 153-156, 162-163
golf matches, 19-22, 147-150, 153,
156-158, 160-161, 184-191
Fresh Meadow (New York) match,
187-190, 192-202
Grosse Ile Golf and Country Club
(Michigan), 228-233
Newton Commonwealth Golf
Course (Massachusetts), 178-182
Grosse Ile Golf and Country Club
(Michigan), 225-227
health of, 119, 120-121, 235-236
hitting strategy, 48, 58-59, 66, 75,
80-81
Hodgson, Claire, 124-126
intentional walks, 63, 80, 106
lifestyle of, 59-60, 103-104, 118-119,
123, 125, 175, 224
media, 70, 72-73, 74, 185-187, 190,
212-214